The Myth of American Exceptionalism

There can be no deep disappointment where there is not deep love.

Martin Luther King, Jr.

To all my friends in America

Contents

Preface ix

ONE A City Set upon a Hill 1

TWO Myth and Reality in the Birth of a Nation 30

THREE From Civil War to Cold War 62

FOUR From Liberal Consensus to Conservative Ascendancy 99

FIVE The Other Exceptionalism 128

SIX The Corruption of the Best 155

Notes 191

Index 205

Preface

I am not American, but I have been thinking about the United States, reading about the United States, and experiencing American history all my life. I belong to that generation of Europeans who saw Americans as our saviors: I was eight years old when the GIs arrived in my native Britain. As soon as I could, I went to Philadelphia to study as a graduate student, and I jumped at the opportunity when my boss, David Astor, editor of the London *Observer,* sent me to Washington as his correspondent.

By sheer accident, when I was a graduate student I met Martin Luther King, Jr., then just coming to prominence in the Montgomery bus boycott. When, six years later, I returned to Washington as a reporter, I spent as much time as I could covering the civil rights movement and was present at many of its most dramatic moments, from the Meredith riot at Ole Miss to King's great speech at the Lincoln Memorial to George Wallace's stand "in the schoolhouse door" and the confrontation in Selma. In 1967 I made a television documentary, which included a long interview with Dr. King, about the way the racial crisis was moving to the North, and I wrote a book about the Reconstruction era.

During a critical period in the 1960s I was able to watch American politics from an unusually privileged vantage point. I was allowed to work from a desk at the *Washington Post,* although I was never an employee there. From the Kennedy assassination to Watergate, I was in close contact with friends at that great newspaper, who taught me much about journalism and about how the political game is played in the nation's capital. Because of close friendships with several highly idealistic members of the Johnson administration, I was sympathetic with and excited by Lyndon Johnson's ambition to build, on the foundations laid down by the Roosevelt, Truman, and Kennedy administrations, a Great Society of racial equality and shared prosperity. Like so many Americans I was disappointed when those aspirations were sacrificed to the war in Vietnam.

Together with two colleagues, I wrote a best-selling account of the 1968 presidential election, *An American Melodrama.* That led to my being commissioned to write a history of the 1960s, *In Our Time.* Since then I have written almost a dozen books, published by American publishers, about American history and politics. They include biographies of Henry Stimson, of Senator Daniel Patrick Moynihan, a personal friend, and of Colonel House, Woodrow Wilson's "right hand man."

I also made a television series about Ronald Reagan, which was shown in more than twenty countries around the world, though in the United States it was recut with Garry Wills as the narrator. Although my sympathies have generally been with Democrats and liberals, I am proud that both Richard Nixon and Ronald Reagan complimented me on my work.

I recite so much autobiography because it is important, before judging the ideas in this essay, to know that I have of deliberate choice spent most of my life trying to understand the politics and the history of the United States. My own personal political beliefs were, I used to think, at least until the 1980s, essentially American. By that I mean that my political principles and hopes were closer to those of what was then the progressive mainstream in the United States than to, for example, either of the two main political parties in my native Britain. I never considered myself a socialist, and admired the way the wealth-creating vigor of American capitalism was successfully restrained by regulation, not choked by public ownership. I never had the faintest admiration for the Soviet Union and regarded the various antinuclear movements in Europe as at best naïve and substantially disingenuous. Moreover, like virtually everyone I respect in Britain and in France, where I have family connections, I shared what I believed was a sincere American dislike of imperialism and an American commitment to international cooperation.

I have always felt particularly comfortable with the rhythm and temper of American life. For various personal reasons, I never made the decision to emigrate and become an American. But for forty years I have visited the United States several times a year, sometimes for extended periods, as when I taught at two great American universities, Cal-Berkeley and Harvard, and of course in order to do the research for my books and several television documentaries. I have actually worked in forty-eight of the fifty states—all but Alaska and North Dakota. I have visited every section of the United States and every major city except San Diego, and have spent substantial periods of time in New York, Boston, Atlanta, New Haven, Alabama, Indiana, Texas, and the Bay Area.

Why, then, have I chosen to write a book that is critical of some of the most cherished shibboleths of American national feeling?

For the past quarter of a century I have had what started in the late 1970s as the vaguest of feelings that something was going wrong in American public life. The balance of political and cultural power was shifting, from working Americans to their corporate masters, from ordinary Americans to the very rich, and from the center Left to the far Right. I shared this feeling with many Americans at the time. Indeed, my own misgivings were essentially learned from American friends, of many backgrounds.

This was not simply a matter of being an unreconstructed liberal, left stranded on a shoal as the tide of conservatism rose. For one thing, I regard myself and am, I think, widely regarded by those who know me as temperamentally and politically conservative. My book about the sixties, *In Our Time,* was critical of the assumptions of consensus liberalism, and I wrote a later book about conservatism, *The World Turned Right Side Up,* which gave sympathetic respect to the principles of the new conservative ascendancy, without joining the uncritical chorus of conservative propagandists.

My "take" on the Reagan administration was that Ronald Reagan deserved to be taken far more seriously than was often the case. He had, I thought and wrote, a small number of principles or instincts—distrust of government, belief in the fragility of the Soviet Union among them—

and a truly remarkable gift for moving public opinion in his direction. I remained an admirer of the administration of George H. W. Bush and in particular of his able and civilized management of America's interaction with the rest of the world at the time of the fall of the Soviet Union and the first Gulf war.

As late as the 1990s, then, I remained an "American" in my politics. One trait of American politics, however, had always bothered me, and that was the missionary persuasion. My own political credo started from the principle of popular sovereignty, first taken as their intellectual bedrock by Thomas Jefferson and James Madison. I identified with those who had fought the good fight for justice and equality in every American generation. I admired, and I expressed my admiration at great length, for the unshakable good sense of the American majority and its capacity for righting the ship when foolish or ungenerous movements threatened its equilibrium.

I watched with admiration, for example, the way that, when the integrity of American politics was threatened by the paranoid foolishness of Richard Nixon and his entourage, every single piece of the constitutional system, from the police court and the journalism and a grand jury to the Senate, the House of Representatives and the Supreme Court did its job as it was supposed to do.

During the 1980s and 1990s, it seemed to me, the United States was doing well. It was a great time, almost a Golden Age, for science, for literature, for all the arts that make life good, from music to gastronomy. It was true, however, and I pointed this out in more than one book, that there was, as it seemed to a British mind, a new, an almost Edwardian feel to American society in those years. It was a time not just of growing economic inequality but of a diminished respect for equality except in the raw form of equal opportunity to make very large fortunes.

America was complacently becoming, as I have written, just what we in Britain have struggled so hard to cease to be, a class society. Economic and social equality were being undermined by the sheer cost of health care and education and by residential segregation.

What troubled me more than that, however, was what seemed to me a new insistence that America be admired, almost worshiped. One of the glories of American life, I had always felt, was the readiness to criticize, to ask questions, to challenge shortcomings. Now, in political journalism and especially in the outpourings of new research institutions that made little pretense of open inquiry and unblushingly promoted conservative ideology and the economic interests of the privileged, there was a new intolerance, a new demand for uncritical assertion of national superiority.

"We need to err on the side of being strong," said William Kristol, "and if people want to say we're an imperial power, fine." Fine! When I read that, I thought of the countless occasions when Americans had earnestly explained to me the wickedness, the folly and sheer immorality of the very idea of empire. Kristol's casual boast was, as Thomas Jefferson wrote of the Missouri Compromise, "a firebell in the night." It "awakened and filled me with terror." My generation in Britain rejected from the bottom of our souls the pretension to empire. To do so in the name of spreading democracy was to repeat the hypocrisy that we had despised as soon as we could read the empty boastings of imperialists. To hear this from the very people who had taught us the anti-imperial principle caused an emotion that went beyond anger, to contempt.

There was, too, it seemed to me, in this new—and as I thought profoundly un-American—discourse an unpleasantly Prussian tone. There was a glorification of military power, a demand of obeisance to a nationalist and anti-internationalist creed, a xenophobia. I winced, for example, when people spoke derisively, as they routinely did in Washington, of Africa as a "basket case"—a metaphor drawn from men and women without arms and legs. I was startled by the open contempt expressed for the United Nations. Had not an American ambassador to the UN actually anticipated an imaginary 9/11 of his own by saying that he would not mind if ten floors of the United Nations building were volatilized?

It was obvious, too, that this sneering contempt for the "lesser breeds without the law," as Kipling, in his American phase, called the peoples of Africa and Asia, was not just an attitude toward foreign policy. It was an integral part of an arrogance that did not begin at the water's edge. It was the worldview of what was becoming a class society, where power came not from the sovereignty of the people but from the skilful deployment of private wealth, the deployers', or that of those who could be persuaded to stump up for them.

An aggressive strand in American attitudes toward the rest of the world, I knew, was not wholly new. From the very beginnings of American history, the commitment to freedom had been mixed not only with the "damned inheritance" of slavery but with ambitions and interests—for land, for wealth, for military glory—that were scarcely different from those of other peoples and other rulers in other times.[1] And why should they be different? Americans, after all, were not angels. They were men and women. They were not, *pace* the man who called himself Hector St. John de Crèvecoeur (more of him later), new men and new women. They were men and women of the same clay as the rest of us, and specifically they were, in their great majority, Europeans who brought with them to America European hopes, European fears, European ideals, European prejudices, and a European worship of the nation state.

Following this train of thought, I began to ask myself whether a vital part of the explanation of what seemed to me, and to many Americans, to have gone wrong, might lie in a corruption of the doctrine that is called American exceptionalism.

Trivial anecdotal incidents strengthened this suspicion. There was the veteran American academic, male, who explained to me at a conference in London with what was clearly passionate sincerity, as if to a backward child, that while other countries have something bad called nationalism, America alone has something good called patriotism. There was the American "scholar," female, who on a radio debate snorted with derision when I reminded her that the Soviet Union and the British Empire had also played roles in defeating Nazi Germany. There was the constant diet of sneering from the Bush administration and its acolytes at the United Nations, at "old Europe," at the French, at anyone in the world who failed to join the chorus of adulation of what was, after all, a largely imagined exceptional America. A new anti-anti-American industry had grown up. It demanded of foreigners that they should be far less critical of America than Americans routinely were of their various countries.

These, however, were mere irritants. What was substantial was that the country had fallen into the hands of people who seemed to me to have departed, coldly and with calculation, from much of what I had seen as the best of the American tradition. It was not just that they were boastful, often fatuously so. They worshiped the golden calf of a largely mythical and certainly short-lived "New Economy." They were at once aggressive and hubristic in their attitude to the rest of the world, and strangely lacking in confidence in the sound sense and gyroscopic stability of the American people, of whom, in fact, beyond the axis from Harvard Yard to the Pentagon, which they professed to despise, but from which they drew their influence, many of them seemed to know curiously little. In short, they seemed to have lost faith in what I loved about their country.

By 1994 such people seemed to be taking over the Congress, and seeking to impose their dogmas on the public life. They were laying siege to the judiciary. And in the year 2000 they succeeded, by a whisker, in taking over the executive branch of the federal government as well. They had managed to establish a sort of hegemony over the media.

How much of this turn of events, I asked myself, could be put down to the strand of exceptionalism? Certainly that strand has run through American life, as one among many traditions, since colonial times. Was I mistaken in imagining that the hubris and the undemocratic instincts I saw so widely deployed were somehow the consequence of the triumph of this exceptionalist tradition, or of a debased version of it? Certainly the early twenty-first century was hardly the first time that intolerance and chauvinism had appeared in American public life, as they have appeared in the politics of most nations, democratic and undemocratic, in history. Was I wrong in seeing the seeds of what seemed to be going wrong in the illusion, or at least the exaggerations, of American exceptionalism?

I had always read American history avidly and with pleasure. Now I began to reread it through a more critical lens. Two coincidences may have influenced me. I spent several years working on a life of Colonel House, which drove me to confront the strange figure and contradictory opinions of Woodrow Wilson. I observed two things: that Wilson had no difficulty in assuming that the rest of the world, though not himself, ought to conform to his own specifications, and that both the Clinton administration and the administration of George W. Bush never ceased to proclaim that, however much they differed about almost everything else, they were both "neo-Wilsonian."[2]

The second coincidence, so to speak, was a commission to write a

history of Thanksgiving. There again two contradictory observations were to be made. I loved the spirit of Thanksgiving, a holiday I have been privileged to share more than once with American friends. And I was startled to find how much the historical story had been used by successive generations and kneaded into a patriotic myth.

As I read and reflected, I came again to conflicting conclusions. It was true—it seemed and still seems to me—that American history has been forced into a distorted and selective narrative of exceptional virtue. It is not wholly untrue. But important truths have been left out. In particular, an exceptionalist tradition has exaggerated the differentness, the solipsistic character of American history. The uniqueness of the American political tradition has been overstressed. The values that were derived from and are still shared with Europe have been underestimated. The sheer historical connections between America and the rest of the world had been wiped from the slate.

The successive phases of American history, it had always seemed to me, were special cases of great events and transformations that stretched far deeper and wider than the history and the boundaries of the continental United States—oceanic trade, the Reformation, the Enlightenment, migration, democratic government, Romantic nationalism, industrialization, the scientific revolution, the creation of a global economy and the clash of global ideologies. All these titanic processes and forces were presented, in much of what Americans were brought up to believe, in ways that falsified or trivialized the genuinely great story of America's birth, growth and success.

There was another side to this too, I am aware. The ideals of American exceptionalism, in themselves, are neither mean nor trivial. At their best they have been incontrovertibly noble. The sovereignty of the people, the rule of law, the subordination of political conflict to constitutional jurisprudence and the protection of rights: these great principles have protected the United States from many of the worst of the political catastrophes that have plagued other great nations. They have frustrated bad men and women and motivated wise and courageous conduct. In that sense, the American conviction that the United States has a special duty and destiny has in the past worked, as other religions have done, to make those who believe in them wiser and more virtuous.

Even so, it is not good, my whole experience tells me, for individuals or nations, to believe things that are not quite true. It is not healthy to congratulate oneself, or to exaggerate how much one excels others. It is not wise to imagine that one is called upon, by God or history or some other higher power, to rule others by superior force. It is wise, and it has been the better part of American wisdom in the past, to resist the temptation to dominate merely because one has the power to do so. It is dangerous, for oneself and for others, to create a myth that seems to justify, even demand, domination, whether it is called empire or not.

Those have been the lessons of history, and in particular of the largely disastrous imperial ventures of the European peoples over the past three centuries. If you look around the world—at Palestine and Iraq, at the nuclear rivalry of India and Pakistan, at Burma, Cyprus, Kenya, the Sudan, Lebanon, Vietnam, the Congo, Rwanda, Zimbabwe, the Caucasus, the list is agonizingly long—the most intractable problems and the most appalling suffering are precisely in the places where European imperialism left its bloody traces. They are lessons that in the past American governments have not needed to be taught. If the United States leaves the same legacy, in Iraq and Afghanistan, and who knows where else, is that "fine"?

It is not the contention of this book that the tradition of American exceptionalism is the sole or even the principal cause of the things that have "gone wrong" in American political life and foreign policy. It is a plea for looking with a skeptical and humble eye at the many and subtle dangers of self-praise.

O•N•E

A City Set upon a Hill

It has been our fate as a nation not to have an ideology, but to be one.

Richard Hofstadter

Wee shall finde that the God of Israell is among us, when ten of us shall be able to resist a thousand of our enemies, when hee shall make us a prayse and glory, that men shall say of succeeding plantacions: the lord make it like that of New England: for wee must Consider that wee shall be as a Citty upon a Hill, the eies of all people are uppon us."[1]

The sermon, "A Model of Christian Charity," delivered by John Winthrop on the eve of the Massachusetts Bay Company's sailing for New England in 1630 has been called "the greatest sermon of the millennium" and "a kind of Ur-text of American literature," though curiously there is not a single contemporary reference to anyone's having heard it delivered, and in fact the precise circumstances under which it was delivered are therefore unsure.[2] It has certainly become one of the sacred texts of that account of American history known as "American Exceptionalism."[3]

In recent years, Winthrop's sermon has been made popular by President Ronald Reagan, who quoted it, to the thrilled approval of his political partisans, in one of his most successful speeches, to the Conservative

Political Action Conference in 1974. He returned to the theme in his last address from the White House in January 1989. The image clearly meant a great deal to him, and it has meant a lot to his followers. "In my mind," he explained as he left office, "it was a tall proud city built on rocks stronger than oceans, wind-swept, God-blessed, and teeming with people of all kinds living in harmony and peace, a city with free ports that hummed with commerce and creativity, and if there had to be city walls, the walls had doors and the doors were open to anyone with the will and the heart to get here. That's how I saw it and see it still."[4]

Reagan and others have spoken and written as if John Winthrop had a vision of a republic that would be an exemplar and a model to the world. That is, however, a serious misunderstanding of who Winthrop was, of what he was saying, and of what he probably had in mind. Of course, if it is seen as a prophecy of the history of the United States, it is an anachronism. Winthrop was not an American. He was an Englishman, albeit one whose religious beliefs put him at odds with the contemporary government of King Charles I and his domineering archbishop of Canterbury, William Laud. Winthrop later went out of his way to emphasize that he saw himself as a loyal subject of the English king, and that the colony he helped to found was, by his wish, subject to the laws of England.[5] Winthrop and the political party to which he belonged decided to fight a king whom they saw as a "man of blood," and they defeated and killed him. That did not make them any the less Englishmen. The values they fought for, freedom and justice, are not exceptionally American values.

Reagan imagined Winthrop preaching on board the *Arabella* off the coast of Massachusetts. In fact the ship was called *Arbella.* The sermon was probably preached in the church of the Holy Rood in Southampton, England, or perhaps on board the good ship *Arbella* in the nearby port. It was certainly preached before Winthrop ever set foot in North America.

More important, he was of course not preaching to Americans about the future of the United States of America. There were no Americans then, and the foundation of the United States was a century and a half in the future. Most historians would agree that there was no distinctively American consciousness for at least a century after Winthrop's sermon. Winthrop could not therefore have anticipated that the United States would be as a city upon a hill. He could not possibly have imagined a United States. He was preaching to Englishmen, and expressing his determination that the colony, or in contemporary language the "plantation," that he and his friends were setting out to found, would be an example to other English colonies, in North America and elsewhere. At the time, it is interesting to reflect that those British colonies included those settled by Scots Protestants in northern Ireland. We have no means of knowing whether Winthrop was thinking specifically of them. But in their context and their real meaning the sermon that Winthrop preached and the sermon that Ronald Reagan used to inspire a conservative shift in American politics some 350 years later have virtually nothing in common.

Another of the beloved texts of American exceptionalism also looks a little different when its context is examined. "What then is the American, this new man?" asked J. Hector St. Jean de Crèvecoeur in a book first published in 1782, just before the triumph of the American Revolution. He answered himself in words that have resonated for generations of American patriots. "He is an American, who, leaving behind all his ancient prejudices and manners, receives new ones from the new mode of life he has embraced, the government he obeys, and the new rank he holds." Ringing words, indeed. But knowledge of their author and their context significantly alters their meaning.[6]

Crèvecoeur (his real name was Michel-Guillaume Jean de Crèvecoeur) described himself as an "American farmer," and it is safe to say that ninety-nine of a hundred Americans who have encountered his famous statement have assumed that he either was, or in due course became, an immigrant to the United States and lived the rest of his life in Jeffersonian simplicity in America. Yet that was not the case. He was a French nobleman who had lived in England and in Canada and who before the Revolution bought an estate of some three hundred acres in upstate New York, which he farmed with the help of slaves, though he implies in his writing that he disapproved of slavery as an institution. He was naturalized there in 1764, not, therefore, as an American, but as a British subject. In 1769 he married an American woman, Mehitabel Tippett, by whom he had three children. In 1780 he returned to France, as he said, to secure his inheritance and his estates to his children. That inheritance, incidentally, included a title of the kind that is forbidden by the United States Constitution.

After independence, through the influence of the countess of Houdetot, the former mistress of Jean-Jacques Rousseau, he was made the French consul in New York and remained for seven years a Frenchman in New York. In 1790 he returned to France for good, and there frequented the most aristocratic society. His friends included the king's former minister Turgot and Turgot's sister, the duchess de Beauvilliers, as well as the La Rochefoucaulds, Rohan-Chabots and the rest of the *gratin*, the "upper crust," of French royalist society. Crèvecoeur was a friend of Franklin's and an acquaintance of Jefferson's. He loved the American wilderness and wrote a delightful travel book, which he dedicated to the Abbé Raynal as if it were written by "a simple cultivator of the earth." He was sympathetic to the poor immigrants from Scotland or from Germany he met, and emphatic about how much better their life would be in America than in Europe. But he did not join them.

So far from deciding himself to become "this new man," he chose to spend the last twenty-three years of his life in Paris and on his estates, in the heart of that aristocratic milieu whose corruptions he had pretended to reject. In this he was not alone but was writing in the then-fashionable tradition of praising the simple life of the backwoods. In the age of the French Revolution other writers from aristocratic backgrounds, such as Bernardin de Saint-Pierre, the author of *Paul et Virginie*, and the great Francois-René de Chateaubriand, not to mention in the next generation Alexis de Tocqueville, praised the simplicity of the frontier but managed to resist its temptations.

A few years after the death of Crèvecoeur, John Quincy Adams, son of the second president of the United States, made a bold claim on behalf of the settlers who later came to be known as the Pilgrim Fathers, which has also entered the litany of exceptionalism. William Bradford, in his wonderful account of the settlement of Plymouth Plantation, describes how he and his friends decided to make what he called a "combination," or as we might say a compact or a covenant, "occasioned partly by the discontented and mutinous speeches" let fall by some of the "strangers"—those among the passengers, that is, who were not part of the separatist congregation that had traveled first from England to Leiden, in Holland, and then to the coast of New England.

There is reason to believe that there was another reason for this "combination." The *Mayflower* had been navigating for a landfall around the mouth of the Hudson, but its skipper had been forced to turn back by heavy seas at Pollock Rip, the dangerous shoal off the southern elbow of Cape Cod. That meant that the Pilgrims would be obliged to settle north of the boundary of the English colony of Virginia, which might lead to trouble. So William Brewster, Bradford, and the other leaders of the expedition made virtually all the adult males on board the Mayflower sign the following declaration:

> We whose names are underwritten, the loyal subjects of our dread Sovereign Lord King James, by the Grace of God of Great Britain, France and Ireland King, Defender of the Faith etc.
>
> Having undertaken, for the Glory of God and advancement of the Christian Faith and Honour of our King and Country, a Voyage to plant the First Colony in the northern parts of Virginia, do by these presents solemnly and mutually in the presence of God and one of another, Covenant and Combine ourselves together in a Civil Body Politic, for our better ordering and preservation and furtherance of the ends aforesaid; and by virtue hereof to enact, constitute and frame such just and equal Laws, Ordinances, Acts, Constitutions and Offices, from time to time, as shall be thought most meet and convenient for the general good of the Colony.[7]

That is the text of what has come to be called the Mayflower Compact. Now listen to what John Quincy Adams had to say about it. It was, said the sixth president, "perhaps, the only instance in human history of that positive, original social compact, which speculative philosophers have imagined as the only legitimate source of government."[8]

In other words, Adams was presenting the Mayflower Compact as a real, historical example of the imaginary "social contract" posited by political theorists, from Hobbes by way of John Locke to Rousseau, as the foundation of political society. With all due respect to the sixth president of the United States, that is anachronistic nonsense.

Brewster, Bradford, and their friends were not penning a state paper, still less prefiguring a future constitution. Caught, as they emerged from a storm-tossed voyage across the Atlantic, between the danger of mutiny from some of their own party and the possibility of legal difficulty because the weather might force them to settle where they had no legal right to do so, they had taken the precaution of getting the members of their party, half of whom would be dead of disease within three or four months, to agree to stick together. In it, they went out of their way to proclaim their loyalty to the king of England. It was a practical business document, and it also no doubt reflected the custom among separatist churches like the one the Pilgrims (as Bradford called them in retrospect) meant to found somewhere near Cape Cod Bay, of binding its members to a covenant. That was not nothing, but that was all.

Even more extravagant is the interpretation put by one of the greatest of modern historians of the religious and literary culture of New England, the Harvard professor Perry Miller. In 1952 Miller gave a lecture at Brown University for which he borrowed his title, *Errand into the Wilderness,* from a sermon preached by the Reverend Samuel Danforth in 1670. Miller explains that his thinking on the subject of "the massive narrative of the movement of European culture into" what he interestingly called "the vacant wilderness of America" began in Africa, where he found himself supervising the unloading of drums of American oil. (That was, of course, in the days when Africa imported oil from America, rather than exporting it to America.) In 1952 it might have seemed pedantic to point out that the wilderness was not quite vacant. That is not the case now. Miller's massive erudition in the literature of Puritan New England led him to conclude that the founding of the Massachusetts Bay Company was "not just an organization of immigrants seeking advantage and opportunity." It was "an essential maneuver in the drama of Christendom."

> The Bay Company was not a battered remnant of suffering Separatists thrown up on a rocky shore; it was an organized task force of Christians, executing a flank attack on the corruptions of Christendom. These Puritans did not flee to

> America; they went in order to work out that complete reformation which was not yet accomplished in England and Europe. . . . This was the large unspoken assumption in the errand of 1630: if the conscious intention were realized, not only would a federated Jehovah bless the new land, but He would bring back these temporary colonials to govern England.[9]

Now this is not as baldly anachronistic as many modern citations of John Winthrop's *Arbella* sermon or John Quincy Adams's interpretation of the Mayflower Compact. Miller was correct in pointing out that the Massachusetts Bay Company was very different in its personnel and its motivation from the Pilgrim Fathers who founded Plymouth. The Pilgrims were a tiny band of impoverished provincial zealots, driven out of England by fear of persecution first to liberal Holland, and then out of Holland mainly by fear that, after the twelve-year truce ended, Spanish victories in Holland would hand them over (the unhappy word *rendition* comes to mind) to the mercies of the Spanish Inquisition. The "great migration" of the Bay Company, on the other hand, was backed and led by some of the most powerful and incidentally the wealthiest members of the Protestant and parliamentary party that actually would, within little more than a decade, challenge the king, defeat him in the field, and eventually put him to death on a scaffold outside the banqueting hall of his own palace of Whitehall. Miller was a learned and talented historian. But it is profoundly unhistorical to wish "unspoken assumptions" onto groups of long-dead actors without evidence.

Ideology was involved, however, and power politics, not only in 1630 but also in 1952. Perry Miller was writing at the height of the Cold War, when it was important to equip Europe with an ideology to rival that of Soviet communism. In fact, with contemporaries like Daniel Boorstin and the Canadian SacVan Bercovitz, Miller was one of the founders of the academic discipline of "American Studies," which in its early days did indeed seek to supply the United States with an official ideology to combat the influence of communism.[10] It was all the easier, too, in 1952 to emphasize the exceptional character of American civilization because at that time the United States was, more than ever before or since, incomparably more prosperous than any other nation on earth, untainted, thanks largely to Franklin D. Roosevelt, by any serious kowtowing to fascism, and virtually unchallenged in its economic and military power.

Even so, the claims of 1950s American intellectuals, most of whom thought of themselves as liberals, read extravagantly today. Max Lerner published in 1957 a book, more than one thousand pages long, called *America as a Civilization.* In dithyrambic rhythms he lauded the exceptional American:

> He is the double figure in Marlowe, of Tamerlane and Dr. Faustus, the one sweeping like a footloose barbarian across the plains to overleap the barriers of earlier civilization, the other breaking the taboos against knowledge and experience, even at the cost of his soul. . . . Thus the great themes of the Renaissance and the Reformation are fulfilled in the American as the archetypal modern man—the discovery of new areas, the charting of skies, the lure of power, the realization of self in works, the magic of science, the consciousness of the individual, the sense of the unity of history.[11]

John Winthrop, William Bradford, and their two companies "footloose barbarians"! What can he have meant? Dr. Faustus was not an American, nor was Christopher Marlowe, still less Tamburlaine. And exploration, astronomy, ambition and self-expression, let alone consciousness and historiography, are hardly American monopolies.

Like many liberal American intellectuals in the 1950s, in fact, Max Lerner shared the conviction that drove Perry Miller, from his moment of epiphany as he watched the oil drums being unloaded on the quayside at Matadi: a conviction of "the uniqueness of the American experience." To put it mildly, that is a subjective truth.

The Puritans who sailed to Massachusetts Bay were not unique in their desire for religious and political freedom. All over Europe, in the century and a half after Luther nailed his theses to the Wittenberg cathedral door, there were communities courageously striving for precisely those two freedoms. If those who emigrated to New England were more fortunate—and after all New England was hardly the home of total religious tolerance—it was in part simply the freedom of the wilderness. Those seeking such freedom in Europe were all too likely to be persecuted out of existence, often with hideous cruelty. That hardly means that they had no desire for freedom. The society and the institutions the Puritans built in New England, too, were far from unique. (There are, for example, striking parallels with Dutch Reformed South Africa and with Presbyterian Ulster.) Half of England, in the 1640s, took arms to fight for the Puritan cause and for the freedom to pursue it. Half of Europe, since the Reformation, had been seeking to do the same. By the day the Bay Company arrived in Massachusetts, the Thirty Years' War between Protestants and Catholics, to its protagonists a war at least as much about religious freedom as the migration to Massachusetts, was already a dozen years old.

John Winthrop, Richard Saltonstall, and the other founders of Massachusetts were not impelled by a unique or exceptional American impulse. On the contrary, they were products of European education, European culture, European piety, and they were engaged in a great European quarrel. One hundred forty years later some of their descendants did, with others, create an American state, and they did so indeed in part, but only in part, as a result of the differentness (though scarcely the "uniqueness") of their American experience. The principles of the American Revolution, however, were deep rooted in European origins: in the beliefs of the English Revolution and the Whig tradition, in the English, Scots, and French Enlightenments, and in the ancient principles of the English Common Law—in short, in the core beliefs of a European civilization.

The purpose of this book is precisely to challenge the assumptions of what Miller called "the uniqueness of the American experience." Of course there have been rich and redemptive elements of the American experience that are characteristically American. But the thesis of this essay is not simply that history, as used for political purposes by John Quincy Adams, or Perry Miller, or Ronald Reagan, is bad history. It is also now proving dangerous, to the United States and to the world, to overemphasize the exceptional nature of the American experience and the American destiny.

That belief does have roots that go back to the very earliest era of European settlement in North America. To some extent, it did guide the Founding Fathers and their early-nineteenth-century successors. In the nineteenth century Americans believed that theirs was what Jefferson called "the empire for liberty" and instinctively applauded when Lincoln said that their country was "the last, best hope of earth." American exceptionalism was nourished by the spectacular success of the United States in the twentieth century, and especially by the way in which America, alone, emerged strengthened by two world wars. It was encouraged by the ideological struggle with communism. For many, it was confirmed by the collapse of the Soviet Union in 1991 and the subsequent discrediting of socialist ideas. Sadly, in this century it has been soured and exacerbated by the shock of the atrocities of September 2001 and their consequences.

This tradition has sometimes been called Americanism, though that term has often been associated with ultraconservative and nativist prejudices. Sometimes it occurs to foreigners that this tradition has matured into something akin to an American political religion of liberty, with its trinity of George Washington, the father of the Republic; Thomas Jefferson, its spirit; and Abraham Lincoln, its martyred son. Certainly it has its apostles and disciples, its sacred texts, its festivals and its rituals.

It is more accurately called American Exceptionalism. The core of that belief is the idea that the United States is not just the richest and most powerful of the world's more than two hundred states but is also politically and morally exceptional. Exceptionalists minimize the contributions of other nations and cultures to the rule of law and to the evolution of political democracy. Especially since Woodrow Wilson, exceptionalists have proclaimed that the United States has a destiny and a duty to expand its power and the influence of its institutions and its beliefs until they dominate the world. In recent decades an economic dimension has been added to this traditional faith in the American Constitution and in the principle of government with the consent of the governed. For many American leaders and publicists today, capitalism, in the particular form it has taken in the United States, must be spread alongside freedom, democracy, and the rule of law.

There are, on close inspection, significantly different views of what precisely constitutes the exceptionalism of America. Sometimes it is seen simply as a matter of resources and material opportunity, and in particular of opportunities for immigrants to attain wealth and position that, it was claimed, they could never have aspired to elsewhere. Not for nothing was *der Onkel von Amerika,* the uncle from America, the phrase in a dozen European languages for the fellow who had struck lucky. Generations of immigrants have taught their children that their successes could happen "only in America," and that belief had credibility because, for European peasants—from the Hebrides or county Cork, from Sicily and the shtetls of the Pale of Jewish settlement—America really did open a golden door of opportunity. Sometimes it has been more subtly argued that what was exceptional in America was not prosperity itself but certain traits in American society or in the American psyche that made Americans more likely to be materially successful. (This was the thesis of a book, highly influential in the 1950s, by the historian David Potter, called *People of Plenty.*)[12]

One particular form of this interpretation, promoted in a famous thesis by an earlier historian, Frederick Jackson Turner, stressed the cultural influence of the frontier of settlement that rolled steadily forward from a few miles inland from the Atlantic beaches to the Willamette Valley of Oregon and the goldfields of California. On the edge of the wilderness, it was said, men and women automatically acquired egalitarian and democratic instincts and a unique brand of individualism. "This, at least," said Turner, "is clear: American democracy is fundamentally the outcome of the experiences of the American people in dealing with the West."[13]

More recently, many historians have challenged Jackson's frontier thesis.[14] They have highlighted the violence, the racism and the undemocratic practices that tainted the frontier experience, and have pointed out that the egalitarian, Protestant culture of the Old West of family settlements was only one episode in the successive phases of the frontier experience, which included the far less democratic spirit of the ranching and mining frontiers.

Often, too, it has been claimed that the exceptionalism of America lay in its absence of class divisions. Feudalism, it has been claimed, never took a grip on American society, though in fact, as we shall see, there were times and places—from the Hudson Valley by way of the South Carolina Tidewater and the Mississippi Delta to the sprawling Texas ranches—where something not very different from feudalism in the making could be found. So great were the opportunities of success in America, this school of thought claimed, that no American could be trapped in class disadvantage for more than one generation except by his or her own fault. In a society that allowed slavery and later racial segregation, it was always hard to argue that opportunity was universal. But many of the claims made on behalf of the equality of opportunity in America have either passed in silence over the great racial exceptions, African-Americans and Native Americans, or averted their attention from other inconvenient truths.

Sometimes the argument has been rather that, even if social class did exist in America, it did not permeate American politics as it did European politics, and there was in the past some truth in that. Specifically, scholars, exaggerating only slightly, argued that socialism, such an important factor in European politics, played no part in America.[15] Again, we shall see that if socialism was a marginal and alien creed, social democracy, in the shape of the New Deal, was central to American politics for half a century.

Alternatively, the emphasis was on the "unique" contributions of American political philosophy: "only in America," it was claimed, did men believe that government must always have the consent of the governed; only in America did a political culture of rights predominate. More recently, a new dimension has been added to the definition of the American creed: America, to many, though not to all, is defined by a particular version of virtually unregulated capitalism as well as by democracy.

At other times, freedom or liberty have been the banners of the American creed, though it is hard for a society that retained slavery so long and still deprives an exceptionally high proportion of its citizens of freedom in the penal system to claim a unique attachment to personal liberty as such. Liberty, for Americans of the revolutionary generation, seems to have meant first and foremost freedom from the English king, and it is true that for a few years the United States was a rare example of a republican government with broad territory. Second, freedom meant freedom from a feudal landlord, and it was quite true that, once the land had been cleared of Native Americans and Mexicans, it was easier for men to acquire and own land in America than anywhere in Europe. Equality, too, meant social equality, an end of forelock tugging and curtseying, and the sense that the poor man was the equal of his rich neighbor in personal dignity, even if there was always substantial inequality in America. European observers as different as Alexis de Tocqueville and Anthony Trollope commented on the way Americans providing personal services nevertheless seemed to see themselves as the equals of those they were serving.[16]

Most of these propositions contain, or have at times contained, a sufficiently large element of truth that it was tempting to see America as exceptional not only in outcomes but in its very principles. It is certainly true that the United States has often led the way. That was true of the establishment of a constitutional republic on a large scale. It was the first state to be explicitly founded on the consent of the governed, and on the principle of equality, even if that principle has so often been denied in practice. The United States was the first large country where the right to vote was available for a substantial proportion of adult white males, though as we shall see, that proportion was in reality lower, for longer, than has been generally supposed, and efforts to withhold the vote have been constant. Free or almost free public education was also accessible for a higher proportion of the white and especially the white male population earlier than in some, though not all, parts of Europe. Religious tolerance, though by no means universal, was also more widely observed, earlier, in America than in Europe. Certainly there was no state religion. The Constitution, and specifically the Bill of Rights, not only guaranteed important civil and human rights by law, even though in practice these were denied to many Americans: a culture of rights prevailed, and could often be successfully appealed to, and the scope of those rights expanded steadily.

That is only the barest list of the American contributions to social and political progress. Observing the sheer diversity of the claims made for the uniqueness of the American experience and the exceptional qualities of American society, however, it is hard to avoid the suspicion that they are motivated at least in part by a wish to believe in them. Exceptionalism, it would seem, is not so much a disinterested view of the American past as a dimension of American patriotism.

As the examples I cited at the beginning of this chapter suggest, American history has been encrusted with accretions of self-congratulatory myth. Much of the history Americans are taught in school, as we shall see when we glance at high school and even college textbooks, for example, is not so very different from Parson Weems's discredited but beloved story about George Washington and his father's cherry tree. That is no accident. Americans have felt so proud of their nation's achievements that they have wanted to socialize their children, and their immigrants' children, with that national pride. Increasingly they have felt called upon to share their beliefs, including their belief in their own exceptionalism, with a wider world. It is, after all, one thing to believe in one's own exceptionalism. That can be morale-building and invigorating. It is quite another to arrive in another country—Iraq, for example—of whose history one knows little and whose language one cannot speak, and expect the inhabitants to accept one's claim to exceptional virtue, especially if one's actions do not immediately confirm it.

There is, of course, nothing exceptional about this exceptionalism. All great nations cherish national myths. They tell their children improving or encouraging stories, about Romulus and Remus being suckled by a she wolf, or about Joan of Arc. The Scots cherish the legend of King Robert the Bruce and the spider who taught him to "try and try and try again." The Germans believed that in the hour of danger the long-dead kaiser, Frederick Barbarossa, would awaken from his tomb under the Kyffhaüser mountain and ride to the rescue of the *Volk*. Most nations, too, have believed in their unique qualities and their historic destinies, as the Serbs take pride in having saved Europe from the Turks and the Irish in having converted the British Isles to Christianity. Spanish pride is proverbial, and so is the attachment of Russians to the soil of the Motherland. The English have not always been free from self-admiration. This sense of special destiny, too, is not confined to nations that at one time or another have had mighty power and universalist ambitions. Today, for example, many citizens in such different countries as both Israel and Iran have exceptionalist feelings about their own history. Most, in fact, in one way or another, insist on the exceptional nature of their historical experience, in the past and the future, and even those whose size or situation preclude convincing dreams of military glory cherish the idea that what they have is special. That is of the nature of nationalism, and if American nationalism is unusual in its pretensions to universality, a product of the sheer size and resources of the continent Americans have "overspread" and of the multiplicity of the immigrants to America, American exceptionalism is nonetheless essentially a form of nationalism.

In modern times, those with power in Spain, France, Britain, Nazi Germany, and Soviet Russia and many other places have all at one time or another defined their national character and their historical role in terms of a mission to spread their ideas to the rest of the world. They were by no means the first to do so. In the ancient world, the Greeks called the countries where they settled the ὀικουμένη, the "inhabited earth": sometimes they contrasted it with the external "barbarians"; sometimes they just assumed that their world was coterminous with the world. The Romans spoke of Pax Romana, the Roman peace, and other ancient civilizations, from China to the Byzantine Empire, had universal claims or ambitions. Both the medieval papacy and Islam, under many dynasties, have seen the world in this "ethnocentric" fashion. Each nation or empire or civilization, in its way, claimed a *mission civilisatrice,* as the French put it; each saw itself as what the Chinese call Chung Kuo or Zhongguo, which we usually translate as the Middle Kingdom, but which is perhaps more accurately rendered as "the kingdom at the centre." Now it is the turn of the United States to see itself as the Middle Kingdom. Indeed, just as British cartographers once placed the Greenwich meridian at the center of the map on the schoolroom wall, now many American maps put America at the center of the world.

Another argument is sometimes brought forward by the champions of American exceptionalism. The United States, they say, is a world society, because of the unique variety of peoples who have immigrated to America. There, too, the case for American exceptionalism may be weaker now that it used to be. London, Paris, São Paulo, Sydney are also the goals of migration from many places, and no doubt that will be true of Shanghai and Mumbai before long. In any case, the professed goal of immigration to America is integration. Wherever immigrants come from, as they and their children become Americans, they cease to be representative of the whole world.

The purpose of this essay is absolutely not to minimize American achievements or to demean the quality of American civilization. It is simply to argue two cases: that the American experience has been less exceptional than is often claimed; and that such claims are dangerous, because they are the soil in which unreal and hubristic assumptions of the American destiny have grown.

American history, and therefore American society, has always been part of a larger reality, first European, then oceanic, and now global. Of course the American experience has been unique: but then every nation's experience is unique. That is how it becomes and remains a nation. What I will argue is that from the beginning, and still today, it makes more sense to keep in proportion, and not to exaggerate, those elements of the American experience that are relatively exceptional.

Two propositions correct the exaggerations of exceptionalism. The first is that, as a matter of historical fact, the history of the United States has always been, and remains to this day, far more intimately connected with the history of the rest of the world, and in particular with the history of Europe, than is generally assumed in the United States, even if the character of that connection is complex. The second is that the evolution of modern American social and political beliefs, including especially the core beliefs in liberty and democracy, has been more problematic than patriotic rhetoric claims. Freedom and democracy have not developed as smoothly or as easily as the preachers of American exceptionalism like to suggest. In America, as elsewhere, they had to be fought for, and not only against foreigners.

From the very start, America was less "exceptional" than the political prophets of American nationalism subsequently claimed. The first English settlements on the Atlantic Coast constituted only one tiny part of the vast expansion of Europe that began in the fifteenth century with the oceanic voyages of exploration. The Texas historian Walter Prescott Webb called this "the great frontier." He pointed out that "Europe had a frontier . . . more than a century before the United States was settled. Europe's frontier was much greater than that of the United States."[17]

The American colonies, and then the United States, were always part of an Atlantic or oceanic world, sharing many of the same intellectual and cultural currents and experiencing most of the same historical movements and conflicts as European and other countries. Gradually, over the centuries, as America began to match and eventually, at least for a time, to surpass the economic and cultural energies of Europe, the traffic became reciprocal. It is still more truthful and more realistic to see America as a vital part of an Atlantic and eventually also of a Pacific world, than to see it as isolated. Americans have by and large been taught to contrast their own expansion as benign, and to contrast it with the malign experience of the rest of the—imperial—expansion of Europe. Yet the settlement, the development, and the culture of English-speaking North America was an integral part of the broader history of European imperial expansion from approximately 1500 to well past 1900.

By the end of the fifteenth century, roughly a hundred years before the first permanent English settlements in North America at Jamestown, Plymouth, and Massachusetts Bay, two vast changes had transformed medieval Europe. The first was the exploration that opened Europe to the world and brought Europeans to trade and settle in Africa, Asia, and the Americas. The second was that religious and intellectual upheaval that became a political and military conflict, which we call the Protestant Reformation.

The rise of the Ottoman Empire in the course of the fifteenth century cut off the merchants of the Italian cities, and especially the Genoese, from the Black Sea trade that linked them, via the Silk Road, to the East. (That explains why so many of the early explorers in America, including Columbus, Amerigo Vespucci, and the man whom we call John Cabot, were from Genoa.) With the Mediterranean a war zone between Christians and Turks for more than a century, the axis of European trade shifted towards the west and eventually to the north; first to Spain and Portugal, then to France, the Low Countries, Britain, and Germany.

Gradually, over the second half of the fifteenth century, the Portuguese pushed farther and farther southward along the west coast of Africa, joining in the already existing trade in slaves as they did so. Just before the end of the century, they reached the Cape of Good Hope and began to trade directly by sea with India, the Spice Islands (in modern

Indonesia), China, and Japan, speeding up contact that previously could be made only slowly and directly overland. By the early years of the sixteenth century, the rulers of Spain, France, and England were all interested in finding a shorter route still to the Orient. America was discovered because Europeans already knew that the world was round and had calculated that China must be closer if you went westward than by the eastward route.

Within a generation of Columbus's landing in the Caribbean, Europe had been torn in half by the Reformation. What began as the last of a long series of rebellions against the pride and corruption of the Roman church became an intellectual revolution, a spiritual awakening. It was also the source and justification of cruel persecutions and bloody wars, from the eastern marches with Russia and the Ottoman Empire to the Atlantic. The voyages of discovery, to the east and then to the west, upset the belief system of medieval Europe, and before long the wealth the voyagers brought back upset the economic and social systems of Europe as well. After the middle of the century, Catholic Europe, led by the Habsburg dynasty and the Jesuits, was fighting back. Those tiny settlements sprinkled along the Atlantic shores of North America were only part of a Great Frontier that reached from the Portuguese and Dutch trading colonies at Colombo, Canton (now usually transliterated as Guangzhou), and Nagasaki, by way of the English and French "factories" in India and the slaving ports of West Africa, to the Spanish silver mines in Mexico and Peru, the great slave market in Havana, and the missions of Jesuits seeking converts from the valley of the St. Lawrence to the plains of Paraguay.

The passionately held beliefs of the Englishmen who settled in what is now Massachusetts were formed by the Reformation. Whether they had stayed inside the Church of England as "Puritans" or broken with it as "separatists," they were Protestants. Their emigration was an episode in the struggle over the future religious practice and obedience of the British Isles, itself only one of the many battlefields of the religious and ideological conflict between Protestants and Catholics that tore the European peoples and their rulers apart in the sixteenth and the seventeenth centuries.

By the eighteenth century, that struggle had largely morphed into the imperial contest between Catholic France (and its Spanish ally) and Protestant England. What Americans know as the "French and Indian War" was one theater in what the English and the French called the Seven Years' War. It could also be called the first world war, because it was fought not only on land in Germany, India, and North America but also on the oceans. It was the need to pay for the cost of that war that drove the government in London to make the North American colonists pay for the cost of their defense against the French and their Indians—and of course it was those demands that made the colonists to raise the banner of no taxation without representation.

The American Revolution itself was hardly unconnected with the quarrel between the British and French monarchies. Without the French fleet, the American army would not have won the decisive victory at Yorktown, where almost as many French as American soldiers fought on the winning side. Even though the ultimate success of the American revolution was arguably never in doubt, it remains true that the birth of the United States was an event, pregnant with consequences, in the history of Europe.

It was also an event whose root causes went back deep into the political and intellectual history of Europe. The political ideas of Benjamin Franklin, Tom Paine, James Madison, and Thomas Jefferson were hardly American ideas, even if the founders of the American republic were both compelled by the revolutionary conflict to announce those ideas with clarity and enabled by their military success to explore their implications as they could not have done with impunity in Europe. The Founding Fathers staked out noble and forward-looking propositions in the Declaration of Independence, and they hammered out a Constitution that has effectively protected the essence of those ideals for more than two centuries. But their ideas were not original. They had literally been to school to the Common Law of England. They were the intellectual heirs of the "commonwealthmen" and radical Whigs who had kept alive the principles of the English Revolution. They were also the children of the English, Scots, and French Enlightenment, of John Locke, David Hume, and Adam Smith, and of Montesquieu, Voltaire, and Diderot.

Even after independence and after the ratification of the Constitution, the United States did not cease to be a vital part of the European world, either politically or economically or intellectually. The party politics of the new republic expressed many interests and many conflicts, not least the primal incompatibility of the slaveholding and the freesoil states, that "irrepressible conflict" which Jefferson heard "like a firebell in the night" as early as 1820. But those politics at first were poured into the mold of an opposition between Republicans, who favored France, and Federalists, who preferred good relations with England.

The decisive events of the first half of the nineteenth century were the gradual expansion of American territory on the western frontier and the immigration from Europe it permitted. While of course at one level that represented the aspirations of millions of individual settlers, speculators, and frontiersmen, it was also undeniably made possible by the politics of Europe. The Louisiana Purchase was an opportunity seized by Jefferson but presented by Napoleon, as a result of certain contingencies of the long war between revolutionary France and its enemies. Even the independence of Texas, though demanded by American settlers, was also made possible by the British government's commitment to the abolition of the slave trade.[18]

The Mexican War and the acquisition of vast territories from Mexico were made possible by the Mexican Revolution of 1810, which in turn was the consequence of the collapse of Spanish power as a result of the French invasion of Spain in the Napoleonic Wars. The Monroe Doctrine, on the face of it a bold proclamation of American independence from European interference, was occasioned by the prospect that the restored French monarchy might also restore the Spanish colonial empire; indeed, it was the British foreign secretary, George Canning, who urged the United States to join with Britain in opposing European intervention in Latin America.

It is not my purpose to diminish the importance or the originality of the great developments that led to the emergence of the United States as a great world power by the end of the nineteenth century. I would merely insist that the United States did not emerge like Athena from the brow of Zeus, or by a kind of geopolitical virgin birth.

The expansion of the United States before the Civil War was made possible by many causes, among them the high birth rate of settlers of European descent, given access to land and other resources denied to them in contemporary Europe; the sheer abundance of resources in America and the attraction that presented to Europeans; and the expulsion of the indigenous inhabitants.

Commercially and economically, at least until the 1860s, the American West was part, a very vigorous part, of a European system. The transcontinental railroads, the crucial infrastructure necessary for what Frederick Jackson Turner meant by the frontier, were largely paid for with British and European capital. Rapid as industrialization was in the United States in the second half of the nineteenth century, to the point that before the century's end the United States had overtaken both Britain and Germany in industrial production, still, until the beginning of the next century, more than 70 percent of American exports were agricultural, and the great majority of them went to Europe.[19] American cotton, wheat, corn, beef, lumber, copper, and other primary products were exported to Europe, and Europe in return supplied labor, capital, and—until toward the end of the century—much intellectual property and technology as well.

In the twentieth century, the relation of America to Europe changed dramatically, largely as a result of the propensity of the European nations to fight viciously destructive wars with one another. It was during World War I that the American economy unmistakably surpassed the manufacturing, as it had long surpassed the agricultural, production of Europe. By 1916, when Woodrow Wilson struck a severe blow to British credit, New York was replacing London as the financial capital of the world.[20] Britain and France, at war with imperial Germany, were desperate for American food, fiber, copper, and munitions. After the war, New York banks financed the recovery of Germany, not as an act of international benevolence but as hard-headed business propositions, though as a result of the Great Depression of 1919, many of those investments were lost. Loans to Britain, too, were excellent business, even if not all the capital was repaid.

Over the course of the twentieth century the United States acquired incontestable military and economic superiority over its former rivals, the European powers and Japan. American business and American civilization came to influence the world more and more. At the same time,

Americans were increasingly attracted to a national ideology that cast them as redeemers of a sinful world. This view was never universal or uncontested in American public opinion, but it was increasingly influential. Between the two world wars, isolationism was a formidable political force, even though on analysis it turned out to hold not that the United States ought to be isolated from the world so much as that the United States should not involve itself with the affairs of Europe. To expand American influence in Latin America and the Orient was quite another thing. Indeed, isolationism often amounted, on inspection, to the reluctance of Irish-Americans to be allied with Britain, the refusal of German-Americans to be drawn into opposition to Germany, and the resentment of the agrarian South and West toward what was (justifiably) seen as the linked money power of Wall Street and the City of London.

Yet the vision of the United States as an international knight errant, riding to the rescue of the victims of oppression and injustice, strengthened steadily over the course of the twentieth century. Woodrow Wilson disapproved of the motives of all the European powers in World War I. To the despair of his advisers, Wilson repeatedly inserted into his speeches language about how the United States alone had no selfish motives in that war.[21]

Wilson refused to allow Britain and France to be called "allies"; they were only "associated powers." He explained to his colleagues that the British and French prime ministers were not representative of their peoples as he was of the American people, even though they had been recently and massively endorsed by elections and by Parliament, respectively, and his party had been defeated in the midterm elections of 1918. Wilson saw the war as ideologically motivated. It was a war for democracy, a war to end war, and America's motives, as proclaimed in his Fourteen Points, included the desire to create a new open diplomacy, to establish the principle of self-determination of peoples (or perhaps of nations, not at all the same thing), and to establish the "freedom of the seas."

If World War I disarmed America's competitors and turned its creditors into debtors between 1914 and 1929, the second war more than confirmed American financial and industrial supremacy. France, Belgium, and Holland were shattered. Britain was impoverished, and the determination of the Roosevelt administration to hasten the disappearance of the British Empire, reinforced by the American acquisition of Middle Eastern oil fields and by the Eisenhower administration's angry response to the Suez invasion by Britain, France, and Israel, accelerated the removal of Britain as a political and economic rival. The German economy was in ruins, and so for a time was that of Japan. Those two former enemies were also discredited by the appalling crimes both had committed. They were only too glad to court rehabilitation by accepting American hegemony and constitutional arrangements more or less dictated by the United States.

Franklin Roosevelt (a subcabinet member of the Wilson administration) was similarly motivated by a Wilsonian ideology. He saw it as a matter of national security that the United States must inevitably be drawn into World War II against fascism. But he also held an ideological rationale of the postwar world America must fight for. Almost a year before Pearl Harbor, he told Congress that Americans ought to be willing to fight for the Four Freedoms: freedom of speech, freedom of worship, freedom from want, and freedom from fear. Until the war was all but won he muffled, if only in the interest of avoiding unnecessary rows with the British, a belief he made unambiguously plain to intimates: that America was also fighting to end imperialism. Roosevelt also actively disapproved of monarchy. He urged Churchill that if the British government should be forced out of London, it should move to Bermuda, not to Canada, as monarchy was to be kept out of the American continent.

Still before the United States had entered the war, in August 1941, he laid down another set of ideological principles in the "Atlantic Charter" that he proclaimed with that unrepentant imperialist, Winston Churchill, at their meeting in Placentia Bay, Newfoundland. It was, he said, "a joint declaration laying down certain broad principles which should guide our policies along the same road." The charter enunciated "common principles" on which he and Churchill based "their hopes for a better future for the world." The eight propositions they announced included self-government for all peoples, a commitment that Churchill must have made with mental reservations, given his known and enduring opposition to decolonization.

After 1945 the United States was generous with its help for the recovery of Western Europe and Japan. Churchill has been much commended for calling Lease-Lend "the most unselfish act in history," but the Marshall Plan was equally unselfish. It was also, however, an act of enlightened self-interest. At Bretton Woods and Dumbarton Oaks and in the creation of the United Nations, it was made plain that the postwar world was to be modeled on American ideas and tailored, albeit in generous interpretations, to uphold American interests.

Eventually the economies of Europe did grow until collectively they now slightly exceed that of the United States in size. But for at least two decades after the end of World War II the American economy had no serious competitors. It has not been considered polite to say so, but American exceptionalism owes much to war, and specifically to the fact that in the twentieth century the American economy was twice left undamaged and indeed enriched by war, while all its potential competitors were transformed into pensioners.

The one European power that seemed for a time to be at least a potential rival was the Soviet Union, if only because its population, land area, and natural resources seemed more of a threat to American geopolitical strategists than the less spacious countries of Western Europe. Within a matter of months after the end of World War II the Soviet Union had become a military and ideological enemy. The Cold War may have concealed the essential bankruptcy, incompetence, and corruption of the Soviet system, and the Soviet government concealed the appalling damage done by the Great Patriotic War.

From the 1950s on the Communist powers, the Soviet Union and China and their more or less captive allies, gradually gave up on the attempt to challenge the United States and its alliance system directly in Western Europe and Southeast Asia. Instead of driving their tanks across the north German plain, Soviet strategists now dreamed of besieging the United States and its European allies in a global envelopment that would cut them off from their sources of raw materials and energy supplies. Almost ignoring the developing rivalry within the Communist bloc, the successive American administrations of presidents Truman, Eisenhower, Kennedy, Johnson, and Nixon allowed themselves to be drawn into what was intended to be the support of democracy against the threat of totalitarian communism. All too often it involved attempting, from a weak strategic position of external lines, to uphold authoritarian regimes (Syngman Rhee in South Korea, the shah of Iran, the Diem family in South Vietnam, and a sorry array of dictators in Latin America among them) whose rulers had little patience with anything that resembled democracy.

That road ended in the hills and rice paddies of Vietnam. Only on a far-fetched interpretation of the then-fashionable "domino theory," which presupposed that any communist victory must lead to others, did it make any sense to send more than half a million American troops and massive naval and air resources to a country so marginal to American interests. No doubt there were those when the adventure began who saw it as an unselfish crusade to bring democracy to Indochina. By 1975 there were few who talked like that. But even before the United States had extricated itself from that least rational of imperial adventures, Washington found itself deeper and deeper embroiled in the Middle East.

By the 1970s the United States was no longer self-sufficient in energy, and the oil resources of Saudi Arabia, the Gulf, Iran, and Iraq were by no means a matter of indifference to American policy makers. But the fatal quality of American involvement in the Middle East was not due only, or even primarily, to a hardheaded determination to safeguard access to a vital economic asset, oil. Nor was it caused primarily by cold strategic pragmatism. Far more decisive was the commitment to the survival of Israel.

This, too, no doubt, had its hardheaded side. The champions of Israel wielded great influence in the United States, in politics and in the news and other media. But the real source of the policy that led from alliance with the shah of Iran against Iranian nationalists to support for supposedly moderate pro-Western governments in Egypt and Saudi Arabia, to interventions in Lebanon and in Libya, and finally to the disastrous adventure in Iraq was neither a materialistic search for oil nor yet a calculation of strategic influence. It was more idealistic, more generous. The American public and their political representatives had fallen in love with a vision of Israel as a democratic model and a replica of the pioneering American past. For two decades after 1945 there was comparatively little interest among the American public generally in the fate of the European Jews. But then, as a result of a series of events we will examine later, the Holocaust became for many Americans, Gentiles as well as Jews, a powerful myth of redemption, in which the United States was cast as the redeemer.

The war against German, Italian, and Japanese fascism was fought and won by a Grand Alliance that was ideologically incoherent. The United States was allied to Stalin's communist Soviet Union and to the British Empire. Even before Roosevelt's death it was plain that the United States intended, tactfully but with determination, to press for the dismantling of the British, French, and Dutch colonial empires, and plain, too, that the days of alliance with the Soviet Union were numbered. Over the next forty years the United States forged and maintained a coalition against the Soviet Union, and gradually refined an ideology for that coalition to fight for if need be. Especially in the early years, the military and economic predominance of the United States within the alliance was so overwhelming that it was easy for successive generations of postwar Americans simply to assume that they were the hegemonic power, and easy, too, to assume that "the allies," a term that often came to be used in Washington with a nuance of irritation or even irony, accepted American leadership in terms of democratic principles, as well as in matters of military hardware, strategy, and diplomatic style. The president of the United States awarded himself—or was awarded by journalists—the title of "leader of the Free World," rather as European monarchs once called themselves "defender of the faith" or "the most Christian king."

The collapse of communism in Eastern Europe, beginning with the fall of the Berlin Wall in 1989, and the subsequent disintegration of the Soviet Union constituted not just a culminating political and ideological victory. It felt to many Americans like final confirmations of American Exceptionalism. Now the United States was "the lone superpower." The phrase, with its semicomic overtones of the Lone Ranger, was incessantly repeated in American news media as the end of the twentieth century approached. Military predominance was unquestionable: by the end of the century the United States was spending more on its armed forces than the next dozen powers put together—arguably, indeed, more than all other nations. Political influence (or "soft power," as it became fashionable to call it) was apparently irresistible, especially after the failure of the European nations to respond effectively to the Balkan wars after the break-up of Yugoslavia.[22]

There was even, as the twentieth century ended, a welcome flutter of economic vitality, especially in the stock market, after years of relative stagnation. President Clinton, in the first State of the Union address of the new millennium, was able to congratulate a country basking in prosperity and peace. All manner of things, it seemed, would be well.

Trouble came, as it will, out of a clear blue sky on the morning of September 11, 2001. At first, a common American response to the evidence that the United States was not, after all, universally loved was an inverted exceptionalism. "Why do they all hate us?" It turned out, of course, that it was not only America that they hated. Even in the danger of terrorism the United States was not exceptional. The fanatics of Islamic jihad had already mercilessly vented their rage against the perceived enemies of their own ideology, in Saudi Arabia, Kenya, Tanzania, as well as in a first abortive attempt in New York City. Before long they had brought death to Bali, to Madrid, Casablanca, Istanbul, London. Once again, as in 1914 and 1939, it turned out that the United States was more involved in the fear and anger, the struggles for survival and domination, of the outside world than the comforting, if patronizing, assumptions of exceptionalism had taught.

The great American liberal historian Richard Hofstadter once wrote that "it has been our fate as a nation not to have ideologies but to be one."[23] Each phase of American history has strengthened the perception among many Americans that the United States is not just one nation among many but a nation marked by the finger of destiny, the land that Lincoln called the "last, best hope of earth."

That sense was present long before the United States was the most powerful single nation on earth. It was there even before the United States existed, in the days of the earliest colonial settlements. Chiefly it took the form of a religious conviction, a Protestant adaptation of the ancient Jews' belief that they were a "chosen people." The American Revolution was no simple struggle between good and evil, and it can certainly be understood only in the context of events in Europe. Yet it did powerfully reinforce the belief that Americans were embarked upon an almost unprecedented voyage of social and political experiment.

In the early nineteenth century the United States expanded into what contemporary Americans saw as a vacuum left by the conquest of Native Americans and Mexicans. They saw their society as a bold experiment in democratic government, and also as the field of unprecedented equal opportunities, at least for most white males. After confronting and resolving in the Civil War the dilemma presented by slavery and the powerful forces that defended the slave system, the United States swiftly became a model of capitalist development, at first almost unregulated. By the end of the nineteenth century, the United States had become the most productive of the world's nations, and potentially the most powerful. American leaders like Theodore Roosevelt and Woodrow Wilson were conscious of that fact. They were able to persuade many of their fellow citizens to share their conviction that it was time for the country to make its wishes felt in the world.

By the beginning of the twenty-first century, thanks in no small part to American reactions to the reckless aggression of German and Japanese militarists, the global ambitions of Soviet communists, and the desperate rage revealed by the Al-Qaeda attacks on New York and Washington, the American government had come a long way from the positions it had occupied a hundred years earlier. A strong civilian tradition had come down from earlier generations. As late as 1940 the United States was bound by the neutrality acts, and American military forces were no larger than those of such minor European powers as Bulgaria or Portugal.[24]

By the end of the twentieth century, that ancestral suspicion of militarism had gone irrevocably. There were more than seven hundred American military bases around the world. Parceled out into the operational responsibility of half a dozen military commands which between them spanned the world, American armed forces had the capability to reduce any city in the world to rubble. To a remarkable degree, what was in effect, if not in intention, a form of world domination, had the support—albeit for the most part the somewhat passive and unenthusiastic support—of the American people. Only partly in jest, President George W. Bush saw himself as the world's sheriff.[25]

The political support for the unilateralist and interventionist doctrines of the American government at the beginning of the third millennium came in part from a paradox of public opinion. Stronger than ever, Americans felt more vulnerable than ever. But this new mood also derived from the widespread acceptance of an ever more exceptionalist interpretation of their own history. That led to a "Wilsonian" philosophy, underlying the foreign policy of both the Republican administrations of Ronald Reagan and the Bushes, father and son, and also, in essentials if not in style, of the Democratic Clinton administration.

That tradition is by no means unchallenged. Almost every strand of it has been unpicked and tested by historians and others. Yet the idea that the United States is morally exceptional, and that it must fulfill a unique historical destiny, remains immensely powerful. It is time to go back to examine the gradual development and historical metamorphoses of the exceptionalist idea and the American ideology.

T•W•O

Myth and Reality in the Birth of a Nation

A general and tolerably equal distribution of landed property
is the whole basis of national freedom.

Noah Webster

The Revolution," wrote the historian Gordon Wood, "made possible the anti-slavery and women's rights movements of the nineteenth century. . . . The Revolution not only radically changed the personal and social relationships of people, including the position of women, but also destroyed aristocracy. . . . It made the interests and prosperity of ordinary people—their pursuits of happiness—the goal of society and government. . . . In short, the Revolution was the most radical and most far-reaching event in American history."[1]

"Around 1776," wrote Howard Zinn, "certain important people in the English colonies made a discovery that would prove enormously useful for the next two hundred years. They found that by creating a nation, a symbol, a legal unity called the United States, they could take over land, profits, and political power from favorites of the British Empire. In the process, they could hold back a number of potential rebellions and create a consensus of popular support for the rule of a new, privileged leadership."[2]

The first of those two statements, by Professor Gordon Wood, of

Brown University, articulates what is now perhaps the orthodox view of the Revolution. It is, of course, a classically exceptionalist position. It is also a considerable exaggeration. To say that the American Revolution "made possible the anti-slavery movement" of the nineteenth century ignores the fact that there was already an antislavery movement in Britain before and quite independent of events in America. As early as 1772 a British judge, Lord Mansfield, abolished slavery in England in the famous Somerset judgment.[3]

By 1787, the year the Constitution went into effect, Granville Sharp, Thomas Clarkson, and British Anglicans and Quakers had founded the Society for the Abolition of the Slave Trade. In that same year William Wilberforce began his long parliamentary campaign for the abolition of the slave trade. Of course, many of the leaders of the American Revolution, including George Washington and Thomas Jefferson, were slave-owners, if in some cases more or less reluctant ones, and the Constitution, the culminating statement of the Revolution's values, not only did not abolish slavery but legitimated it. Indeed, many slaves appear to have felt that their prospects were preferable under continued British rule. Black slaves were offered their freedom if they would fight for the British governor of Virginia's "Ethiopian Regiment," and thousands of them left with the British when they withdrew.[4]

Similarly, it is simply unhistorical to suggest that there would have been no movement for women's rights if there had been no American Revolution; there already was a movement for women's rights in both England and France before the beginning of the nineteenth century that owed nothing whatsoever to Washington, or Jefferson, or Madison. It is true that the power of monarchy and aristocracy was still great in early-nineteenth-century Europe, and at the margin the movements to reduce that power were encouraged by American experience. But the movement to enhance the interests and prosperity of "ordinary people" was one of the great themes of nineteenth-century politics, thought, and literature in Europe. Wood ends with a strange anticlimax. Just when he seems to be claiming universal achievement for the American Revolution, his peroration makes only the relatively provincial claim that the American Revolution was the most far-reaching event in . . . American history.

"How far the greatest event in the history of the world, and how far the best!" exclaimed Charles James Fox, the great champion in Britain of the American Revolution. He was speaking of the Revolution not in America but in France, which to him and to other European radicals was incomparably the bolder and more inspiring event, however much its goals of liberty, equality, and fraternity were later tarnished by the Terror and by Napoleon's wars of aggression.

Howard Zinn, a more radical American historian than Wood, wrote with his tongue firmly in his cheek when he suggested, without personally endorsing the idea, that it is possible to see the American Revolution as merely a struggle between two elites, whose effect was to repress more populist upheavals. That interpretation, like Wood's in the opposite direction, goes too far. No doubt, as many historians have long pointed out, the immediate beneficiaries of the Revolution were overwhelmingly wealthy, if disgruntled, members of the existing colonial elite. But that does not mean that no real social and political change took place. And it ignores the extent to which the Revolution encouraged a dynamic, if gradual, process of change that really did allow new groups and classes access to political power.

It must always be remembered, though, that just as there was constant change in America, mostly in the direction of greater democracy and broadening liberty, in Europe, too, the nineteenth century was an age of liberty, progress, and liberal thought. In Europe, as in America, the franchise was steadily enlarged. New classes and groups were steadily, if slowly, included in the political society. Progressive ideas in every field—in education, in medicine and public health, in law and penal reform, in feminism, and in every area of social policy—made steady progress in Europe, just as they did in America. It is tempting for Americans to contrast the prerevolutionary Europe of George III's England with their own ideas as they had been refined by the thought and experience of the nineteenth century; easy to forget that, for all their differences, nineteenth-century America and nineteenth-century Europe were essentially two parts of the same progressive, liberal capitalist civilization.

The historical significance of the American Revolution is obscured, as a third historian, Bernard Bailyn, saw, by the fact that in one important respect it had essentially happened before the fighting began.[5] Quoting

John Adams in a letter to Jefferson, Bailyn wrote, "What do we mean by the Revolution? The war? That was no part of the Revolution; it was only an effect, and consequence of it. The Revolution was in the minds of the people, and this was effected, from 1760 to 1775, in the course of fifteen years before a drop of blood was drawn at Lexington."[6]

What Bailyn meant was that the consciousness of the American people, their "mentality," had been changed. Their circumstances, as Europeans possessed of unused and unexploited resources of land and minerals on a scale that had not been freely available in Europe for centuries, if ever, inevitably changed the character of American society. So, too, did the relative absence of "sitting tenants" of this vast estate: where in Europe most land was owned by long-established families (or by such institutions as the Crown, monasteries, churches, or colleges) and there was a surplus of landless men to work it, in eighteenth-century America a continent lay open to be exploited, and men to do the work were at a premium.

The growth in the colonists' numbers, to the point where by the time of the Revolution a quarter of George III's subjects lived in America, and the prosperity of their trade gave them increased practical independence of London.[7] They felt greater security from the French and their Indian allies after the "French and Indian War" ended in 1763. Most of all, the sense of opportunity felt by Englishmen, Scotsmen, Irishmen (both Protestant and Catholic), and some Germans made it seem wrong for them to be ruled by men who lived several weeks' sailing away and could neither share their interests nor understand their feelings. They were, after all, living on the edge of a continent only weakly held by Native Americans who had been more than decimated by European diseases to which they had no immunity. What Bailyn could say, after his profound immersion in the pamphlets and journalism of the prerevolutionary period, was that, before the "shot heard round the world," a majority in the colonies had already come to accept that it was time for them to govern themselves.

That process of change in the colonists' mentality, as Zinn and many historians before and after him perceived, began with a local elite, with Boston merchants and lawyers who knew that a Parliament in London would never shape its tax policy with their interests first in mind, and with Virginia gentlemen who chafed at their mounting debts to the Liverpool merchants who bought their cotton and tobacco and sold them their French wine and their English guns. It spread to the craftsmen and sailors of the seaports and the farmers and frontiersmen of the back country, many of whom, as a series of disturbances and rebellions would show, were already dissatisfied not only with British rule but also with the dominance of the seaboard elite.

The story has been polished and buffed until it shines as the founding myth of the American Republic. It is an inspiring story, of courage and wise statesmanship. The Americans of the revolutionary generation and their successors in the first half of the nineteenth century built well. But their history deserves to be scraped clean of myth, exaggeration and self-congratulatory propaganda.

These new Americans, placed as they were, no longer seriously threatened (as a result of the British victories and then of the French Revolution) either by France or by Spain or by any Indian confederacy, enjoyed a favorable situation. They had already begun the process of acquiring if not yet a revolutionary consciousness, at least a new sense of self-worth and confidence. They were divided in many ways, but they had already begun to articulate their political beliefs and aspirations in clear and eloquent tones, in the language of Jefferson, Paine, and Madison, among the most persuasive political writers of any time or place. They had shown the courage to stand up and take on the most formidable military power of their age, and, not easily but in the end decisively, they had prevailed.

When we come to the Revolution we are no longer looking at the later, self-pleasing whimsies of the exceptionalist tradition. We are not writing back twentieth-century patriotic rhetoric into the sermons of seventeenth-century English Puritans, or fantasizing about flank attacks on the corruption of Old Europe. We are talking about real and important historical events, about solid change and the building of lasting institutions. The American Constitution was indeed an exceptional document, "the most wonderful work," the great British Liberal leader William Gladstone said, "ever struck off at a given time from the brain and purpose of man."[8]

It created institutions that have endured, and that in part because the Framers shaped their design so that it was, not easy, but possible, to adapt it to a society changing at times with riotous speed. The Constitution was exceptional not only in its intrinsic skill and wisdom but also because it was almost unique in its historical contingency. Rarely, if ever, had men been able to sit down and devise de novo, on a clean sheet, a new political system for a territory as extensive and as rich in resources as the new United States.

The American Revolution did indeed create a state that was in significant ways very different from any that the world had seen before up to that time. There had been, to be sure, republics before. The republic had been a recognized, if generally unstable, European political institution since the ancient world. Most republics, however, like Athens or the merchant cities of the ancient world, the city states of the Hanseatic League, the imperial cities of medieval Germany, or Geneva, or Venice, Florence, and the other republics of Renaissance Italy, were geographically restricted and responsible for a small, more or less homogeneous population.[9]

The exceptions, among them Venice, with its empire in the eastern Mediterranean, and Holland, one of the most powerful states in the world in the seventeenth century, and also a successful colonizing power, were run by commercial oligarchies. Neither made any serious claim to have brought broad swaths of the population into political power. For a few years, England had been ruled by a republican Commonwealth, but to Americans of the revolutionary generation, who knew the story so well, that was the exception that proved the rule, because it took so short a time for Oliver Cromwell to become a monarch without the name, and because the monarchy was so quickly restored by Charles II.

So the American Revolution did create the world's first large republic, though within a few years an equally or even more daring experiment would be made in France. The American Revolution did more than that, however. It created a state based on a political ideology of republicanism. Its principles had been hammered out in the trial of revolutionary war and in years of thoughtful debate to which men of the various elites made the decisive contribution, but in which many others had a voice. That ideology was proclaimed in the bold language of Jefferson's Declaration, in assertions both of universal human equality and universal human rights. It rested on the proposition that the republic would be governed with the consent of the governed. It replaced divine right, and hereditary right, and customary legitimacy, with the supreme authority of the people.

None of these ideas was wholly original. They came from a stock of European thinking that dated back at the least to the religious conflicts of the sixteenth century and the Enlightenment. To the extent that they did not triumph earlier in Europe, that was because the established political powers, monarchies and aristocracies, had every interest in repressing them, sometimes with savagery. It was the military victory of the American colonists, helped by their French allies, that ensured that the progressive idea of the European Enlightenment could be adopted in the new republic.

Until the American Revolution, the British constitution was generally admired by liberals everywhere as the best in the world. It is commonly said to have been an unwritten constitution, but in fact it was written in hundreds of statutes and many thousands of judicial decisions, as well as in libraries of law books, all well known to the Framers of the American Constitution. It was admired because it distributed power between the monarch, representing the historical nation; the House of Lords, representing wealth and power; and the House of Commons, representing those of the common people whose interests—to the mind of the time—deserved to be represented. The revolutionary ideology of the Declaration was refined, and to some extent balanced and nuanced—but not contradicted—by the compromises of the constitutional convention. Both were grounded in the changed mentality recorded by Bernard Bailyn in the language quoted above, which reflects the judgment of no less a contemporary authority than John Adams: that the real revolution lay in the changes of heart and mind that changed Britons who lived overseas to Americans who lived in their own country.

Even that did not express the full originality of the Revolution's new politics. For Americans were not simply carrying out the first rebellion by white settlers against metropolitan rule. Historians still argue about how far the Revolution transferred power to those who had before been powerless. But two propositions are clearly true: that the circle of those with political power did widen after 1787, and that a process began with the Revolution that would steadily expand the distribution of political power.

The Revolution, in fact, opened what was the most exceptionalist period in American history. In several specific ways American government and society were arguably more truly exceptional in the half-century after the ratification of the Constitution than at any time since. The political ideology was more nearly unique. The participation in voting and in other political activity was more widely distributed than anywhere else at the time: by the end of the nineteenth century many other countries had caught up in respect of the inclusiveness of the franchise. Indeed, where votes for women were concerned, the United States (1920) lagged many years behind such countries as New Zealand (1893), Australia (1902), and Finland (1906); Norway (1913) and Denmark (1915) also enfranchised women before America, as did Austria, Canada, Hungary, Ireland, Germany, Poland, Russia, and the United Kingdom (all in 1918).

Nowhere else, in the early nineteenth century, did so many citizens own land and other assets that conferred full citizenship. Public education was more generally available in the early decades of the United States than in many parts of Europe.[10] Ideology, franchise, landowning, and public education: American achievement in those four areas are enough to stake a strong claim for American exceptionalism in the first half of the nineteenth century.

It was Noah Webster of the dictionary who pointed out that the success of republican institutions depended in the first place on a sufficiently equitable distribution of land. "A general and tolerably equal distribution of landed property," he wrote, "is the whole basis of national freedom." He went further. "All the rest," he argued, "—The liberty of the press, trial by jury, Habeas Corpus writ, even Magna Charta itself— . . . are all inferior considerations."[11]

It was certainly easier to provide this prerequisite of freedom in the America of 1787 than in Europe, or indeed in the America of later generations. There was land, and to spare. There was plenty for poor farmers on the frontier, and for craftsmen and modest shopkeepers in the longer-settled districts.

Land ownership was not, however, quite as widespread in early-nineteenth-century America as popular mythology would have it. Obviously large sections of the population—women, slaves, free blacks, indentured servants, day laborers, hired hands, and what were called the "strolling poor" in town and country alike—either could not or were very unlikely to own land. George Washington owned a few thousand acres at Mount Vernon and had his eye on many millions of acres on the Ohio and the Kanawha. His friend Lord Fairfax had four million acres in the Northern Neck of Virginia before he was driven out by the Revolution. Dutch "patroons" long survived the Revolution in the Hudson Valley. The van Cortlands, Schuylers and van Rensselaers owned manors of which a Hungarian prince or an English absentee landlord in Ireland might be envious. Until the middle of the century, farm tenancy was common, especially in the Hudson Valley and western New York State. But if the chances of owning land in America are compared with the pattern in Britain and in western Europe generally, the comparison is telling. In nineteenth-century Britain, including Scotland and Ireland, most land was part of more or less big estates, owned by wealthy noblemen or squires, who worked some of the land "in hand" and rented the rest to tenant farmers, many of whom had worked it for generations. Virtually all land there was firmly held, and while men who made money—as increasing numbers did, in commerce or manufacturing, at the law, at sea, or in the colonies—often invested in land, the chances of a typical working man acquiring land were minimal. By the nineteenth century, a high proportion of the land in England was owned by a few thousand families. The situation varied from one part of western Europe to another, but in general it was the same as, or worse than, in Britain. Indeed, the oppression of rural tenants was one of the principal causes of the French Revolution and of the subsequent upheavals elsewhere. After the French Revolution there was a wide redistribution of land. The word *peasants,* which simply means countrymen, is usually interpreted pejoratively in English-speaking countries. In reality, since the Revolution, French peasants have been free proprietors, many of them prosperous.

In America land had always been more available than in Europe, and the urge to acquire land was one of the strongest impulses that drove Englishmen, Irishmen, and other Europeans to cross the Atlantic from the beginning. On the first anniversary of the Pilgrims' arrival in Plymouth, one of their leaders, Robert Cushman, in a sermon on the text "Let no man seek his own: But every man another's wealth," chided those of his companions who had crossed the sea not to find God but in order to be "Gentlemen, Landed men."[12]

It was a hopeless cause. Not only did colonial Americans dream passionately of landowning. They speculated furiously in land, and so did their descendants after the Revolution. It is impossible to say precisely what proportion of Americans did own land in 1800. It was, however, substantial. Not only did most Americans live on the land. The territory was expanding, especially after the Louisiana Purchase of 1803, the acquisition of east and west Florida, and again after the Mexican War. The frontier rolled steadily forward, bringing millions of acres of forest and prairie, once inhabited by Native Americans, onto the market. Many urban artisans or other citizens of modest prosperity owned some land. More important, a far higher proportion of Americans than of Britons thought that in the future they might be able to acquire land, which was extremely plentiful and relatively cheap. After the Northwest Ordinances of the 1780s, as a matter of federal as well as state policy, land was subdivided and offered for sale in the Ohio Valley and the rest of the "Old West" at affordable prices, and the same pattern was followed as the frontier expanded westward.

From the start, Congress was besieged with petitions for free land. In 1797 one came from the Ohio Valley settlers, and the early settlers in the Mississippi Valley did the same two years later. In 1812 Representative Jeremiah Morrow of Ohio argued that every American was entitled to a piece of free land, and in 1825 Senator Thomas Hart Benton of Missouri proposed a law to give free land to settlers. The first Homestead Act was passed in 1846, but it was not until 1862 that Andrew Johnson, later Lincoln's vice president, proposed the act that gave every American the right to a "quarter section," or one-quarter of a square mile, for free, plus additional land at $1.25 per acre. That was unimaginable prosperity for most European peasants, who flocked to take advantage of the offer in the fertile plains of the Middle West.

By the Civil War hundreds of thousands had acquired farms in this way. Yankees, frustrated by the rocky soil and long winters of New England, had poured into the Western Reserve of eastern Ohio, then into

Indiana, southern Michigan, and Illinois. Southerners colonized Kentucky, Tennessee, and southern Indiana and Illinois, and poured down the Natchez Trace toward Texas, while the rich lands of the Alabama Black Belt and the Mississippi Delta began to fill up with Carolinians and Georgians and their slaves, as the Cherokee were pushed westward along the Trail of Tears. By 1840 there were few organized Indian tribes east of the Mississippi. Old-stock Americans were joined by immigrants, at first mostly from England and Ireland, but then also Germans, who settled especially densely in Ohio and Missouri and—after the 1848 revolutions in central Europe were crushed—in Wisconsin and the Hill Country of central Texas. At about the same time the first Scandinavians began to push into the landscapes—familiar to them, with their lakes and their hard winters—of Minnesota.

The agrarian dream did not always live up to the hopes of either the dreamers or their legislative sponsors. Land in some places turned out to be more fertile than land elsewhere, and there were parts of the new lands that were too arid for 160 acres or even a square mile to be enough to feed a farm family. In most places and at all times from the Revolution until the end of the nineteenth century, debt was a reality, and often a nemesis for individual families. Life on the frontier was hard, even when successful communities took root. But the chief reason why public land was not parceled out earlier and more widely was the same as the reason for so many disappointments in the America of the first half of the nineteenth century: slavery. Southern representatives in Congress steadily opposed the Free Soil movement. They did not want their "peculiar institution" to be challenged on the ground by white farmers or in Congress by the votes of their representatives. The Union victory in the Civil War established the reality of Free Soil. But before long the process of industrialization and the growth of cities meant that the proportion of Americans, as opposed to the number, who owned land entered into a slow but steady decline.

One of the ways in which America seemed genuinely exceptional to many European observers in the first half of the nineteenth century was in the unusual distribution of that necessary condition of participation in democratic politics, the right to vote. Tocqueville, for example, was under the impression that "as a general rule" Americans voted for their representatives every year, and that "universal suffrage" was the rule.[13]

It is true that the right to vote was far more widely distributed in early-nineteenth-century America than in contemporary Europe. But it is also true that the right to vote was not in practice universal, and that, so far from being taken for granted, it was contested in many ways and on many grounds. Even before the Revolution, the franchise was far commoner in America than it would be in England for almost a century. The best estimate is that close to 60 percent of adult white males voted toward the end of colonial times. It was not until the second great Reform Act in Britain, in 1867, that anything like that proportion of men could vote there.[14] By the middle of the nineteenth century, according to Professor Alexander Keyssar of Harvard, the author of a massively erudite study of the history of the right to vote in America, "the nation had taken significant steps in the direction of universal white male suffrage."[15]

More surprising, Keyssar found, the broadening of the franchise does not tell the whole story. As American society changed, especially under the impact of immigration and urbanization, an "antidemocratic reaction" set in. Some groups, among them women, free blacks, paupers, felons, and migrants, actually lost the right to vote.[16]

To a modest degree, the Revolution did increase the number who could vote, in part because of the gradual dismantling after 1790 of the property qualifications that, in colonial America as in Britain, had limited suffrage. But those gains were surprisingly modest, in part because as the new century went on, the proportion of propertyless men increased. After 1830 the right to vote was increasingly limited by the imposition of a requirement to register. Whigs, and later Republicans, sought to deny the vote to Irish and later to other non-Protestant voters (German, Hungarian, Polish, and Italian Catholics and eastern European Jews). One reason why it seemed safe to American politicians in the decades after the Revolution to allow men with little or no property to vote was that then, but not later, they were seen as unthreatening.

Until the eve of the Civil War, except in an incipient way in New York City, in Philadelphia, and in the new Massachusetts textile towns, there was no such thing in America as the industrial proletariat that alarmed the owners of property in England. It was this, rather than any national commitment to extending suffrage, that accounts for the relatively high proportion of American men who could vote in the first decades after the Revolution. "Put simply," Professor Keyssar sums up, "to the extent that the working class was indeed enfranchised during the antebellum era (and one should not ignore that women, free blacks, and recent immigrants constituted a large portion of the working class), such enfranchisement was largely an unintended consequence of the changes in suffrage laws."[17]

Traditionally historians have cited, as one of the reasons for the exceptionalism of American political development, the absence of class politics. Keyssar does not agree. He concedes that "the history of suffrage in the United States is certainly distinctive in many ways. . . . [It was] the first country in the western world to significantly broaden its electorate by permanently lowering explicit economic barriers to political participation." However, he makes the point that the democratization of politics in the United States was a good deal less exceptional than has usually been assumed, both in America and elsewhere. "Indeed, almost all of the forces and factors that shaped the history of the right to vote in the United States were present in other nations." In America, as elsewhere, class interests and class tensions restricted the suffrage, while war tended to favor its expansion. "The American story, contrary to popular legend," Keyssar sums up, "was not a unique amalgam of the frontier, the democratic spirit, and egalitarian principles; it was not an exceptional example of democratic destiny and idealism."[18]

The proposition that in the United States politics developed free from the rancor of class conflict is dear to the hearts of exceptionalists. The sociologist Seymour Martin Lipset interpreted American exceptionalism almost wholly in those terms. In his second book on the subject, written with Gary Marks, he observes that "for radicals, 'American exceptionalism' meant a specific question: Why did the United States, alone among industrial societies, lack a significant socialist movement or labor party?"[19]

He concedes that the Great Depression "Europeanized American politics and American labor organizations." Lipset and Marks conclude, cautiously, that either the political gap between the United States and other western democracies will narrow or "the seemingly universal shift to support for capitalism and the free market may be of short duration." Lipset and Marks cite H. G. Wells and many other observers writing in the early twentieth century to the effect that the United States developed without an aristocracy or a "subservient" peasant class, and it is clearly true that the absence of an aristocracy with privileges guaranteed by law explains why there is no "Tory" or traditionalist conservative party in America. The rural poor in the United States were certainly not "subservient," but their resentment of and struggles against economic privilege provide one of the main themes of nineteenth-century American politics, up to and beyond the silver politics of the populists.

Lipset's view, though widely held, goes too far. European observers of the United States may have been too ready to mistake what were really self-congratulatory or aspirational accounts for literal description of American realities. They may also have seen American attitudes as reinforcing their own struggles for equality in their own countries. But the best recent historical research concludes that it was far from the case that class conflicts played no part in American democracy. It is true that in the late nineteenth and early twentieth century, when various versions of socialism were influential in Europe, explicitly socialist parties in America were less successful than in, for example, Germany, where the Sozialdemokratische Partei Deutschlands, the social democratic party, was powerful in parliament and in civil society. But that does not mean that working-class politics were absent from the political scene in America between 1865 and 1920, or indeed earlier.

Between the Revolution and the Civil War, working-class movements were strong in America, and the idea that politics was the arena for a contrast between the interests of the Few and the needs of the Many was almost as endemic in America as in Europe.

A handful of examples make the point. There were only half a dozen cities in antebellum America with a substantial concentration of working people: Boston, New York, Philadelphia, Baltimore, Charleston, and New Orleans, then after the war St. Louis, Cincinnati, and Chicago. The two cities of the Deep South were different, if only because the presence of numbers of free and unfree black workers created what was known as "master race democracy"; white workers saw themselves as sufficiently identified with the maintenance of the slave system that they were less ready to struggle against the power of the rich.

Radical artisans in Boston, Baltimore, New York, and Philadelphia, however, had played their part in the Revolution itself. By the 1820s and 1830s, in a time of economic depression, working-class movements like William Heighton's Mechanics' Union of Trade Associations and the Working Men's Party—the "Workies"—led by Thomas Skidmore and George Henry Evans in New York, were forces to be reckoned with. During the bank crisis of 1833 the Massachusetts Whig Edward Everett told a British banker, "The present contest is nothing less than a war of Numbers against Property."[20]

Two years later William Seward, later Lincoln's secretary of state, complained that it was utterly impossible to defeat Martin Van Buren. "The people are for him. Not so much for him as for the principle they suppose he represents. That principle is Democracy. . . . It is with them, the poor against the rich; and it is not to be disguised that, since the last election, the array of parties has very strongly taken that character."[21]

To simplify some rather complicated political cross-currents, Jacksonian democracy was an alliance between southern and western farmers and the working men of the East. If the agrarian element in this coalition was predominant, it was because before the Civil War the United States was a primarily agrarian society: in 1860 half of all Americans still lived on farms. That does not mean that there was no element of class conflict in the politics of rural America. Even before the Revolution the farmers of the western counties, from the Green Mountain Boys of what became Vermont to the Regulators of both Carolinas, resented, resisted, and sometimes rebelled against the men in silk stockings in Boston, New York, and Philadelphia who held their mortgages and other debts.

The economic issues of the young republic, from the two Banks of the United States to the tariff, set class against class in a way that is now deemed to be un-American. Nor did rural resentment and rebellion end with the ratification of the Constitution. In every state that stretched west to the Appalachians—in the Carolinas and Virginia, in Pennsylvania, New York, and Massachusetts—agrarian class conflicts erupted. In 1786 Daniel Shays led a mob of farmer debtors against the courthouses in two counties in western Massachusetts. In 1795 President Washington had to send fifteen thousand militiamen to put down the Whiskey Rebellion in western Pennsylvania. From 1839 to 1860 the Hudson Valley, even as it was being glorified by great American painters like Albert Bierstadt, was the arena of constant antirent rioting against the vast feudal estates of the van Rensselaers and their fellow patroons.[22]

Even in coastal Rhode Island in 1842, Thomas Wilson Dorr led a private army with two cannons against the Providence arsenal. He had been elected governor under a "People's Constitution" in protest against the state's lawful constitution, which dated back to 1663 and withheld the franchise from more than half the adult white male population. Dorr was found guilty of treason and sentenced to solitary confinement at hard labor for life. He was released after a year, and in general rebels in early-nineteenth-century America were treated with more mercy than in Europe. But the Dorr War ended in defeat. For a little longer the Irish immigrants who were pouring into Rhode Island's textile industry remained disenfranchised.[23]

The Dorr War was an isolated event, an unusual example in early-nineteenth-century America of a landed ruling elite stubbornly defying all moves in the direction of democracy. In general the tide did flow steadily in the direction of greater democracy, at least in terms of the right to vote. And while in Massachusetts, New York, and Pennsylvania the city gentry of bankers, merchants, and lawyers continued to be over-represented in the personnel of American politics, still, as the century went on, that aspect of the nation's life, too, was progressively democratized. Even so, the cherished traditional view, that in democratic America, in contrast with corrupt and reactionary Europe, class conflicts had no place in politics, simply does not hold water. Looking not just at the antebellum period but at the whole sweep of American history from 1790 to 1920, Professor Sean Wilentz of Princeton, the leading authority, has demonstrated to this reader's satisfaction, at least, that contrary to the exceptionalist thesis, there has been a "history of class consciousness in the United States comparable to that of working-class movements in Britain and on the Continent."[24]

Thomas Jefferson wanted to be remembered after his death for the Virginia Bill for Religious Freedom, the Declaration of Independence, and the foundation of the University of Virginia. But in his lifetime he was inclined to rate the Bill for the More General Diffusion of Knowledge as equally important. Washington, Adams, Madison all agreed that a republican people, if they were to remain free from the evils of monarchy and aristocracy, must be educated. Jefferson even specified what he thought a republican people ought to be taught. He distinguished between the laboring and the learned classes. For those who would do the republic's work, it would be enough "to give every citizen the information he needs for the transaction of his own business," to know his rights, and to play his part as a voter. Such a citizen would need to study only reading, writing, and arithmetic, along with "mensuration" (surveying), geography, and history.

For the "statesmen, legislators and judges, on whom public prosperity and individual happiness" would depend, however—or in other words for a group already destined in early life to be a political class, the planter aristocracy to which he belonged by birth—Jefferson prescribed a more imposing curriculum, starting with no fewer than eight ancient and modern languages, including Hebrew and Anglo-Saxon, theoretical and practical mathematics, an exhaustive array of the natural sciences, together with law, political economy, and "ideology," in which he included grammar, ethics, rhetoric, literature, and the fine arts. President Kennedy once quipped to a dinner of Nobel laureates at the White House that no greater array of human talent had been gathered there since Thomas Jefferson last breakfasted there alone. Jefferson seems to have wanted the public men of the young republic to be educated to his own superhuman standard. "No theme was so universally articulated during the early years of the Republic," wrote one of the leading historians of American education, "as the need of a self-governing people for universal education."[25]

Yet it has to be said that though the ideal of universal education—at least for white, Protestant males in the common, public school—was widely held between the Revolution and the Civil War, it was then still an aspiration, not an accomplished reality. There had been public schools, some of them free, since the earliest days, especially in Massachusetts and Connecticut. After the Revolution there was a powerful movement for "common schools," on the grounds that the citizens, or at least the male citizens, of a free republic ought to share an education. The Northwest Ordinance of 1787, which marked out the plan on which the westward expansion of the nation should developed, proclaimed that "religion, morality and knowledge being necessary to good government and the happiness of mankind, schools and the means of education shall forever be encouraged." Men like Noah Webster and Horace Mann labored mightily to bring about universal public education. Thousands of women devoted their lives to teaching. Yet the high hopes of the founding generation, and the faith of those who believed that common schools would breed an equal generation of republican citizens, were not fulfilled by midcentury.

Education was a state and in some respects a local responsibility. So inevitably provision was patchy. In some places, such as southern Michigan, where New England influence was strong, free public high schools prepared students for a free state university, though even there it took a celebrated court case in Kalamazoo in 1858 to establish that there should be a single, free system, paid for by state funds, for both students going on to higher education and those wanting only vocational education. In other states, especially in the South, there was far less agreement than in New England on the desirability of state provision, and consequently less provision.

Horace Mann became secretary of the new Massachusetts board of education in 1837 and threw himself into popularizing the idea of the common school and doing his energetic best to see his ideal made real. "The common school," he said, "is the greatest discovery ever made by man." Yet by the coming of the Civil War universal free public education was still no more than an aspiration in both North and South.

Although Jefferson, Mann, Webster, and many others saw education as the key to the creation of a republican society, there was not yet agreement, as perhaps there never can be complete agreement, about whom should be taught what and by whom. In general terms, most American schools accepted that they should teach a nondenominational but emphatically Protestant religion; that they should inculcate national and nationalist pride; and they should teach a mixture of practical skills and high culture. But when it came to the details, the common purpose was impeded by disagreements and divisions.

No one, for example, was more influential on educational ideas in the early years of the century than the Reverend Lyman Beecher, who moved from Boston to the Lane Seminary in Cincinnati; and no one could have been more exceptionalist. "If this nation is," he wrote, "in the providence of God, destined to lead the way in the moral and political emancipation of the world, it is time she understood her high calling, and were harnessed for the work."[26] Yet Beecher thunderously denounced the pernicious influence of the Roman Catholic Church, its priests, and their congregations, flooding in from Ireland and Germany to threaten America's lofty, Protestant, destiny. No one could have cared more for education or fought harder to establish educational institutions than Bishop, later Archbishop, John Hughes of New York. Yet Hughes was so appalled by the effect of what he saw as the Protestant influence of the common schools that he fought the Public School Society and delayed the foundation of a public school system in New York as long as he could.

Nor could it be said that the content of American education in this period was exceptional, in the sense in which the visionaries of the revolutionary generation had hoped it would be. There was, to be sure, a practical bent to some curricula, and an emphasis, derived from the religion of self-help taught by Benjamin Franklin and Horatio Alger, on "getting on." Yet until long past the middle of the nineteenth century, American education was essentially derived from European models, imitative of European curricula, and recognizably similar to education in contemporary Europe. John D. Pierce, for example, the first superintendent of public instruction in Michigan, and one of the architects of that state's progressive public education system, admitted that he had drawn the "fundamental principles" of his Michigan's system from the Prussian model. Even Noah Webster, whose heroic labors were inspired by the belief that "as an independent nation our honor requires us to have a system of our own, in language as well as in government," relied heavily on English models: "the very essence of his educational outlook rested on contemporary British sources."[27]

The fact is that the ferment of enthusiasm for education in early-nineteenth-century America was not exceptional but swept across the world on both sides of the Atlantic as a consequence of the Enlightenment and both the American and French revolutions. In Europe there had been schools, including schools open to poor people, for centuries, and free schools spread in many countries in the eighteenth century. Scotland had had public schools, partially subsidized with public money, since the sixteenth century, as well as a developed university system that had contributed substantially to the Enlightenment. By 1872 Scotland had a universal system of free primary schools. The situation in England was more chaotic, with a variety of different schools, some Episcopalian and some run by "Dissenters," many of them charitable foundations. Universal elementary education was made mandatory in England in the 1870s, though it was not wholly free until 1890. The public school systems in France and in Prussia, which by the nineteenth century was by far the largest of the German states, dated back to the Napoleonic period, after the French Revolution had destroyed the Catholic Church's monopoly of educational institutions. In 1833 the "Guizot law" provided that every commune in France with more than five hundred people should provide free education for boys, extended three years later to girls.[28]

Napoleon was an authoritarian and a dictator, but he too, like his American contemporaries, "wanted the schools to train the creators of a new type of society." He laid the foundations for a French state-run educational system, with lycées (elite secular secondary schools) in every major city and collèges in smaller towns. He did not so much destroy Catholic education as fit it into his state system. He created a national corps of educators, from the humblest village schoolteacher to the illustrious professor. His system, like that of the more enlightened American states at the time, was capped by a reformed university, and by the then unique engineering school, the Polytechnique. Napoleon was certainly no believer in freedom of thought. His system was centralized and statist, though it was also antiaristocratic and open to talent. His reforms ushered in a period of great achievement in theoretical and applied science and in the social sciences in France.

The Swiss educational reformer Johann Heinrich Pestalozzi was concerned with ordinary children, not only the children of the rich or cultivated. He taught that the poor man's child needed better instruction than the rich man's, not worse. His ideas were adopted by the brilliant generation of young Prussian officials and intellectuals—among them

Immanuel Kant's pupil the nationalist Johann Gottlieb Fichte; the philosopher Georg Wilhelm Friedrich Hegel; the government minister Freiherr Karl vom Stein, and the Humboldt brothers, Wilhelm and Alexander—who responded to Napoleon's defeat of Prussia by determining to reform both Prussian government and society. They saw education as the key tool for their purpose.[29] Martin Luther had already called for universal free education, and by the eighteenth century the kingdom of Prussia had universal free primary education in the eight-year *Volksschule.* During and after the Napoleonic wars (1810–1815) the Prussian reformers created an impressive national educational system based on the *Abitur,* the qualification for higher education. German higher education was later to have the decisive influence in creating the great American research universities through the influence of men like Daniel Coit Gilman of Johns Hopkins and Charles W. Eliot of Harvard. They returned from studying at German universities in the mid-nineteenth century determined to introduce the German graduate school system built around the research seminar and the Ph.D.

Education, in short, is one of many fields in which American exceptionalism has been nourished by ignoring both the interdependence between America and Europe and the fact that Europe, in the course of the nineteenth century, was changing as fast, if not in precisely the same ways, as the United States. "America's noble experiment—universal education for all citizens—" proclaimed the Web site for a PBS series about education, "is a cornerstone of our democracy." The implication is that universal education was an American ideal alone. But in fact, throughout the nineteenth century, European nations, too, understood the value of education and the need for it. They had different obstacles to overcome, but in Germany and Scandinavia, in France and England and Scotland, pioneers were expanding educational opportunity in much the same spirit as in America, and in some cases earlier.

In its July–August issue in 1845 the *United States Magazine and Democratic Review* of New York published an anonymous article calling boldly for "opposition to the annexation of Texas to cease." Historians argue whether its author was the paper's editor, John O'Sullivan, one of the leaders of the Young America group of aggressive nationalists and expansionists, or his editorial writer, the flamboyant Jane Eliza McManus Storm, better known by the nom de plume "Storms," once allegedly the mistress of the aged Aaron Burr, and one of the first women political writers in America. The article became famous because of a single phrase. It denounced England for standing in the way of "our manifest destiny to overspread the continent allotted by Providence for the free development of our yearly multiplying millions."[30]

The availability of free land, as we have seen, was a major factor in the relatively open and equal society of early-nineteenth-century America. You do not have to be an uncritical disciple of Frederick Jackson Turner to see that the frontier was one of the things that differentiated the United States from the old societies of Europe, where, since the *Drang nach Osten* (the "drive to the East") of the German Middle Ages and the thirteenth-century "assarting" of the woodland, the frontier had been overseas. But the collective American memory has underplayed the extent to which the westward expansion took place as a result of events in European history, and of the nimbleness with which American statesmen took advantage of shifting advantage in European power struggles to offer opportunities to acquire territory.

The United States acquired the land between the crest of the Appalachian Mountains and the Mississippi, then almost uninhabited by Americans, as a result of the way Franklin, John Jay, and John Adams were able to exploit the differences between the European diplomats they negotiated with in 1782.[31] The nation added the vast territories of the Mississippi and Missouri basins as a result of Napoleon's decision to sell "Louisiana"—in effect the entire catchments area of the Mississippi and its tributaries, including the mighty Missouri—almost immediately after he had acquired it from Spain. (Indeed it is questionable whether he actually had title to these lands.) Napoleon's decision to sell was taken for short-term reasons, largely as a result of the disastrous French expedition to put down the slave rebellion in Saint-Domingue, but also with wider calculations in his mind about his priorities in the great war France was fighting against most of the rest of Europe.

In the 1820s American settlers could push the planting of short-staple cotton into "Florida," which for the purpose then included the rich soils of the Alabama Black Belt and the Mississippi Delta, as a result of the Adams-Onís treaty with Spain; they had already been moving into Spanish territory for a generation by then, often with the approval of Spanish governors who liked the trade they brought and in any case, with their homeland prostrated by the Napoleonic wars, could not do much about them if they wanted to.

The weak Mexican republic whose territories the United States annexed after the Mexican War of 1846 to 1848 by the treaty of Guadalupe Hidalgo was itself made possible by the Mexican revolution against Spain at a time when Spain was conquered by Napoleon's armies. And the "manifest destiny" to "overspread" the North American continent from the Atlantic to the Pacific was finally fulfilled by diplomatic negotiation with Britain, which gave the Oregon Territory to the United States but left British Columbia to Canada. American expansion was driven by the animal spirits of the frontier and by the rapid American population growth. But it was also a product of events in Europe.

Americans have always remembered Washington's warning, in his farewell address, against "entangling alliances." (Washington did not in fact use that phrase. He said it was America's true policy "to steer clear of permanent alliances"; he added that we may "safely trust to temporary alliances for extraordinary emergencies.") They have not always understood the context of that speech, or what Washington, and Alexander Hamilton, who worked on the speech with the president, were really saying. Even such trusted historians as Henry Steele Commager and Samuel Eliot Morison interpreted the farewell address as meaning that "a new power in the West considered herself outside the European system."[32]

On the contrary, Washington and Hamilton were positioning the United States for advantage within that system. They were not saying that the United States should never entangle itself with those corrupt Europeans. They were taking a stand in what was the burning political question of the time: whether the United States should side with Britain, from whom they had just become independent after a cruel and destructive war, or with France, which had been their ally when it was an absolute monarchy, but had now been transformed by revolution, terror, and the emerging militarism that was replacing the original purity of the revolution's aims.[33]

In context, Washington was saying that the United States should not for the present side with France, but was also warning that American interests might change with changing circumstances. This was not simply a speech about "foreign policy," seen as a detached and marginal concern for the nation. At one level, it was about hard politics: it was intended to influence the forthcoming presidential election. It was also about sectional metapolitics, because it was a warning that France still had ambitions on the North American continent and might try to detach the West and dismember the Union. At the deepest level, it was about ideology. Washington and Hamilton were warning the nation against what they saw as the dangerous naïveté of Jefferson and those Republicans who were sentimentally attached to the ideals of revolutionary France, ideals that were already being abandoned.

From the very start, in other words, American politics were intertwined with those of Europe, just as the American economy, heavily dependent on foreign trade, was interconnected with the booming industrial revolution in England and the fortunes of the revolutionary and Napoleonic wars. Foreign relations were essential markers for the parties as they developed in the new republic. Republicans favored revolutionary France, though the French often proved difficult allies. England, too, could be an awkward ally when the Royal Navy "pressed" American sailors and the Orders in Council closed European markets to American merchants, but Federalists favored good relations with England, principally for commercial reasons but also because, as England became the organizer of the great coalition against Napoleon, it was ideologically the champion of traditional values, including those of religion and of the international balance of power. Blood, too, was thicker than water. As Alexander Hamilton said, "We think in English, and have a similarity of prejudices and of predilections."[34]

From the outbreak of the French Revolution, the young republic had constantly to confront the possibility of war with one or another of the two great powers, England and France, who had been disputing the hegemony of the world since the beginning of the eighteenth century. Conflict between England and France had led to the taxation that had provoked the American Revolution. It had motivated French support for the Revolution. Before the farewell address was two years old, the United

States was entangled in a "quasi-war" with France; and in 1812 it was engaged in actual war with England.

The declaration of the Monroe Doctrine, too, has traditionally been seen in the United States as a bold warning from republican America to the monarchies of Europe to keep their hands off the New World, and so from one point of view it was. From another aspect, however, it is yet another example of the way America was caught up in the web of European conflicts and alliances. In 1808, just five years after selling off Louisiana to Jefferson, Napoleon invaded Spain. For the duration of the French occupation, bitterly contested by Spanish nationalists and by Wellington's Peninsular Army, Spain's vast territories in the Americas were in effect free from Spanish rule. The small Creole elites who dominated millions of Indios and hundreds of thousands of slaves from Mexico to the River Plate took advantage of events in Spain to make themselves independent. Where in 1812 there were only two independent republics in the whole of North and South America, the United States and Haiti, by 1820 seven Latin republics had proclaimed their independence.

After the defeat of Napoleon, Europe was ruled by a coalition of conservative monarchies—Russia, Prussia, Austria, and France under its restored king—which called itself the Holy Alliance. Britain, with its constitutional monarchy, its liberal public philosophy, and its very different economic interests, stood aside from this conservative grouping. But in 1823 the French king invaded Spain. He announced that he proposed to rescue his royal brother, Ferdinand VII, from the constitution imposed on him by the liberals. But immediately strong rumors began to circulate that he intended to restore the Spanish monarchy's authority over the South American republics.

It was at this point that George Canning, the British foreign secretary, made an astonishing suggestion to the American minister in London, Richard Rush. British foreign secretaries had not been in the habit of making friendly overtures to American ministers. But now, suddenly, in August 1823, Canning asked whether the United States was ready to join with Britain in warning France against intervening in South America. Rush replied, skillfully, that the United States would join in this démarche—provided that Britain was willing to recognize the threatened republics. This, as Rush had correctly surmised, a British Tory government, albeit a liberal Tory one, would not be ready to do.

When Rush's account of this exchange reached Washington, John Quincy Adams was suspicious. His information from Paris was that the French did not plan to send a force to the Caribbean, and if they did, Adams knew that the British Royal Navy could prevent it. Canning had said, in a famous phrase, that he wanted to "bring the New World into being to redress the balance of the Old." Adams fastened on the language of Canning's note, in which he suggested that both Britain and the United States should pledge that they would not acquire previously Spanish territory in the Americas. He suspected that what Canning wanted to achieve was to prevent the United States from acquiring either Texas or Cuba. (There were rumors that Cuba might become independent, and many Americans, then and long afterward, wanted to annex Cuba to the United States. John Quincy Adams himself had hinted broadly that within half a century the annexation of Cuba would be "indispensable to the continuance and integrity of the Union itself," and for good measure he threw in Puerto Rico as another suitable case for annexation. He openly warned that the United States could and would prevent Britain from annexing Cuba, "if necessary, by force.")

Adams persuaded Monroe to send a dusty answer to Canning in the shape of the passages about foreign relations in Monroe's annual message to Congress in December 1823, and it was Adams who drafted the language of what came to be called the Monroe Doctrine. "The political system of the allied powers," ran the key passage, "is essentially different in this respect from that of America."

> This difference proceeds from that which exists in their respective Governments. And to the defense of our own, which has been achieved by the loss of so much blood and treasure, and matured by the wisdom of their most enlightened citizens, and under which we have enjoyed unexampled felicity, this whole nation is devoted. We owe it, therefore, to candor, and to the amicable relations existing between the United States and those powers to declare that we should consider any attempt on their part to extend their system to any por-

> tion of this hemisphere as dangerous to our peace and safety. With the existing colonies or dependencies of any European power, we have not interfered and shall not interfere. But with the governments which have declared their independence and maintained it, and whose independence we have, on great consideration and on just principles, acknowledged, we could not view any interposition for the purpose of oppressing them, or controlling in any other manner their destiny, by any European power in any other light than as the manifestation of an unfriendly disposition toward the United States.[35]

The background to Canning's approach was, however, rather different from Adams's suspicions. Whether or not there were any in Britain who seriously contemplated acquiring Cuba as a British colony, the economies of Britain and the United States were already intimately connected at that period through the importance to both of them of trade, and especially of the cotton trade. American settlers were pouring into the lower Mississippi Valley. Eli Whitney's invention in 1793 of the "gin" made it possible to mill the short-staple cotton that would grow in these newly acquired lands. Cotton provided the staple crop needed to assure the prosperity of these new settlements. By the 1820s sixty million pounds of cotton a year was being shipped to Europe. It was cotton that was transforming the United States and Britain—in spite of the revolutionary memories and republican suspicions of the likes of J. Q. Adams—from enemies into business partners. By 1820, thanks to cotton, Britain was the United States' biggest customer, and the United States was Britain's biggest customer too. By 1830 raw cotton made up 50 percent of American exports, and manufactured cotton made up 48 percent of Britain's exports to the rest of the world. "By means of cotton," a distinguished British historian wrote, "the United States and Britain were so closely bound together that it is appropriate to speak not of two separate economies but of two sectors, one 'colonial,' the other 'metropolitan' of a single Atlantic economy."[36]

Canning, it is reasonable to assume, was not primarily interested in slipping in a text that might or might not inhibit a future American annexation of Cuba. He wanted to improve diplomatic relations between two countries that, however testy their previous relations, were now economically so powerfully dependent on one another. American fears of European and especially British machinations in the second quarter of the nineteenth century were linked to the powerful thrust of settlement and to the belief, as widely held among frontier settlers as it was among their representatives in Washington, that it was, indeed, the "manifest destiny" of Anglo-Americans to "overspread" the continent. Two foreign powers, at least, seemed to stand in the way of that hunger for land and resources.[37] One was Britain, the old enemy. Everywhere, in Canada, in the Oregon Territory, in Texas, and in the Caribbean, Americans saw, or thought they saw, the long arm of British interference.

The other was Mexico, heir since Mexican independence in the second decade of the century to the sparsely settled Spanish possessions up the Pacific Coast as far as San Francisco Bay and into the arid provinces of what is now the American Southwest. Both powers became involved in the question of Texas. Andrew Jackson, unchanging and unforgiving in his resentment and suspicion of Britain, told Francis Blair in 1844 that Texas was "the important key to our future safety." He believed that the British would recruit armies of Indians and escaped slaves and invade the American West from Texas as the prelude to a British reconquest of the United States. "Take and lock the door," Old Hickory preached, "against all danger of foreign influence."

Jackson's fears were the paranoid imaginings of an old man who, as little more than a child, had been badly treated by British soldiers and, as a mature soldier, had cemented his reputation by defeating the redcoats at New Orleans. But it was true that the British government encouraged the settlement of Texas as an independent, slave-free republic. After the Texas revolution of 1836 reintroduced slavery, the British prime minister, Lord Aberdeen, told Parliament that "every effort" would be made by the British government to end slavery in Texas. It is possible, though it cannot be proved, that it was in Canning's mind that an independent Texas would, by restricting American growth, serve Britain's long-term interest.

In the same treaty in which he secured east Florida for the United States, John Quincy Adams renounced all claims to Texas. (West Florida had already been annexed.) In the 1820s the Mexican republic encouraged Anglo settlers in Texas, though the Mexican foreign secretary, Lucas Alamán, warned presciently that the American colonists, in collusion with the federal government in Washington, would prove the cuckoo in the nest, and push the fragile Mexican chicks out.[38]

So in 1830 the Mexican government attempted, without success, to ban Anglo immigration into the province of "Tejas." The only result was the Texas revolution of 1835, which set up an independent republic of Texas. By the 1840s John C. Calhoun, as secretary of state in the Tyler administration, openly sought the annexation of Texas in order to protect southern slavery. In 1845 James K. Polk became president of the United States as a direct result of his advocacy of taking Texas. He was chosen by the Democrats in place of Martin Van Buren, previously assumed to be the Democratic candidate, because southerners could not accept Van Buren's opposition to slavery. Polk came to the White House committed to annexation, and by the year following his inauguration, as a result of some deft manipulations, he delivered the successful war against Mexico.[39]

The partisans of "manifest destiny," led by John O'Sullivan and his *Democratic Review*, wanted to annex the whole of Mexico, and O'Sullivan's ally, Moses Yale Beach, owner of the *New York Sun*, went to Mexico, accompanied by Jane Eliza Storm, to negotiate the annexation of "all Mexico." Beach also sought to negotiate the right to dig an interoceanic canal across the isthmus of Tehuantepec in southern Mexico, thus anticipating the Panama Canal by more than half a century. In the end, Polk's emissary Nicholas Trist, married to a granddaughter of Thomas Jefferson, negotiated the treaty of Guadalupe Hidalgo, which delivered almost as much territory to the United States as Jefferson's purchase of Louisiana.

The United States annexed only one-third of Mexico's territory. The principal reason for this comparative moderation was not any inhibition about annexing the territory of foreign states but the reluctance of many in Washington, not least of Calhoun, to burden the United States with eight million inhabitants, many of them of mixed or nonwhite blood. "I protest against the incorporation of such a people," said Calhoun. "Ours is the government of the white man."[40]

The United States had fulfilled its manifest destiny. It had acquired in these possessions an empire by any standards, rich with Texas land,

California gold, and Nevada silver, the orchards and farms and ranches of California, Arizona, and New Mexico, all taken at gunpoint from Mexico. But the Manifest Destiny movement was not only about Mexico. It was also about the remaining British territories in North America. Canada had recently been reconstituted as an independent dominion of the British Crown by the reforms introduced by the great Governor-General Lord Durham, who saw that if the colonies were given as much freedom to govern themselves as the people of Great Britain, they would become more loyal instead of less so. Britain also had a claim to the virtually unoccupied Oregon Territory.

The partisans of Young America called for the border between the United States and the British Empire to be pushed northward. "Fifty-four forty or fight!" was their slogan, invoking a line of latitude level with the southernmost tip of Russian Alaska. Michigan alone, said one of that state's representatives in Congress, could take Canada in ninety days. It was generally assumed that Canadians were impatient to embrace liberty by becoming citizens of the United States. Indeed, one New York newspaper predicted that Canadians would soon "become ashamed of their state of slavery, and casting off the yoke of England, set up for themselves."

In the end Canada was spared the blessings of this liberty. Even so the United States had acquired another vast swath of land, much of it at least potentially fertile once irrigated, and rich in many minerals. The continental United States, between the Rio Grande and the forty-ninth parallel of latitude, was now complete. But that was not the end of the American appetite for land. Abraham Lincoln's secretary of state, William H. Seward, was a convinced expansionist. In a speech during the 1860 campaign, he revealed that he had dreamed of a United States stretching from the Canadian north to the tropics, with its capital on the site of the city of Mexico. In 1867 he had the gratification of having Alaska all but thrown at him by the czar of all the Russias, for whom it was a territory too far.

That was the northern version of Manifest Destiny. Before the Civil War there was a southern version as well. Southern statesmen dreamed of balancing the expansion of Free Soil states by creating a great slave empire in the Caribbean. Southern leaders supported Narciso López's ill-fated attempt to raise a rebellion against Spain in Cuba, and after his execution a governor of Mississippi, John Quitman, repeatedly tried to annex Cuba by filibustering expeditions. William L. Cazneau and his wife, the former Jane Eliza McManus Storm, tried to draw the Dominican Republic into the slave empire. William Walker was executed in Honduras in 1860 as a result of repeated attempts to extend American rule in several of the Central American republics. The mission to expand the "empire of liberty" had become strangely confused, in the minds of at least some powerful American leaders, with the mission to expand the empire of slavery.

To summarize my argument so far: The period between the American Revolution and the Civil War was the time when the United States was most clearly exceptional. Voting, the ownership of land, and educational and economic opportunity were far more widely available than in even the most successful European societies, though in the case of education at least not perhaps by as wide a margin as Americans have traditionally been taught. To be sure, those successes, immensely valuable for millions of individuals and families as they arrived in America and set about making their way in a new society, owed much to circumstances and events that had little to do with the superiority or otherwise of American institutions or ideology. Above all, the expansion of nineteenth-century America was due to the gigantic accretions of territory and resources taken from European powers and from the Native American tribes.

Even more exceptional was the fact that a new and dynamic republic was coming into existence under the banner of a political ideology that was genuinely new in its adherence to the principle of government by the consent of the governed. This was seen by Americans as an ideology of liberty.

To be sure, this ideology involved a certain amount of deception and self-deception. As Dr. Johnson had pointed out so pungently before the American Revolution, the empire of liberty depended to a substantial extent on the literal and brutal deprivation of liberty for millions of African Americans: "How is it," Johnson asked, "that we hear the loudest yelps for liberty among the drivers of negroes?"[41]

In ethical or philosophical terms, the manifest destiny of white Protestant Americans to "overspread" a continent that was far from empty is not by modern standards so easily distinguished from the contemporary expansion of czarist Russia from the steppes above the Black Sea across the Caucasus, Central Asia, and Siberia to the Bering Strait. It is even morally comparable to the nineteenth-century conquests of Britain and France in Asia and Africa, which were also motivated in part by a sense of mission to bring Christianity and civilization to peoples seen by nineteenth-century white men as benighted, as well as by the same hunger for land and resources that drove Americans westward.

Americans found it easy to believe that what they were building was an "empire of liberty," a far, far better thing than what the Europeans were up to, and in some specific, measurable respects they surely were. Yet the expansion of the frontier was driven by self-interest as much as, or more than, by the dream of liberty.

In short, even in this most genuinely exceptional age, the American experience was less exceptional than patriotic history has maintained. The American Revolution was occasioned by European ideas and by events in the history of Europe, from the seventeenth-century English Revolution by way of the rivalry of Britain and France and the European Enlightenment in the eighteenth. The American economy was tightly tied to the European and in particular to the British economy. Even the cause of liberty was no American monopoly. This was an age when European political struggles—in France and Germany in 1848, in Poland and Ireland throughout the period, and from Greece in the 1820s and Spain in the 1830s through Italy in the age of Garibaldi—were also explicitly about liberty.

No doubt that goal was harder to achieve in Europe, where powerful and ruthless vested interests opposed its attainment, than in land cleared of its native inhabitants. But even from 1776 to 1862, America was comparatively, not absolutely, exceptional.

T•H•R•E•E

From Civil War to Cold War

Political democracy evolves most quickly during the initial
stages of setting up a new community.
Stanley Elkins and Eric McKitrick

After the defeat of the Confederacy, the population of the recreated Union was slightly more than 30 million, including the recently freed slaves and the defeated Confederates. By 1917 it was 103 million. At the beginning of this period, in other words, the United States was a distracted, largely agricultural nation, its population no greater than that of Britain or France, and dispersed over vast distances with imperfect communications. By the date of the United States' entry into World War I, it had a larger population than any European power except Russia, and those people had been forged together into an increasingly unified modern nation.

Already, by the time of the centennial, a dramatic process of industrialization and urbanization, triggered by the demand of the war itself, had begun to transform the nation, and that transformation continued with irresistible momentum into and throughout the twentieth century. One constant was the conviction of most Americans that their nation was exceptional, in its moral purpose and destiny as much as in its power and success.

Throughout the last third of the nineteenth century settlers puffed westward in railroad cars where once they had plodded in Conestoga wagons. Their plows broke the plains, while spindles clattered and forges roared in the new industries from Massachusetts to Missouri. But in reality, this diverse, dynamic society, in spite of its explosive pace of development, in spite of its conviction of its own special providence, did not on the whole develop in the direction of being more "exceptional." On the contrary, one of the most striking characteristics of late-nineteenth- and early-twentieth-century America was the degree to which it was becoming less different from Europe. The reason was simple. The United States was feeling the impact of essentially the same forces that were also transforming Europe and eventually large tracts of the world: the forces of steam, steel, and money, of intellectual skepticism and social discontent.

"American democracy," wrote Frederick Jackson Turner, "is fundamentally the outcome of the experiences of the American people in dealing with the West."[1] The most distinctive fact of Western society, Turner believed, "was the freedom of the individual to rise under conditions of social mobility, and whose ambition was the liberty and well-being of the masses." The same ambition, though Turner did not seem to be aware of it, was transforming Europe, not to mention other parts of the world, such as Australia, where Europeans had also settled. Turner conceded that "the democracy of the newer West is deeply affected by the ideals" of a million Germans and more than a million Scandinavians out of the seven million inhabitants of the Middle West at the end of the nineteenth century. Yet he seems not to have noticed the contradiction between that observation and his quotation of the poet James Russell Lowell:

> Nothing of Europe here,
> Or, then, of Europe fronting mornward still,
> Ere any names of Serf and Peer
> Could Nature's equal scheme deface
> . . . .
> New birth of our new soil, the first American.

In the same breath, so to speak, he quoted—of all writers—Rudyard Kipling, and—of all his poems—"Song of the English":

On the sand-drift—on the veldt-side—in the fern-scrub we lay
That our sons might follow after by the bones on the way.
Follow after—follow after! We have watered the root
And the bud has come to blossom that ripens for fruit!

Explicitly, the great prophet of frontier democracy was quoting the great poet of British empire to equate the adventure of the American frontiersman with the English imperial settlers in the sandy heart of Australia, the South African veldt and the fern-covered hills of New Zealand.

The point should not be exaggerated, but in many ways the bustling, expanding capitalist America of the last third of the nineteenth century was going through very similar experiences to those of the bustling, expanding capitalist Europe that was invading and invigorating the entire world at the same period. On both sides of the Atlantic, industry, the spread of railroads and steamships, and the application of science and technology were transforming society, raising living standards, but at the same time painfully increasing inequality. Both in America and in Europe cities were growing bigger than had ever been seen before, and from Texas to the Ukraine farmers were in trouble.

This was the first age of globalization, and American and Canadian wheat, Australian beef and horses, South African gold and diamonds were finding world markets alongside textiles from Lancashire, Lille, and Massachusetts, German machinery and chemicals, British coal and steamships, and American oil, typewriters, safety razors, and sewing machines.

Not surprisingly, it was an age of bursting commercial optimism, in Britain and Germany as much as in America. But it was also a troubled age, in which traditional religious beliefs were challenged, especially for intellectuals, by textual analysis of the Bible, by the discoveries of geologists, and by the theory of evolution. In New York, just as in London and Paris, it was the age of classic liberalism, governed by a faith in progress and freedom. But under the stress of social tensions and conflicts, it was, both in Europe and America, more and more an age of skepticism and doubt.

Both Europeans and Americans were breaking out beyond their traditional boundaries in an age of exploration and settlement. The

Americans of the generation of Theodore Roosevelt, like their British, French, German, and Russian contemporaries, had few doubts about their right to expand or the superiority of the civilization they brought with them. The obvious difference was that where Europeans were settling in new lands in Africa, Asia, and the Pacific that lay beyond the borders of their nation-states, the United States had helped itself to so much land in the course of the nineteenth century, and so effectively cleared that land of its indigenous inhabitants, that until the very end of the century, Americans could settle in a frontier that was contained within their national borders. Many studies, however, have drawn parallels between the society of the American West and similar frontiers in Australia, Argentina, and Canada.[2]

Indeed, while this was the classic age of the frontier, that was not as exceptional as the followers of Frederick Jackson Turner would have us believe. All the major and some of the smaller European nations were expanding in similar ways in the later nineteenth century. Russian farmers were expanding eastward as Americans were going west. This was the time when British engineers were pushing the railways across the Argentinean pampas and the Canadian prairie, and dreaming of linking the Cape and Cairo by rail. Germans were planning to construct the Berlin-to-Baghdad railway. It was the age of the struggle for Africa and the competition for the trade of the Chinese treaty ports, in which American merchants competed as eagerly as any of their European counterparts. The Australian Gold Rush of the early 1850s mirrored the California boom of 1849, and the mining frontier of late-nineteenth-century Montana was more than matched by the fabulous wealth extracted from the South African Rand. It was also the age of the submarine cables, the Lloyd's stations, the steamer lines, and banking, shipping, and import-export agencies that were linking a whole world commercially.

No doubt to many Americans there is something shocking about comparing the conquest of the American West with European colonialism. But the impulses and the outcomes in the late nineteenth century were in truth not wholly dissimilar. If European colonialism often pillaged the resources and oppressed the peoples of colonial territories, in Canada, Australia, and New Zealand, emigration from Britain produced vigorous economies and vital democracies. If democracy was of slower growth in Latin America or the Indian subcontinent, there too eventually democratic institutions and the practice of democracy took root. At the same time, the American frontier was hardly the idyll of untroubled democratic freedom that Frederick Jackson Turner and his disciples portrayed.

In America, immigration on an unprecedented scale, impelled almost as much perhaps by the push of hard times and deprivation in Europe as by the pull of the American West, drove a prosperity that was as alluring as it was uneven, both over succeeding phases of boom and bust and as between individuals in what was no longer by any standards an exceptionally equal society. During that first rough half-century, from the end of the Civil War to the onset of World War I, the most striking fact in American life, and the salient question in American politics, was essentially the same as in Europe. It was what was known as the "social question," or rather the whole range of economic, social, and political problems posed by the impact of industrialization and urbanization in an era of virtually unregulated capitalism.

That story unrolled differently in Europe and in America, but it was essentially the same story. By the eve of the First World War it was hard—*pace* the Turner thesis—to insist on the exceptional nature of an American society uniquely egalitarian and democratic. However exciting the economic expansion of the American West, an expansion largely fueled by European investment and European markets as well as by European immigration, in that period the old continent and the New World developed in harness.

In the years on either side of the Civil War, millions of settlers did buy family farms and create in the Middle West, or transplant from New England, the characteristic American small town. But farther west, in the later nineteenth century, as in Australia, development was not so much a matter of family farms as on the one hand stock raising and the mining frontier, and on the other the rapid development of large, sophisticated cities. Denver, Seattle, and San Francisco were creations of a similar history to that of Sydney and Melbourne, Toronto and Vancouver.

In the late nineteenth century Europe and America were interdependent, as they had always been. They shared the experience of the first globalization. International shipping, trade, and migration were fed by new technologies, new institutions, and a confident, even arrogant, sense of new opportunities. That exciting time of capitalist enterprise and international cooperation, that first age of "globalization," was abruptly ended by the outbreak of World War I. That took most people by surprise. Few realized that the rulers of Germany, in some ways equal to the United States as the most modern state of the age, were so afraid of the future power of Russia that they were determined at all hazards to strike before Russia was too strong.

The war was the starting gun for a period, which lasted at least until the mid-1970s, when Europe and America were tied together by a chain reaction of shared disasters: war, revolutions, recession, dictators, war again, and the long struggle of the Cold War. In that period, in contrast to the late nineteenth century, the United States was indeed exceptional in that, where everyone else experienced impoverishment, hunger, destruction, and political and social disruption, Americans, almost alone, did well out of two world wars.

The United States did not enter the first war for two and a half years, and did not enter World War II for two years and a quarter. While large American forces fought in both wars, American casualties were relatively light. (In World War I the British Empire lost about 900,000 military dead, France nearly 1.4 million, Russia 1.8 million, and Germany more than 2 million, while the United States lost just 117,000. In World War II, the British Commonwealth as a whole, including large Australian, Canadian, and Indian forces, lost fewer than 600,000 military dead, and France, out of the war from 1940 to 1944, 212,000. Germany lost 5.5 million and the Soviet Union 10.7 million, just from 1941 to 1945. U.S. military dead were 417,000.)[3]

Europe, where the first war was principally, and the second largely, fought, was all but crippled, while the United States thrived. It took only a matter of months—from 1914 to 1916—for the war to have ruined the Austro-Hungarian, Russian, and Turkish empires. The downfall of the German empire took only a further two years. By the midpoint of the European war both Britain and France had become heavily dependent for war munitions, for food, and for any reasonable prospects of victory on American wheat, copper, machinery, and weapons, and therefore on American goodwill.

When the murder of the archduke Franz Ferdinand at Sarajevo touched off the war, America was the newest and in military (though not in naval) terms the weakest of the Great Powers. The resources, the vitality, and the skills of the American economy, and above all the fact that the United States stood aloof from the conflict until it could enter the war on its own terms, meant that America emerged from the war as its greatest and in reality its only beneficiary.

During the interwar period the United States at first continued to forge ahead industrially and economically. American preponderance in the 1920s was far greater than it would be in the later years of the twentieth century. To take a single, telling example, though the internal combustion engine had been developed in Germany, Detroit was by the end of the 1920s manufacturing about eight times as many automobiles a year as Britain, France, and Germany combined.[4] Almost overnight, by the end of the first war, New York had replaced London as the financial capital of the world. In the 1920s American loans enabled the recovery of Germany. The new technologies—automobiles, machinery of every kind, industrial chemistry, and the oil and gas industries, even the crucial technique of photography (which revolutionized every technique from cartography and artillery to surgery), radio, and film—were largely invented in Europe but commercially developed in the United States. After 1918 in mass production the United States had no real competition until the 1970s.

Between 1919 and 1939 the United States was exceptionally powerful, yet hardly exceptional in the moral dimension. By 1940 the United States was not only self-sufficient in energy, in agriculture, and in minerals, it was out in front on its own. The American economy was, however, sufficiently closely linked to a world financial system that when a middle-sized Austrian bank failed in 1929, the American economy all but collapsed with it. The United States, in spite of its titanic strength, had once again been hit by the same economic as well as political waves as Europe and the countries that lived by supplying both with raw materials. (Those countries, such as Australia and Argentina, were hit even harder than the industrialized countries in the 1930s.)

By the end of that decade it was plain that however passionate the wish of many Americans to be free from the maladies of the rest of the world, the United States would not be able to live in isolation from the miseries of what the poet W. H. Auden called a "low dishonest decade": mass unemployment, poverty, beggar-my-neighbor politics, and fascist brutality.[5] And in the New Deal, the American federal government had no alternative but to address the economic crisis by adopting what was understood to be a variant of European social democracy.

To revert to the beginning of this period, the American Civil War was indeed an exceptional event. It was the biggest and the most lethal war the world had yet seen. The armies deployed dwarfed even those assembled first by Napoleon and then by the posse of European powers assembled to arrest revolutionary France. It was the first great war in which armies were deployed by rail, the first in which innovative military technologies—new explosives, rifled gun barrels, ironclad warships—were used on so murderous a scale. It was even more an exceptional war in that it was fought not over territory or dynastic ambition or national pride, but over principle, or rather over two distinct though related principles: over whether the Union could endure "half-slave and half-free," and over the issue of human bondage itself.

At Gettysburg, Abraham Lincoln anointed the war in a speech that lives with the noblest passages in the English language. Those earlier masterpieces, from the King James Bible and *The Pilgrim's Progress*, coming from the seventeenth century, drew their power from religious belief.[6] Lincoln, as a man of the nineteenth century, was evoking the emotional power of what amounted to a political and nationalist religion. He ended with a political promise: "that this nation, under God, shall have a new birth of freedom—and that government of the people, by the people, for the people shall not perish from the earth." A year earlier he had told the Congress, in a speech that is even more at the heart of the exceptionalist canon, "In giving freedom to the slave, we assure freedom to the free—honorable alike in what we give, and what we preserve. We shall nobly save, or meanly lose, the last, best hope of earth." Ringing words in a noble cause, but what were those to think who had already "given freedom to the slave"?

In the war, triumphantly, but also in the puzzled, angry years of a failed Reconstruction, the United States did indeed live through a drama of high moral purpose that can meet some of the claims of exceptionalism. Yet what is most striking about the rest of the nineteenth century, and the early years of the twentieth, is precisely that the United States underwent essentially the same experiences as the rest of what is now called the "developed world." After the transactions that are euphemistically called the "redemption," meaning the reimposition—by southern politicians with northern complicity—of ruthless political and social control over southern blacks, the United States became in many respects a nation not dissimilar from the contemporary liberal, industrialized states of western and central Europe—on a bigger scale very like the new nations of overseas Europe such as Australia, Canada, Argentina, and Brazil. One difference from the European nations was that its colonial hinterland, supplier of raw materials produced by cheap labor, lay within its own frontiers.

Its politics, like those of Europe, revolved around the impact of industrialization, the belief in "progress," and the effort to reconcile the social cost of capitalist economic development with liberal aspirations to social justice. (Of course I refer to the nineteenth century liberalism of Gladstone or Cavour, rather than to the "liberalism" of modern usage, a euphemism for the socialist Left.) Where Tocqueville in the 1830s had found equality the most striking characteristic of America, fifty years later what was salient was the gross disparity between the wretched conditions of the immigrant slums of New York, Boston, and Chicago and the luxury and ostentation of Park Avenue, Saratoga, and Newport.

Once the Civil War was over, there was massive immigration, reaching a peak in the first decade of the twentieth century. Much of it was living proof of the interconnected character of the European and North American economies. The massive migration of European farmers, from the British Isles to the Ukraine, was a direct consequence of the import of cheap North American grain, exacerbated by the impact of the economic depression of 1873. Some of the new Americans went directly to the family farms of the Midwest. Most were not so fortunate. Many more crowded into the great cities, just as Europeans in the same decades were pouring from the countryside into London and Glasgow, Paris and Berlin, Vienna and Budapest, Moscow and St. Petersburg.

These were the peak years of industrialization, which was transforming Britain, France, and Germany in much the same way at the same time. The railroads—financed, like the West generally, largely with British and European capital and built largely with Irish and other immigrant labor—needed coal, steel rails, machinery. So at last the United States, surrounded by a protective tariff, acquired an industrial work force, a proletariat, of the kind Americans had been proud to believe existed only in the wicked Old World. No doubt in the future, people hoped, American workers would have greater opportunities to progress. It was that hope, after all, that had motivated the immigrants. But in the here and now it was not so obvious to their inhabitants that the slums of New York or Chicago were so very different from those of Paris or the East End of London.

It was a time of growing inequality, something that, as Tocqueville had pointed out, had seemed alien to Americans before the middle of the century. Great fortunes were made, and great poverty came into existence. Increasingly, thoughtful Americans, like their European contemporaries, came to ask themselves whether these two phenomena might be two sides of the same coin. In America, as in Europe, the great preoccupation of the late nineteenth century was with what was called "the social question"—the question, essentially, of poverty. Many of the political and intellectual movements that stirred men's souls in the 1880s and 1890s addressed one aspect or another of that question.

The various agrarian rebellions that flamed in the heartland, from the Grange to the People's Party, challenged assumptions about the justice and even the economic viability of the American farmer's life. That was an old theme in American history. But now in the cities, too, one movement after another asked hard questions about economic and social justice. The Social Gospel, the settlement house movement, trust-busting, the mainstream of progressivism itself, all these facets of the Progressive Age were in the main the responses of the comfortable to the manifest inequalities and injustices of the great industrial cities. But no one should underestimate the vehemence of the rebellions from below in the shape of labor unions, insurrectional strikes, various forms of socialism, and even anarchist violence.

Many of the books that touched a nerve in the Gilded Age and in its successor, the Progressive era—William D. Howells's *Hazard of New For-*

tunes, and Jacob Riis's *How the Other Half Lives,* to cite just two out of many dozens—derived their power and popularity from the fact that they came to terms with the reality that even in fortunate America there was poverty, misery, and injustice. Not only that: the social conscience of middle-class America in the late nineteenth century sprang both from deeply rooted moral and religious beliefs and from a mood of disappointment and even foreboding. The promise of American life (the title of a book by Herbert Croly that was immensely influential with progressives, including both Theodore Roosevelt and Woodrow Wilson) seemed under threat from a new inequality and a new social injustice.

In January 1903 Samuel McClure made the discovery that made his fortune. Hitherto he had been publishing literature, specifically the work of such writers as Rudyard Kipling and Mark Twain. He had also celebrated the success of industrialists like the meat packer Philip Armour and the Scottish-born steel king, Andrew Carnegie. He had hired a talented staff of what came to be called investigative journalists, or—in Theodore Roosevelt's contemptuous epithet—muckrakers. They included Ida Tarbell, Lincoln Steffens, and Ray Stannard Baker. Now, McClure found, to his surprise, a single issue of his magazine containing Steffens's "The Shame of Minneapolis," and Baker's "The Right to Work," and the first part of Miss Tarbell's monumental and devastating "History of Standard Oil" was immensely popular. His countrymen, McClure realized, were so dissatisfied with the price paid by ordinary citizens for the opulence of the Gilded Age that they wanted to read not about what had gone right for some, but about what had gone wrong for the many. In *McClure's Magazine,* economics and sociology were suddenly what people wanted to read. Indeed, much of the literature of muckraking and social concern, and much of the political ferment of the Progressive Era, amounted to a kind of exceptionalism of the Left. How could it be, asked the muckrakers and their middle-class readers, that these failures, these corruptions and shortcomings, could come to pass even in America?

Yet in America, just as in Europe, though in a somewhat different way, the great political questions of the late nineteenth and early twentieth centuries were essentially the same. There was the social question, defined by the experience of unregulated capitalism, rampant industrial expansion, and urban squalor. There were the issues of equality for women, of freedom from official or unofficial censorship, of municipal and state corruption, of excessive power in the hands of business or other elites. And there was the response to those problems, pressing the political system to use the power of government and collective solutions to reform what seemed to have gone wrong, and could not be put right by any agency weaker than government.

One element of the exceptionalist theory as it has developed over the decades is that posed by Werner Sombart and developed by Seymour Martin Lipset, among many others: that the United States differs from the developed democracies of western Europe because socialism never took root in the United States. Even that claim is not wholly true. An imported version of socialism did play a certain part in American political life in the late nineteenth and early twentieth centuries. But if the definition of socialism is expanded to include what is known as social democracy, as it should be, then the Democratic Party in the New Deal years, and as late as the presidency of Lyndon Johnson, was a social democratic party, albeit one tied in unhappy marriage to racially and socially conservative Democrats in the one-party South. Certainly conservatives, both in the Republican Party and in the South, had no doubts that the New Deal and the policies of subsequent Democratic administrations were leading the United States down the primrose path to socialism. As late as the 1950s the supporters of Senator Robert Taft rarely made a speech without repeating that charge.

From the 1870s at least to the 1930s and arguably until the 1950s, the salient question of politics both in western Europe and in North America was precisely the "social question": how government should respond to the social problems caused by economic change, and in particular by industrialization and its impact on how people worked, and lived. These were not merely technocratic issues, either. For thoughtful people in America, just as in Europe, they were vital, unavoidable questions of ethics and justice, and therefore of politics.

This can be traced in three separate but connected fields. First, empirical studies—some striving for scientific objectivity, others frankly emotive—of conditions in, for example, the Lower East Side of Manhattan, the East End of London, and such wretched Paris neighborhoods as the Goutte d'Or, described essentially similar conditions and proposed

strikingly similar remedies. Second, theoretical analysis of how conditions might be alleviated followed closely parallel tracks. And third, political proposals for reform, though not identical, were similar enough at that period that to stress the exceptionalism of American conditions is evidence of ideological preconception or patriotic rhetoric, rather than an accurate representation of the essence of what was taking place.

On both sides of the Atlantic, reporters and social commentators of every kind ventured into the cities and came back with shocking tales of poverty, disease, demoralization, and immiseration. Jacob Riis, a Danish immigrant turned muckraking journalist, explored *How the Other Half Lives* in the noisome tenements of the Lower East Side. He went into "Blind Man's Alley," "the Bend," and "Bandit's Roost," places where child abuse, child mortality, robbery and murder were endemic. Riis documented what he saw with flash photography. The primitive flash equipment of the day occasionally set on fire the tenements he was trying to bring to light.

William Dean Howells, urbane novelist, editor, and man of letters, explored the Lower East Side and reported his findings in *Harper's* magazine in 1896 and later in a powerful book. He commented on the airless tenements, with dark sleeping "bins," on the scanty food and sordid sanitation. He found the Jewish districts marginally less miserable than those inhabited by old stock Americans or by the Irish, because their inhabitants seemed to have more hope and more self-reliance. But everywhere was misery.

> The New York tenement dwellers, even when they leave their lairs, are still pent in their high-walled streets and inhale a thousand stenches of their own and others' making. The street, except in snow and rain, is always better than their horrible houses, and it is doubtless because they pass so much of their time in the street that the death rate is so low among them. . . . With the tenement dwellers it is from generation to generation, if not for the individual, then for the class, since no one expects that there will not always be tenement dwellers in New York as long as our present economical conditions endure.[7]

Howells did not simply report the appalling conditions he found in lower Manhattan, however. He concluded that they could not be improved by leaving them to the free operations of the capitalist market. Like so many of his serious-minded and thoughtful contemporaries, in the United States just as in Europe, he thought conditions could be improved only by public action, that is, by the state, or by its local and municipal agents: "Upon the present terms of leaving the poor to be housed by private landlords, whose interest it is to get the greatest return of money for the money invested, the very poorest must always be housed as they are now. Nothing but public control in some form or other can secure them a shelter fit for human beings."

The genre is unmistakably the same as that of similar writing from England, such as Arthur Morrison's 1896 novel about the East End of London, *A Child of the Jago.* It echoes the judgment of J. H. Mackay on London: "The East End of London is the hell of poverty. Like one enormous black, motionless giant kraken, the poverty of London lies there in lurking silence and encircles with its mighty tentacles the life and wealth of the City."[8] Mackay was writing, in German, about conditions everywhere that had brought about an international movement, anarchism, that led to terrorism everywhere, from Dostoevsky's St. Petersburg to Conrad's London to the Chicago Haymarket. Because industrial capitalism, industrialization, and city slums developed earlier in England than in the United States, the "condition of England question" had been a familiar subject of British fiction and social reporting at least a generation earlier than in the United States. Benjamin Disraeli defined the chasm between the Two Nations and put it on the agenda of even conservative politicians in his political novel *Sybil,* at the time of the quasi-insurrectionary Chartist movement in 1845. He described "two nations between whom there is no intercourse and no sympathy; who are as ignorant of each other's habits, thoughts, and feelings, as if they were dwellers in different zones, or inhabitants of different planets. . . . The rich and the poor." Dickens tackled the condition of the poor as early as 1836, when he published *Oliver Twist,* and fixed it in the national imagination in his masterpiece, *Bleak House,* in 1853.

In the second half of the nineteenth century the condition of the poor in Britain was the subject of a swelling torrent of sociological investigation. Henry Mayhew's classic four-volume study of *London Labour and the London Poor* troubled mid-Victorian consciences when it came out in 1861. In 1884 the pioneer socialist Henry Hyndman published the results of an inquiry into poverty which claimed that up to 25 percent of Londoners lived in extreme poverty. In 1886 Charles Booth, who had begun to take an interest in analyzing census returns, met with Hyndman and told him he believed that Hyndman had grossly exaggerated the situation. That year Booth began a meticulous study of the London poor that ended only seventeen volumes later in 1903. It confirmed Hyndman's diagnosis.

In France "realist" writers as early as Victor Hugo in the 1830s and 1840s had graphically described the misery of the Paris slums, and in 1877 Emile Zola, who preferred to call himself a "naturalist," published *L'Assommoir,* a powerful study of the effects of alcoholism on the poor in a Paris slum. He followed that with *Germinal* (1885), describing the appalling conditions suffered by deep-seam coal miners in the north of France a generation earlier. Zola's method was to experience for himself something of the horrors he described; for *Germinal* he went down in the cage with the miners.

Urban poverty and the insistence, by middle-class observers as well as by its victims, that it be placed at the top of the political agenda, developed sooner in England and France, and—to the extent that repressive governments allowed it—elsewhere in Europe, before they did in the United States. That was because the conditions had reached critical mass earlier. Yet from the 1880s on the consequences of unregulated industrial capitalism cried aloud for remedy on both sides of the Atlantic. In both fiction and nonfiction evidence was piling up of the terrible conditions to be found in the slums of the great cities from Chicago to St. Petersburg, by way of Dublin, Glasgow, Paris, Berlin, and Naples. Perhaps conditions were no worse than they had been in earlier centuries. But they were now on a far vaster scale, and a new consciousness was pressing them on the attention of reformers, clergymen, journalists, and politicians.

This new consciousness, or conscience, had its origins in the Enlightenment, that great upsurge of ethical awareness that transformed values and attitudes in the eighteenth century on both sides of the Atlantic. In part it also arose from a series of challenges to religious orthodoxy and so to the traditional religious basis of ethical teaching. That challenge took a long time coming. It came first from the deist or agnostic thinkers of the English, Scots, and French Enlightenment, then from the German idealist philosophers like Immanuel Kant, Georg Friedrich Wilhelm Hegel and Johann Gottlieb Fichte. The Romantic movement, in Germany, France, and Britain, offered a new, subjective and emotive basis for ethics. But the challenge to the ethical values of Christianity in all its forms, to American, British, and German Protestantism as well as to the Roman Catholic Church, did not attain critical mass until the double attacks of biblical criticism and natural science in the mid-nineteenth century. Traditional biblical scholarship was shaken by skeptical lives of Jesus Christ like David Friedrich Strauss's *Das Leben Jesu* (1835) and Ernest Renan's *La Vie de Jésus* (1863).

Throughout the nineteenth century scientists were shedding doubt on the Bible's account of the history of the universe and of mankind through the new, or modernized, disciplines of geology and evolutionary biology. Jean-Baptiste Lamarck published his theory of evolution as early as 1800, though his work has been undervalued because of many scientists' rejection of his theory of the inheritance of acquired characteristics. Sir Charles Lyell published his *Principles of Geology* in 1830–33 and *The Antiquity of Man* in 1863. Lyell influenced Charles Darwin, who produced a largely accepted explanation of natural selection as the mechanism by which evolution works in *On The Origin of Species* (1859). Alfred Russell Wallace, who had been working independently on ideas similar to Darwin's, published *The Malay Archipelago,* largely confirming Darwin's ideas, in 1869.[9]

The Sea of Faith—wrote Matthew Arnold in 1867—

Was once, too, at the full, and round earth's shore
Lay like the folds of a bright girdle furled.
But now I only hear
Its melancholy, long, withdrawing roar.[10]

As a young man Ralph Waldo Emerson was a member of the philosophical and political circle surrounding John Stuart Mill, the great philosopher of liberty, in London. A whole generation of Americans of that middle-nineteenth-century generation, including William James, Henry Adams, Daniel Coit Gilman, future president of Johns Hopkins, and Charles W. Eliot, the great reforming president of Harvard, studied for lengthy periods in Europe, mostly in Germany. A new generation of philosophers, many of them the sons of Protestant ministers who could not share their fathers' beliefs, tried to find a middle way between the profoundly disturbing implications of the new science, and the idealist tradition in ethics. This movement happened at about the same time in Britain, in the persons of Henry Sidgwick at Cambridge and T. H. Green at Oxford, in Germany with Wilhelm Dilthey, in France with Alfred Fouilleé, and in America with William James and the slightly younger John Dewey.[11]

The dominant cast of European political thought in the middle of the nineteenth century was liberal, in the sense that John Stuart Mill might have used the word. The collection of political ideas loosely labeled *socialism* dated back to the aftermath of the French Revolution. A series of events in the 1860s and 1870s, including the American Civil War, the forging of new centralized states in Germany and Italy, and the Paris Commune of 1871, were seen as revealing the limitations both of classic "Manchester" liberalism, with its faith in free trade and minimal government, and of the earlier, ethical versions of socialism. For a new generation, the social question—that is, the impact of unregulated industrial capitalism—could not be answered except by the vigorous intervention of an activist, centralized government.

It was in Germany, which had come later to industrialization than Britain, the Low Countries, or France, that this was first put into effect by the "Iron Chancellor," Otto von Bismarck. Between 1883 and 1887 he introduced a whole series of measures, including health and unemployment insurance, to protect the workers. Bismarck's ideas were scarcely liberal. He did his best to ban socialism. Yet he did call in the state to protect the poor on a larger and more imaginative scale than at any time since the very different circumstances of the Middle Ages. He could do so effectively because of the high traditions of public service in the admittedly elitist and authoritarian Prussian bureaucracy. The idea of state intervention to counter the consequences of unregulated capitalism spread gradually across Europe and to the United States, where it took the form of the Progressive movement, and specifically of both regulation and antitrust legislation.

Beginning in the 1880s, in Germany, Britain, France, and the United States, a new generation of social democratic intellectuals began to replace the minimum government liberalism of political leaders like William Ewart Gladstone and John Bright in England, the Democrat Grover Cleveland in America, and the radical Georges Clemenceau in France. The approaches of this new wave of social democratic thinkers varied in detail. Taken as a whole they amounted to an international response to industrialization and its consequent social evils that was common to North America and central and western Europe.

In England the married couple Sidney and Beatrice Webb built a whole series of institutions devoted to gradual change in the social system, to be brought about by the building of pragmatic cases for specific change based on meticulous statistical research. Their work was highly influential in the United States. They worked through determined lobbying of a Parliament whose electorate had been broadened to include almost all male voters by 1884. That year they founded Toynbee Hall, the first of many "settlements," in deprived East London, initiating a movement that was replicated by Jane Addams at Hull House in Chicago in 1889. It subsequently spread to influence policy in many areas nationally by the time of the advent of the Woodrow Wilson administration in 1913. Still in 1884, the Webbs founded the Fabian Society, dedicated to gradual social revolution through parliamentary action to pursue social democracy. In 1895 they founded the London School of Economics, in effect a social democratic university, though by the 1930s its faculty included many economic conservatives, including Lionel Robbins and Friedrich Hayek.[12] In 1913 they founded the influential magazine the *New Statesman,* whose contributors included George Bernard Shaw, H. G. Wells, and John Maynard Keynes.

One of those influenced by the Webbs was Eduard Bernstein, who articulated social democratic theory more clearly than any other writer. Bernstein was a member of the German Social Democratic Party who was driven into exile in England by Bismarck's antisocialist legislation. Lenin's pamphlet *What Is To Be Done?,* the key text of the Leninist version of communism, was written as a rebuttal of Bernstein's insistence that social democracy could be achieved within a parliamentary system, not—as has often been assumed—the other way round. Bernstein's formal exposition of social democratic theory, which drew Lenin's polemic, was written in a series of "revisionist" articles in the Swiss newspaper *Die Neue Zeit* (The new age) in 1896–98.

Meanwhile, in France, Jean Jaurès, too, had been arguing for a social democratic modernization of socialism. The situation in France was different from that in Britain or indeed in Germany, because of the rift—which went back to the French Revolution—between the Right, identified with monarchy and with the Catholic Church, and a republican, atheist Left, a divide that had been deepened by the bloody repression of the Commune in 1871. A bitter miners' strike in 1892 convinced Jaurès, who had resigned from Parliament to teach and write philosophy, that regulatory legislation was not enough. But he remained a believer in parliamentary democracy and in 1899 supported the reform coalition government under Pierre Waldeck-Rousseau. This was not a socialist government, but it did support many of the measures the Progressives campaigned for in America, including protection of women and child workers and the defense of labor unions. Jaurès (and Zola) stalwartly defended Alfred Dreyfus, the Jewish army officer who was falsely accused of treason, and he stood four-square against anti-Semitism. In 1904 he founded *L'Humanité*, later the Communist Party's newspaper but then owned by the Socialist Party. Jaurès was assassinated a few days before the war in 1914. Had he lived, the split between the Socialists and the Communists in France after the Russian Revolution might have been averted.[13]

The politics, the labor movement, and the intellectual climate in the United States between the 1880s and America's entry into World War I were different from the circumstances in Europe, though in truth the differences among England, France, Germany, and Russia were quite as great. From the 1880s on, in the United States as in Europe, a Progressive movement gathered momentum that was based on social democratic thinking. On both sides of the Atlantic the essential problem of the modern industrial state came to be seen as how to protect the workers, both urban and rural, from the deprivation into which late capitalism seemed to be pressing them down.

In the 1880s and the early 1890s, writers such as Edward Bellamy and Henry George offered various solutions to this problem. But as James T. Kloppenberg, the historian of social democracy on either side of the Atlantic, put it, "Social democratic theory in the United States . . . emerged from a background of ethical reformism rather than revolutionary political action."[14] Two key figures were Walter Rauschenbusch, a political radical who was also a Christian socialist, and Richard T. Ely, author in 1889 of *The Social Aspects of Christianity.* Both men had studied in Germany. Rauschenbusch worked in Henry George's campaign for mayor of New York in 1886 and worked with a congregation of German Baptists in Manhattan's Hell's Kitchen, while Ely moved from Johns Hopkins to the University of Wisconsin.

By the second decade of the twentieth century a younger generation of American social democratic radicals had emerged. Herbert Croly traveled in Europe in the 1890s before returning to Harvard in 1895. He worked as a journalist in New York before publishing the immensely influential *The Promise of American Life* in 1909. His 1913 Godkin lectures at Harvard were published in 1914 as *Progressive Democracy.* In 1913 he met the wealthy Dorothy and Willard Straight, who gave him the financial support to start the *New Republic.* The journal supplied much of the intellectual capital of the Wilson administration. It was also closely connected with British progressive, social democratic and pacifist writers like Noel Brailsford (*The War of Steel and Gold*) and Norman Angell (*The Lost Illusion*). The *New Republic* editors, among them Randolph Bourne, were close to the British pacifist and social democratic group, the Union for Democratic Control. The key thinker of Croly's editorial team was the young and brilliant Walter Lippmann. Lippmann came from a German-Jewish family that made annual journeys to Germany. He was a founder member of the (social democratic) Socialist Club at Harvard. He published *A Preface to Politics* (1913) and in 1914 *Drift and Mastery.*

The old nineteenth-century liberalism was grounded in the ideas of writers like John Stuart Mill, who saw freedom as an end in itself, and thought that freedom, and in particular economic freedom, would be enough to liberate citizens from the bonds of the old state. Unlike Mill's generation, late-nineteenth and early-twentieth-century writers lived in a world where aristocratic power, based on land, was less of a threat to most people than the new power of industrial capital. In contrast to the liberals of the Mill school, they saw that Manchester liberalism merely defended the privileges of the rich and did little to help the poor. "Liberalism eventually became a rationale for perpetuating privilege," writes Kloppenberg, "instead of an ideology of radical change." It made "freedom an end in itself, not a means toward the end of virtue."[15]

Increasingly, as industrial strife and political revolution threatened the bourgeois prosperity of the early twentieth century, thinkers in America and Europe alike adopted social democratic ideas, not only out of ethical concern for the condition of the poor under capitalism but also because they were afraid of the consequences of failing to address the social question.[16]

These were, of course, not the only strands of political thought in that age. But they were the dominant ones. The point is that it was an international response, in which a network of common preoccupations, friendship, and controversy tied the most influential thinkers in western Europe and America together in what they saw as a conscious shared effort. America in the age of Theodore Roosevelt and Woodrow Wilson was confident, conscious of its new strength, and occasionally truculent and imperialist—like the societies of late Victorian England, Wilhelmine Germany, and the French belle époque. The predominant current of American culture and political thought in that generation was anything but exceptionalist.

The war and the Paris peace conference brought this optimistic prewar mood to an abrupt end. The Wilson administration was the incarnation of social democratic progressivism (even if its predominantly southern coloration gave it surprisingly conservative instincts in some areas, especially in anything to do with race). But with the defeat of the League of Nations treaty and the illness of President Wilson in 1919, the stage was set for the return of business conservatism in the United States, and something similar happened in Europe in the 1920s. The great war leaders, Clemenceau and Lloyd George, both of whom started as liberals, turned to the right and were succeeded by conservatives, like Raymond Poincaré, Bonar Law, and Warren Gamaliel Harding, who had never pretended to be anything else. The Russian Revolution of 1917, welcomed at first by American progressives, including Wilson himself, darkened into oppression and eventually under Stalin into bloody tyranny.

The European democracies and America responded differently to the crisis of the Great Depression. Where in the United States, Franklin Roosevelt preserved the capitalist system and the constitutional tradition by the social democracy of the New Deal, reinforced by adroit political management, the leading European nations went their different ways. In Britain, Labour governments in 1923–24 and 1929–31 failed to tackle economic failure and were replaced by conservative administrations. In France, the socialist (social democratic) government of Léon Blum in the middle 1930s was brought down, mainly by the international crisis. In Italy, in Germany, and in Spain, and in eastern Europe, economic disaster opened the gate to fascism, which in Germany was called national socialism.

When the second war ended, the United States emerged for a time as the only economically successful society. Only the mysterious and—to democrats—sinister bulk of the Soviet Union, which had done more than American or British efforts to overthrow the Nazi "New Order" in Europe, stood between America and a sunlit future. Dr. Win-the-War, in Roosevelt's phrase, had done what Dr. New Deal could not achieve: it had ended the Great Depression. The immense effort to arm the American economy for total war had doubled the gross national product in five short years and put the unemployed, who had reached one-quarter of the workforce, back to work. In those same years, the economies of all the European nations had been shattered, their plants bombed, their sources of energy and raw materials cut off, their retail systems fettered by rationing, and their labor forces decimated by mobilization and casualties.

With generosity, but also out of a wise calculation of enlightened self-interest, the Truman administration did what it could, through the Marshall Plan and other programs, to revive the economies and the societies of western Europe. There was a need for future trading partners, but there was also an urgent fear that destitution and despair would turn the Europeans towards communism and leave the United States without a beachhead or an outer defensive perimeter in Europe. Elsewhere, American policy rebuilt Japan and used the heavy weight of political and economic pressure to hasten the end of the British, French, and Dutch empires. At Yalta, in particular, Roosevelt seemed to take the view that the Soviet Union would be a better partner than the British Empire in building the postwar world, though there was of course an element of calculation in this.[17] The Roosevelt administration, with more than a dash of exceptionalist overconfidence, hoped to use nationalist China as its ally in building a new, democratic Asia.

Immediately after the end of the war, the United States had a monopoly of the most devastating and most terrifying military weapon ever devised, a weapon it had actually used, twice, on Japan. Both British and French scientists had, however, along with émigré Germans, Hungarians, Italians, Frenchmen, and Danes, played an important part in the work that made it possible to build an atomic bomb.

Far sooner than anyone in Washington anticipated, that monopoly came to an end. First the Soviet Union, then by the middle 1950s even the enfeebled economies of Britain and France, acquired nuclear weapons and some capacity to deliver them.

In a disastrous process of reciprocal fear, the Soviet Union and its client states in Eastern Europe, on one side of an ideological abyss, and the United States and its European and other allies on the other, moved blindly through rearmament to a posture of armed confrontation that could at any moment have burst into war. Probably the Soviet Union, in Stalin's lifetime, had no real intention of marching to conquest in Europe. But the Soviet Union was ruled absolutely by a paranoiac dictator. No one in his realm dared defy or deflect him. He and his party colleagues were afraid that the capitalists meant to surround them. Their antagonists in Washington, especially after the communist revolution in China, were equally convinced that communism was a militant ideology on the march. No wonder that within five years from the high hopes of 1945, those voices—those of Dean Acheson, James Forrestal, and Paul Nitze, among others—prevailed in Washington. They concluded that the nation must prepare for permanent readiness, and if necessary for permanent war.

Stalin was ruthless and mad, but he was also cautious. In 1944, for example, he decided not to support the Greek Communists who were already fighting a British force in northern Greece. But in a manner that was understandably interpreted in Washington as a systematic plan, he supported Communist governments, or governments dominated by Communists, in one country in Eastern Europe after another. The coup d'état in Prague in 1948, in particular, caused an abrupt war scare in Washington and seemed to confirm the entirely reasonable fears of those who believed that Stalin meant to make as much of Europe as he could into a Soviet sphere of influence. When that same summer the Soviet authorities tried to isolate the western sectors of Berlin, American and British air forces were able to supply the beleaguered city by an airlift. The West was strengthened, but the confrontation became more acute.

In the National Security Act of 1949, the Truman administration set to work to build the institutions—a National Security Council, a unified Defense Department, and a Central Intelligence Agency—that would be needed to fight a Cold War. This was, as conservatives of the Robert Taft persuasion protested, a historic break with American tradition. The politics of the Cold War have been persuasively explained not as a contest between liberal Left and conservative Right but as a Great Debate between upholders of traditional values and the partisans of a new, hard-boiled ideology of national security.[18] The traditionalists upheld such established American instincts as suspicion of centralized government, of military influence, and of high taxation. The partisans of the new national security state and its ideology were convinced that the republic must change if it was to gird its loins for an enduring condition of near-war with communism, and it was they who prevailed.

By 1950—five years from a moment when the United States had created, in the United Nations, the World Bank and the International Monetary Fund, the international institutions that were to have guaranteed lasting peace—the Truman administration had accepted the strategy contained in National Security Council memorandum 68. This was a strategy of armed containment of communism. It implied massive rearmament. In a few short years it quadrupled defense expenditure. Over time, it did transform the United States into a "national security state."

In the same year the Korean War broke out. That seemed to confirm the fears of those who saw the Soviet Union as committed to an aggressive drive for world domination. They were not wrong. Recent research, based on Soviet archives opened after the fall of the Soviet Union, has confirmed that Stalin was indeed aware of, and approved, North Korea's invasion of South Korea. The United States, and some of its allies, found themselves at war with Communist North Korea and before long with the People's Republic of China. In Europe, after the Berlin airlift the Soviet Union stepped back. East and West continued to glare at each other over the Iron Curtain for another four decades. In East Asia, however, the Cold War was hot.

The coming of the national security state had profound implications for American society, not only abroad but at home. Fear of communism, in the form of what was called "McCarthyism," threatened traditional American rights, including the First Amendment guarantee of free speech. Abroad, the United States found itself in charge of a worldwide network of bases, eventually at least seven hundred of them in more than one hundred countries. Some were strategic air bases. Others were intelligence bases, including the secret bases for U-2 flights over the Soviet Union. Many were supply bases associated with American military aid. Some came into existence in the course of wars fought against communist or nationalist insurgencies, in the Philippines, in Southeast Asia, or in Central America.

While great care was taken in most cases to preserve the proprieties and represent these bases as established at the request of allies, in practice, given the dependent status of the allies doing the requesting, it was often hard to distinguish them from traditional colonies. Extraterritorial rights were often claimed, so that American personnel were treated more favorably than local people. In some cases, such as the island base on Diego Garcia in the Indian Ocean, leased from Britain, local inhabitants were evicted from their home country. American embassies, built in many supposedly allied capitals like great concrete forts, behaved toward sovereign governments rather like the political "residencies" with which the British Empire controlled territories in the Persian Gulf and elsewhere.

In many instances the U.S. government, often through the CIA, intervened more or less aggressively in local politics, overthrowing governments or preventing what Washington saw as undesirable changes of government. This is widely known to have happened in the Philippines from 1950 to 1953, in Iran in 1953, in Guatemala in 1954, in Cuba in 1961 and 1963, in South Vietnam in 1963, and in Chile in 1973. This roster by no means exhausts the instances of secret Washington intervention. That list includes the Congo from 1960 to 1965, Indonesia in 1965 (where the CIA was deeply implicated in a repression in which at least five hundred thousand and by some accounts two million communist and Chinese Indonesians were killed), Brazil in 1964, and India in the early 1970s. Even in Western European countries such as France, Italy, Greece, and Portugal, the CIA interfered clandestinely at one time or another to influence elections.[19]

If the United States "projected power," as the phrase went, in these and other ways—for example, with the political use of economic and military aid—it is of course true that this world hegemony was different in many ways from the European empires of the past. The style and the rhetoric were anti-imperial, if only because American identity was so historically rooted in opposition to imperialism that conscious efforts were devoted to distinguishing the American way from the colonial past. It is true, too, that in the late nineteenth and early twentieth centuries the United States had pioneered methods of indirect and clandestine influence in the Caribbean and in Latin America that afforded precedents for what was happening elsewhere in the 1950s and 1960s. Yet the establishment of this network of alliances, bases, and systems of influence, and the sheer scale of American intervention—justified by American leaders and publicists by the perception of a worldwide contest against communism—marked a sharp departure from the American past.

It was not only on Diego Garcia or Okinawa, in Norfolk and the Rhineland, that bases were being built in the 1950s. From Thule to the Panama Canal Zone bases were being built nearer home. Senators and congressmen, once content with building post offices or the occasional dam, vied with one another to bring military "pork" to their states and districts. The surest sign of political clout in Cold War Washington was success in bringing massive military infrastructure to a politician's home state. In an age when power in the Washington committee structure went by seniority, which it did until the early 1970s, the advantage held by long-serving legislators from the one-party South was decisive. Georgia, represented by Richard B. Russell, chairman of the Senate Armed Services Committee, and Carl Vinson, his opposite number in the House, was the home to huge bases. The U.S. Army Infantry Center at Fort Benning claims "to provide the nation with the world's best trained Infantry, Soldiers and adaptive leaders imbued with the Warrior Ethos" and to "provide a Power Projection Platform capable of deploying and redeploying soldiers, civilians, and units anywhere in the world on short notice."

Texas, fortunate enough to be represented by Speaker Samuel T. Rayburn, Senate majority leader Lyndon Johnson, and George Mahon, chairman of the crucial House Appropriations Committee, did even better. As well as air force bases like Lackland (the world's biggest military flight training installation) and the vast expansion of the great army bases at Fort Hood, Fort Bliss, and Fort Sam Houston, not to mention Lyndon Johnson's pet project for his friends at Brown and Root, to dig the deepest hole on earth, "MoHole," Texas walked off with the Houston space center.

Military infrastructure transformed the country. But the big military procurement contracts did so even more. Senator Henry M. Jackson of Washington, who started life as a liberal Democrat with reliable union backing, became "the senator from Boeing" and ended up as one of the fiercest hawks in the Washington aviary. Georgia legislators fought for Martin Marietta, New York congressmen for Grumman on Long Island, Californians for Lockheed, Douglas and the futuristic flight research at Edwards and Vandenberg air force bases. Aerospace corporations began to hire retired generals and admirals to smooth their path through the appropriations jungle in Washington, while senators like Barry Goldwater were given rank as generals to keep them loyal to the interests of the Military.

The sheer scale of Cold War investment in military hardware was enough to change the economic geography of the country. Southern California was the conspicuous example. At Burbank in the San Fernando Valley, Lockheed built not only military aircraft like the Hercules, Galaxy, and Starfighter, not to mention the mysterious U-2, but also the new generation of intercontinental ballistic missiles to deliver nuclear warheads. Douglas, at Santa Monica and Long Beach, did the same. But California was not the only state whose economy was boosted by defense contracts. Texas, Washington, Missouri, Florida, and Georgia were industrialized largely as a spin-off from the prosperity of defense contractors. The

Manhattan Project's installations in Washington vied with the investment at Boeing in transforming that state.

Even President Eisenhower, the former supreme commander of allied forces in Europe, famously warned, in his last speech as president, against the dangers of the "military-industrial complex." It was only out of reluctance to annoy members of Congress that he allowed the draft of his speech to be changed: what it originally targeted was the "military-industrial-congressional complex." Eisenhower's speech has often been misinterpreted. He was not denouncing the creation of an American arms industry. He was pointing out that there had been no such thing before World War II, and he was drawing attention to the potential impact of what had come into existence for politics and for society. In effect, he was echoing the concern of 1950s conservatives: that the headlong expansion of the military and the defense industry would create a "garrison state."

"How can we prepare for total war," Hanson W. Baldwin, the *New York Times*'s respected military correspondent, asked in 1947, "without becoming a 'garrison state' and destroying the very qualities and virtues and principles we originally set out to save?"[20]

The answer that the government gave in the 1950s and 1960s was essentially, "We don't believe that in transforming the nation into a national security state, we are in fact destroying our values and our virtues." By and large, the nation agreed—until the Vietnam War.

The coming of the Cold War, rearmament, and the creation of a national security state had a paradoxical effect on politics. The challenge to the Truman administration came not from a pacifist or anti-interventionist Left but from the Right. The political mood and style named for Republican Senator Joseph McCarthy of Wisconsin extended far wider than his vicious but buffoonish attacks. (The mood could just as well have been called "Nixonism," because the thirty-seventh president of the United States first came to prominence by flinging around equally wild and disingenuous accusations, even if in the most celebrated case, that of Alger Hiss, he struck lucky and was right.)[21] It was absurd that McCarthy should insinuate that Dean Acheson, as tough an anticommunist as could be found, was somehow in cahoots with the communists; absurd, in that instance, but the fear of domestic communism was not just the product of the wild raving of an isolated Midwestern alcoholic. If the nation found itself engaged in a life-and-death struggle for the survival of all that America stood for, millions of sensible Americans asked, how can we be sure that we are not being corrupted from inside, like the governments of those countries in Eastern Europe that had been subverted by communist tactics? After all, communists had been influential in the American labor movement. How can we rise to the challenge our leaders say we must confront? "McCarthyism" was a dark chapter in the history of American civil liberties. It was also consciously used by selfish interests of several kinds to justify attacks on labor power and on the intelligentsia of the Left. But wholly irrational it was not.

The impact of the Cold War on American society was all but ubiquitous. At one end of the spectrum was the expansion of educational opportunity. Universities could, for the first time in history, attract federal funding, even for such fields of study as classics and literature. The GI Bill, though not strictly a Cold War measure, allowed millions of Americans whose families had never been able to dream of higher education to go to college. At the other end of the spectrum, the Interstate Highway System, the first national road system and perhaps the most ambitious infrastructure project ever undertaken by any national government in peacetime, was begun by the Eisenhower administration, though it was not completed until the twenty-first century. Whole industries received a boost from the willingness of Congress to appropriate money for a wide range of desirable projects if they could be represented as required for national security. Civil aviation, for example, was subsidized by the manufacture of warplanes.

At the same time American businessmen, traditionally hostile to government intervention in the economy, grew accustomed to depending on lush cost-plus contracts from the Department of Defense and other fountains of federal munificence. High-technology industry—in particular, in nuclear physics, materials science, electronics, computers, and many departments of engineering—was pushed ahead by government research and development contracts. The Pentagon's Defense Advanced Research Projects Agency played a crucial role in developing the Internet, and government poured money into private research labs such as Bell Laboratories and XeroxParc, as well as into universities.

Memory has distorted the actual sequence of economic history. The Cold War was by and large a good time for the American economy and for average income, though not comparatively as good as the years when World War II was ending mass unemployment and pushing up wages. The true Golden Age for the American economy was during World War II. Average disposable personal income (in 1996 dollars) grew from $5,912 in 1940 to $7,920 in 1944. Then, in the late 1940s, before the Korean War boom and before the increase in defense expenditure after NSC-68, disposable income in real terms stood still for a while. It picked up strongly again in the 1950s, rising from $7,863 in 1950 to $9,167 in 1959.

So both war and Cold War were good for the economy, but hot war was better than cold. Still, the economy did continue to grow steadily in the Cold War years. For a time there was virtually no foreign competition. There was massive investment in manufacturing, distribution, and agriculture. (It was not until 1954 that the number of tractors on American farms passed the number of horses and mules!) Prosperity was increasingly widely distributed.

The big industrial unions joined together in the CIO were able to negotiate exceptionally favorable contracts that gave the workers "fringe benefits," including health care and pensions. The 1950 contract signed by the United Auto Workers with General Motors was the benchmark. It heralded the coming of a new era in industrial bargaining, an era of unprecedented prosperity for unionized workers, though the growth in wages was not as spectacular as under the pressures of war, with millions of workers away in uniform. Now tens of millions of American workers were able for the first time to look forward to a standard of living previously available only to executives and professionals. Home owning spread rapidly. By the end of the 1950s it was possible to claim—with some exaggeration and with the help of such devices as official counting of all women as "white collar workers"—that more than half of the American work force had joined the middle class.[22] That claim, too, dubious as it was factually, became the basis of another exceptionalist rhetoric: "Only in America . . ." It was not long before the same was true in much of Europe and elsewhere.

By the early years of the Cold War, American society was certainly exceptionally successful—if only in the sense that, thanks to the catastrophe of war, all potential rivals were not successful at all. By the 1970s, however, that had substantially changed. Whether you measured average income, or gross national product, or productivity, many other nations, in Western Europe and East Asia, were closing the gap. In those early Cold War years, the United States certainly was exceptional in terms of plenty and profusion. That was not, however, what had made the United States exceptional in the first half of the nineteenth century. Then, American society had been exceptional in terms of equality, of opportunity, and of political participation.

A new ideology of exceptionalism was becoming widespread in the 1950s. It defined American exceptionalism, partly in terms of material prosperity and military power, and partly in the name of a contrast between democracy, often assumed to be essentially American, with dictatorship and totalitarian societies, especially, of course, in contrast with the Soviet Union and communism. This was the new and specialized meaning of *freedom,* a value that had been cherished by Americans since the Revolution, but whose precise meaning had changed.

This new American ideology has been called the "liberal consensus," because it represented a grand bargain between liberal values in domestic politics and conservative anticommunism as the guiding principle in foreign policy. Many conservatives, that is, more or less grudgingly accepted the "liberal," or social democratic, goals of the "welfare state"; most liberals signed up for anticommunist foreign policies. This ideology overlapped with that of the "national security state" in rejecting traditional fears of a "garrison state." It assumed a congruence between a constitutional system based on the sovereignty of the people and the rule of law, and the prevalence of free-market capitalism. Later, beyond the limits of the period we consider in this chapter, it became fashionable to restrict the role of government and to emphasize the need to minimize the regulation of the free market. But as John F. Kennedy succeeded General Eisenhower in the White House and redefined the national purpose in terms of a "long twilit struggle" against communism, the American ideology was cast, as never before, in terms of opposition to the Other.

That had always been an element in the national ideology, and therefore in the understanding of American exceptionalism. Only the identity of the Other, and the character of the struggle against it, altered.

In the colonial period, the Other was the Native American, sensed more as a shadowy menace in the woods than as an organized enemy, and the slave, feared as a potential threat on the farm and even within the home. In the Revolution, and for a long time afterward, the Other was the British monarchy, the Established Church, and more generally a hierarchical society that set limits on the freedom of the individual citizen. Soon, in response to Catholic immigration from Ireland and central Europe in the 1840s and 1850s, the Roman Catholic Church itself became for a time the Other. The 1850s, the decade of massive immigration from Ireland, was the time of the Know Nothing movement and of wild nativist paranoia about papal plots in America.

It was not hard to see "Prussian militarism" as the Other in 1917, when the big new German U-boats sank liners and freighters bound for Britain and France with Americans on board. It was even easier in the 1930s and 1940s to see Nazi Germany and its Italian and Japanese allies in the same light. Easiest of all was to cast international communism as an implacable enemy, and one that could be seen as an enemy within as well as without, burrowing into American society through spies, agents, labor radicals, and pink professors.

Soon the exceptionalism of the Cold War period took on a religious flavor. In a famous passage in his memoirs, Dean Acheson describes how he intervened in a meeting with President Truman to persuade him that the United States must take over the defense of Greece and Turkey from Britain, which could no longer afford to keep troops there. Acheson recalled how when his chief, the secretary of state, General Marshall, "flubbed his opening statement," he pleaded in a whisper to be allowed to speak. "I knew we were met at Armageddon," he wrote. As the son of an Episcopal bishop, Acheson knew very well that Armageddon was the place where, in the book of Revelation, the last battle would be fought between the legions of good and evil.[23]

Five years after Dean Acheson stood at Armageddon, as we have seen, the great New England scholar Perry Miller spoke at the opening of an exhibition of Puritan texts at the John Carter Brown Library at Brown University in Providence. He took his theme from a sermon preached in 1670 by the Reverend Samuel Danforth, which gave him a title: New England's *Errand into the Wilderness.* In his speech, Miller made the ultimate exceptionalist boast: "The Bay Company was . . . an organized task force of Christians, executing a flank attack on the corruptions of Christendom."

There had always been a thread of religious destiny in the pattern of American patriotism. Lincoln and Woodrow Wilson infused their great speeches with the language of redemption, election, salvation. But the circumstances of the 1950s wove a new fabric. There was the consciousness of material plenty. There was the sense of victory, with the lurking hope that, whatever the dark powers of the Soviet Union, nuclear weapons might restore invulnerability. Mingling with that hope was a new fear, that America might yet be called to do final battle with the forces of evil. All this came together to forge a new militant sense of exceptionalism. It breathes through the high school and college textbooks of the time as well as through the political oratory, a belief that the United States had been entrusted by God with a mission of bringing light to a darkling world.

The most perfunctory trawl through the high school and college textbooks of the Cold War period illustrates how pervasive was the exceptionalist theme. Americans who were at high school in the 1950s and at college in the 1960s were brought up with assumptions about the exceptional historical destiny of the United States as uncontested as the air they breathed. These texts were not especially arrogant or aggressive in their assumptions. Most were written with a due respect for those past European traditions they saw as contributing to the improved version of humanity that was America. They occasionally made a bow to what were seen as the promising efforts of Latin America to aspire to the same ideals. They were not even wholly uncritical. Slavery is condemned, and some texts even speak sympathetically of the experience of the Native Americans, though others are less sensitive in that regard. What is characteristic of them all is a certain calm assumption of the ethical superiority not only of the American condition but also of American ideals.

A 1948 high school text illustrates this tone.[24] It begins by asking the teacher to invite the students to say which they consider to be the three greatest countries in the world. From the start, then, children are to be taught to put their homeland in a competitive setting. It then lists, in a frankly self-congratulatory tone, ten characteristics of "Americanism" that can be traced from colonial times to the present:

(1) Economic opportunity
(2) Wide participation in politics
(3) Belief in reform rather than revolution (!)
(4) A mobile population
(5) A high position and freedom for women
(6) Belief in education and widespread educational opportunity
(7) Concern for the welfare of others
(8) Toleration of differences
(9) Respect for the rights and abilities of the individual
(10) World-wide responsibility

It is not that any of these propositions, except perhaps the volte-face on revolution, is plain untrue. It is not even that many of them apply to most other developed societies. Are Americans unique in their concern for the welfare of others, for example? Or in respect for education? In their respect for women? What is suspect is that the purpose of beginning a secondary school textbook with a set of self-praising propositions of this kind is not to encourage a thoughtful or analytical understanding of the history of the student's country. It is to inculcate an American exceptionalist ideology, almost, indeed, a theology.

Unit Seven is a good example of this tone. "People from many countries came to America as a land of opportunity. These people developed ideals which one historian has called the American Dream. It is a dream of a richer, fuller, and better life for each person according to his ability and his talents regardless of his race or nationality. . . . The American Dream is slowly coming true." So that's all right, then.

When those high school students (or, in those days, a severely limited proportion of them) reached college, they would be taught history in a similarly ideological vein. A 1960 college text is equally self-congratulatory:

The American Revolution was in part a revolt against the upper classes of European derivation, and as time went on the

> cult of the common man grew until it became the typical American philosophy. The goal of America has been the economic improvement of the masses, and this remains a goal which requires social and economic change. . . . The goal of achieving a decent standard of living for all men, of abolishing poverty and inequality, has come closer to realization in the United States than was dreamed possible. It has largely eliminated those class conflicts which have plagued almost all societies. The 'classless society' which Marxian socialists held up as the goal of proletarian revolution has been largely achieved by American "capitalism," mixed with a good deal of government welfare activity. The American standard of living is many times the world average.[25]

Calm as is the tone, and free from vulgar bombast, this text does read oddly today. The suggestion, for example, that the Revolution targeted "upper classes of European derivation" suggests that it was largely carried out by persons not of European derivation. But Washington's family came from England, and Jefferson's were Irish Protestants. With few exceptions, all the Founding Fathers traced their descent from the British Isles, and so did most of their followers. The only significant populations in the American colonies not of European descent were slaves, who tended to favor the English Crown, and Native Americans, who displayed an infuriating tendency to side with sometimes the English, sometimes the French monarchy. The language imports into the account of the American Revolution anachronistic New Deal–era notions of immigrant populations rising against Boston Brahmin snobs and their unreconstructed habit of insisting that "no Irish need apply." The text has a liberal flavor that is now out of fashion. It would, I suppose, be a bold person who would now maintain that the goal of America is still the economic improvement of the masses, and indeed an unusual teacher who would speak to students of "the masses." As for the abolition of inequality, the United States now comes either near the top or at the top of the list of the most unequal societies among the world's developed industrial democracies, whether measured by income or wealth.[26] Nor, at the time of writing, is the American standard of living "many times" the average of its equals and competitors in the world.

The peroration of this textbook praises American society for its superiority in terms of charity, tolerance, and faith. "No other portion of the globe," the authors write on the very eve of the civil rights revolution and the racial rioting in several hundred cities across the United States in the middle 1960s, "has a comparable record in the peaceful coexistence of so many different kinds of people." Finally, the authors praise their countrymen for their exceptionally pacific character:

> The vision of universal peace continues to exist here. The "true grandeur of nations," Americans have always felt, lies in peace, not in war; in social improvement, not in military glory. . . . This secular version of the Christian ideal of the millennium comes as close as any one thing to summing up the meaning of American history. A land where miracles have happened, and unhappy men have become happy, America is a country with a national faith that this can go on happening, until democracy, in the words of Walt Whitman, has fashioned "a new earth and a new man."

The ideal is endearing. No one can dislike the teachers who offered such an irenic vision to adolescents. Yet this picture was offered in the year when the most successful military man of his generation was warning his countrymen against the dangers of the military industrial complex, and former lieutenant (junior grade) John Fitzgerald Kennedy was riding to power with his warnings of a nonexistent missile gap with the Soviet Union. In his eloquent inaugural he told his countrymen that the trumpet summoned them again—"not as a call to bear arms, though arms we need; not as a call to battle, though embattled we are"—to a "long twilight struggle." It was true that he defined that struggle as one against "the common enemies of mankind: tyranny, poverty, disease, and war itself." But his call was clearly understood, in America and around the world, as a call to renewed militancy against the nation's military enemies in the Cold War. And over the following half-century the United States, for all this vision of "universal peace," accumulated the most formidable military arsenal the world had ever seen by spending more on the military than the rest of the world put together, and used that arsenal on many occasions.

There is no "official history" in the United States as it was known in the Soviet Union or other totalitarian states, though the need for textbooks to be vetted by state authorities can sometimes, in some southern states, approach the reality of censorship. If one American historian can claim a pseudo-official status, however, it is perhaps Daniel J. Boorstin, who served with distinction as Librarian of Congress, and who is widely admired for the learning and originality of his three-volume history, *The Americans.* But the college text that Boorstin wrote with the help of his wife and a colleague has an unmistakably exceptionalist tone, from a "prologue" on the very first page:

> American history, in this version, is the story of a magic transformation. How did people from everywhere join the American people? How did men and women from a tired Old World where people thought they knew what to expect become wide-eyed explorers of a New World? . . . What has been especially American about our ways of living and earning a living? Our ways of making war and making peace? Our ways of thinking and hoping and fearing, of worshipping God and fighting the Devil? Our ways of traveling and politicking, of importing people, of building houses and cities? These are some of the questions we try to answer in this book.[27]

Nothing could be more explicit. The emphasis of a history to be put into the hands of undergraduates is to focus consciously on what is different, what is "especially American," in other words on what is exceptional, about American history. No wonder if at least some of the Americans taught in this spirit out of books like this came to believe that not only their country, but they too—unlike "tired" Europeans—were morally exceptional. In these texts, we can actually watch young Americans being taught a quasi-official exceptionalism that takes little account of inconvenient facts. They could not be expected to see it for the tangle of dangerous half-truths that it was.

F•O•U•R

From Liberal Consensus to Conservative Ascendancy

We shall fight for the things which we have always carried nearest to our hearts—for democracy, for the right of those who submit to authority to have a voice in their own governments, for the rights and liberties of small nations, for a universal dominion of right . . .

Woodrow Wilson, declaring war in 1917

The case for American exceptionalism has long been expressed by a familiar litany. America, generations have reassured themselves, is as a city set upon a hill, its citizens new men and women, its destiny the last, best hope of earth. But as we have seen, on examination the details of the case turn out to have changed a good deal over time.

Many exceptionalists today, starting with the forty-third president of the United States, base their case on religion. It was the deity, according to them, who singled out the United States for his purposes. Yet the Founders, to take an obvious example, were hardly conspicuous for their religious belief; deism, among them, was as common as orthodoxy.

In recent decades, capitalism has taken its place on the podium as an aspect of American exceptionalism almost equal with democracy. For many, however, throughout the Progressive and New Deal years, capitalism rated very low in their reasons for thinking the United States exceptional. Where once Americans, like Alexis de Tocqueville, saw their country as exceptional in its practice of equality, the conservative consensus of the late twentieth century gave equality a far lower place than other values, such as freedom. Empirically the United States has become one of the least equal, indeed probably the very most unequal, of the world's developed democratic nations in terms of the distribution of both income and wealth.

Where once America was exceptional in its contempt for militarism and its suspicion of standing armies—"there is such a thing," boasted Woodrow Wilson, "as a man being too proud to fight"—now the supposedly invincible prowess of American arms is a vital part of the exceptionalist litany. Recent American presidents have not been too proud to fight even quite small nations. Woodrow Wilson's reasons for believing in the exceptional destiny of the United States were different from those of Abraham Lincoln, and John Kennedy's again different in some respects from those of Franklin Roosevelt. Lyndon Johnson won a record mandate from the American people and vowed to build a Great Society. Fifteen years later, the United States was governed by people who admired Margaret Thatcher for saying there was no such thing as society.

So while the sacred texts and the public rhetoric of exceptionalism have drawn on a common bank of ideas and phrases, when the public philosophy of Americans changed, so did the character of their exceptionalism. And between 1960 and 2000 the public philosophy did change decisively, from the liberal consensus to the conservative ascendancy.

If the moral exceptionalism of America's historical destiny remained as much as ever the grand theme of American nationalism, Americans in the last third of the twentieth century praised themselves for being exceptional in very different ways from the way their parents had praised themselves. In a nutshell, Americans used to be proud of being exceptionally liberal. Now many of them are equally proud of being exceptionally conservative.

In 1950, in a book called *The Liberal Imagination,* the critic Lionel Trilling, then perhaps as close as America has known to being an intellectual pope in the French manner, wrote that "in the United States at this time liberalism is not only the dominant but even the sole intellectual tradition. For it is the plain fact that nowadays there are no conservative or reactionary ideas in general circulation." Indeed, he went further and put the boot into any lurking conservatives, who did not, "With some isolated and some ecclesiastical exceptions, express themselves in ideas but only in action or in irritable mental gestures which seek to resemble ideas."[1] Irritable mental gestures? That would not go down well at the American Enterprise Institute.

Nor was this merely an illusion of liberals living within an academic ivory tower. Richard Nixon famously said, "We are all Keynesians now." He could almost as plausibly have said, "We are all liberals now." In far more ways than the conservative faithful of the Bush years might admit, the Nixon administration's domestic agenda was a continuation of the Kennedy-Johnson policy. That is not altogether surprising, if you think that the man in charge of domestic policy was none other than Daniel Patrick Moynihan, profoundly a liberal at heart, even when in a middle period of his life he railed at certain liberals, because of his resentment at what they had said about him and his famous report on *The Negro Family.* The last time I saw Moynihan, I was criticizing Dick Cheney and Donald Rumsfeld over Iraq. "Ah," said Pat in his most puckish manner, "you mean my liberal friends from the Nixon White House!" It is true—if now hard to believe—that in those days rising Republican politicians did not altogether disdain liberal credentials. Certainly the Nixon administration pointed with pride to its achievement in desegregating schools across the South. A generation later the proportion of Americans who call themselves liberals, as measured by one survey, fell from 34 percent in 1970 to 20 percent in 2000.[2]

Those numbers probably exaggerate the change that has actually taken place. What has unmistakably happened, however, is that the center of gravity of American politics has moved decisively to the right. The word *liberal* itself has fallen into disrepute. Nothing is too bad for conservative bloggers and columnists—let alone radio hosts—to say about liberals. Democrats themselves run a mile from the "L word" for fear of being seen as dangerously outside the mainstream. Conservative politicians and publicists, by dint of associating liberals with all manner of absurdity so that many sensible people hesitated to risk being tagged with the label of liberalism, succeeded in persuading the country that it was more conservative than it actually was.

The word *liberal* has had a strange history. It was coined in Spain in the early nineteenth century. Originally, a liberal was not just one who believed in freedom. He was also one who upheld the interests and the values of the bourgeoisie against monarchical and clerical reaction. At the philosophical level, liberals like John Stuart Mill upheld the supreme value of freedom, including economic freedom. Later in the century, as we have seen, critics on the Left argued that what came to be called Manchester liberalism defended the interests of the rich against those of the poor. Many therefore turned to socialism in one version or another. Nineteenth-century liberals were the defenders of laissez-faire, of capitalism, and of business interests. This was at a time when, everywhere in Europe as well as in Britain, businessmen were relatively progressive compared with aristocratic landowners, not to mention the church and the monarchy. In Britain the Liberal Party of Gladstone, Asquith, and Lloyd George was sharply distinguished from Labour and the socialists, though there was a certain overlap on what was called the "Lib-Lab" Left.

To the extent that neither monarchs and their courtiers, nor landed noblemen, nor an established church threatened the freedom of the American bourgeoisie, the United States had no obvious role for Manchester liberals. The closest equivalent in nineteenth-century America was perhaps those New England abolitionist capitalists, Radical Republicans of the piratical stamp of Benjamin F. Butler, who combined a passion for liberty with a commitment to a robust industrial capitalism. It was not until the 1940s that *liberal* came into general use as a euphemism for "Left." The New York Liberal Party was the home of those on the Left who realized that to call yourself socialist in the United States was to risk losing the votes of many natural progressive supporters. So it came about that conservatives could use the word *liberal* to denounce the mildly social democratic ideals behind the ambitious proposals of the New Deal, the Fair Deal, and President Lyndon Johnson's Great Society. They have succeeded in frightening many into avoiding the liberal label.

To generalize about the political mood of a contentious, volatile nation of three hundred million souls is at best unscientific and at worst absurd. If one tries to gauge long-term shifts in that mood, one conventional measure is the proportion of the American electorate that identifies as being Democrat, Republican, or independent. The Louis Harris poll has been tracking these self-identifications since 1969. Changes have been slow, but significant. In 1969 just under half (49 percent) of those asked gave their party affiliation as Democrat, just under one-third (32 percent) called themselves Republicans, one-fifth (20 percent) were independents.[3]

The Democratic percentage has fallen steadily (though with occasional small revivals) to 41 percent in 1980, the year of Reagan's first victory, and 34 percent in 2004. The Republican share fell to 21 and 22 percent in four of the five years after Watergate. It had risen to one-third, 33 percent, by Reagan's last year and held at 31 percent in 2004. Independents reached 32 percent in 1974, the year of Nixon's Watergate disgrace, and touched 29 percent in 1992, the year of Ross Perot's impressive third-party campaign and Clinton's first victory. But by 2004 independents had settled back to 24 percent, just 5 percentage points above where they had been thirty-five years earlier. Most significant has been the erosion of the Democratic margin over Republicans, from an average of 21 points in the 1970s to a bare three points by 2004.[4]

If instead of looking at party identification you consider ideology, as measured by the scale from conservative to liberal, and ask people about their own assessment of their ideological position, the changes in their answers are equally gradual, perhaps surprisingly so. In the 1970s, 32 percent of all adults called themselves conservatives, and 18 percent liberal. By 2004 the number who called themselves conservatives had risen to 36 percent, and the liberal number had held solid at 18 percent. Moderates were 40 percent in the 1970s, and are still 40 percent in the first decade of the new century.[5]

These self-identifications are unsatisfactory, for at least two reasons. For one thing, people like to think they are "moderate," and many who so describe themselves would seem to others extreme to the verge of fanaticism in one direction or another. For another, and this is particularly troubling for our present inquiry, the definitions of political ideologies themselves change over time. What was seen as dangerous conservative extremism in the 1970s may have become almost liberal by the twenty-first century, and vice versa.

There has undoubtedly been a substantial shift in public opinion away from identification with liberalism and toward identification with conservatism. The conservative assault on government has captured much ground. To be at all precise about the size and the timing of this shift, however, is treacherous. It is often forgotten that even in 1936, the high-water mark of the New Deal, more Americans identified themselves as conservative than as liberal. Pollsters and political scientists have long abandoned a binary division between liberals and conservatives. First they favored a tripartite analysis that counts liberals, conservatives, and "moderates." More recently they have looked for more precise, because multiple, categories.

In 1987 the Pew Center, cooperating with the *Times Mirror* survey, produced an elaborate new "typology" that sought to get behind simple categories.[6] The study derived from academic studies dating back to the 1960s of political outlooks and personal characteristics that influenced voter behavior. Some of these were psychological, such as "alienation." Some concerned attitudes toward government and politics directly. Some, such as isolationism or anticommunism, affected foreign affairs, while others dealt with social or moral attitudes, for example, to race, class, or religion, and others again arose from economic or financial circumstances. The researchers then used the statistical tool factor analysis to break the answers of more than four thousand respondents into nine basic value orientations or themes that, they claimed, "provide the motivation for virtually all political behavior in America."

On the basis of this more subtle inquiry, the researchers found that only 27 percent of Americans identified strongly as conservatives and 19 percent as liberal. In terms of traditional party allegiance, 31 percent identified strongly as Democrats, and only 23 percent as Republicans. One possible explanation is the history of southern conservatism. (Many older people who considered themselves loyal Democrats were staunchly conservative, especially on race but also social issues, and no doubt some continue to resist the equation of conservatism with the Republican Party.) The study concluded that although party did not correlate strongly with people's opinions on many issues, it was an important element in the way people arrived at political opinions. If party is combined with the nine basic values, it does improve understanding of Americans' political attitudes. Ideological self-identification as liberal or conservative was not important for most Americans. Self-identification, finally, as liberal or conservative provided a less reliable analytical tool in the opinion of the authors of the survey than did basic values.

Seven years later, the Pew Center revisited these questions and refined its typology.[7] The 1994 typology divided the public into ten groups defined by their attitude toward government and a range of other beliefs. Two of these "value orientations" were party "leanings." The other eight involved attitudes toward environmentalism; religion and morality; social tolerance and social justice; business and the respondent's own financial situation; government; and patriotism. The survey found three groups who identified strongly with the Republican Party ("staunch conservatives," "populist Republicans," and "moderate Republicans"). Four groups identified strongly with the Democratic Party: the survey called them "liberal Democrats, "new Democrats," "socially conservative Democrats," and the "partisan poor." Other groups were independent or politically uninvolved bystanders. This typology certainly made it possible to relate the political ideology of individuals closely to topical issues, such as gay rights, criticism of President Clinton personally or of the Clinton administration, or welfare policies.

The study of ideological and party identification in general has evolved in the direction of more complex analysis. Whether you agree with the approach or its conclusions in detail or not, it has become harder to say that the country is moving decisively or as a monolith from a more liberal to a more conservative orientation, if only because the analysis shows such different strands of opinion within both political parties, and within liberal and conservative thinking. So the flight from liberalism may not have been quite as headlong or as universal as it has suited conservative publicists to maintain.

Yet it remains undeniable, in my opinion, that if the word *liberal* has fallen out of favor, so too have essential elements in the liberal philosophy itself.[8] At the heart of the liberal style in government since the New Deal was a methodology. A problem was identified and analyzed by experts, often academics. A program would be devised for dealing with the problem. Funds would be appropriated, staff hired, the program implemented. Hey, presto! The problem would be solved. Justly or unjustly, the majority of Americans, having watched the efforts of the Kennedy and Johnson administrations to use this method to bring about the earthly paradise, or at least the Great Society, decided that it didn't work. Among intellectuals, that was the basis of the neoconservatives' faith in what they liked to call the law of unintended consequences. Beginning as an undeniable generalization, that most schemes of social reform have consequences not intended by their sponsors, it became an argument against social reform in general, and an attack on the claims of any government to achieve any improvement in society.

Many working-class white Americans, meanwhile, came to a further conclusion. The liberal reliance on government and its bureaucracy was seen as a more or less deliberate bid on the part of a privileged class of persons to give to African-Americans help and comfort that had not been forthcoming to white workers or to their immigrant grandparents. In parallel with this new, or newly reinforced, suspicion of government, was a new acceptance of the idea that business, or—as conservative publicists liked to put it—"the market," could solve social and economic difficulties more efficiently than government. This evolved into what Thomas Frank has called "market populism," the highly dubious belief that businessmen have the public's interests closer at heart than do politicians.[9]

At the same time corporate management itself was moving, so to speak, to the right. In the 1960s the most admired corporate leaders had been those who were willing, in order to avoid labor conflict, to build a corporate welfare state, working closely with union leadership in the process. In the 1970s the combined impact of the energy crisis and renewed foreign competition from first European, then Asian manufacturers evoked a tougher, harder management style.

It did not take the new corporate culture long to break the power of organized labor. The proportion of American workers enrolled in unions fell drastically. In 1965 more than 30 percent of the American workforce were union members. Their number continued to rise, reaching a peak of more than 22 million as late as 1979. By 2007 the number had fallen to 15.7 million, and the proportion had gone down to 12.5 percent: only one American worker in every eight is now a union member.[10] Moreover, union membership in the private sector was only 7.5 percent. Union members were far less likely than in previous generations to be white male family heads. More of them were women and members of ethnic minorities, which ought not to have reduced their political and social power, but probably did.[11]

In other ways, too, corporate management changed. Power shifted from manufacturing to the financial sector and financial markets, from General Motors to Goldman Sachs. A new style of finance capitalism, marked by a fierce new culture of "mergers and acquisitions," hostile takeovers, and corporate raiding, put management under pressure as never before to deliver higher profits, quarter by quarter, to the shareholders. The share of the owners of capital in the revenues of business grew, and the share of the workers' wages declined.

In the quest for higher profit, managements outsourced to plants overseas. More important, they pressed down relentlessly on wages and conditions for their employees stateside, and cut back employment ruthlessly. Increasingly unprotected by politicians or by unions, workers for corporations like McDonald's and Wal-Mart found their personal dignity, as well as their incomes, under constant siege.

Another aspect of the new tone, from the 1970s on, was a subtle but steady "southernization" of American political life. Some observers claimed to trace this in various cultural fields, such as the national enthusiasm for country music or the spread of a supposedly southern passion for sports, including NASCAR racing and hunting, even a southern style in attitudes to the military and to patriotism.[12]

What was not a mere matter of opinion was the growing political influence of southerners and in particular of southern evangelical Christianity. Although this has been denied, it appears that powerful church groups such as the Southern Baptist Union were alarmed and affronted by a threat from the Carter administration to remove immunity from federal taxes from Christian schools.

Politics in general was transformed by southern influence and in particular by the process, itself a consequence of the enfranchisement of southern blacks, whereby the Republican Party came to be dominated by conservative southerners. At the same time, as southern conservative influence largely disappeared from the Democratic Party, and the influence of African-American, female, and Hispanic voters increased, the Democratic Party moved some way to the left.

While in many respects racial attitudes were growing more tolerant and some barriers to economic and social progress by minorities were lowered, in racial matters, too, the rest of the country became in some ways more like the South. The great northern cities became as segregated, in residential and educational terms, as the major cities of the South, and by certain measures even more so. (By both of the two methods of measurement, "absolute clustering" and the Gini coefficient, Chicago and Detroit were by the 1990 census more segregated than Atlanta or Houston.)[13] By the 1990s the general sympathy for African-Americans generated by the civil rights movement had been largely replaced by a resentment fed by the suspicion that liberal elites had favored blacks at the expense of working-class whites. The *Bakke* case was a flag, marking how far public opinion had shifted away from all kinds of affirmative action. Derision of "political correctness," a staple of conservative journalists and polemicists, increasingly made it acceptable to mock the sensitivities of women and minorities.

These are some of the background changes that transformed the political climate and shifted its center of gravity to the Right. To understand the evolution of exceptionalism, it is worth taking the time to recall, albeit briefly, the political narrative of the past forty years. The modern conservative ascendancy in America can itself be seen as an "unintended consequence" of the political and intellectual upheavals of the 1960s. By the later years of that turbulent decade, many Americans had reacted negatively to the libertarian and self-indulgent aspects of what was known as the counterculture. They became what were called "social conservatives." A largely imaginary bacchanal of the 1960s became a historical datum. Lashed on by godless upper-class libertines, younger Americans were given to believe, the decade of the 1960s was consumed with unbridled chemical and sexual experimentation. As early as 1972 Richard Nixon was able to take advantage of this reaction to caricature the Democratic presidential candidate, Senator George McGovern, a sober-living Midwestern former bomber pilot from that bastion of metrosexual debauchery, South Dakota, as if he were a monster of unpatriotic licentiousness.

Well before that time, a new conservative movement had sprung up. It arrived largely unnoticed at the time of Lyndon Johnson's landslide victory in the 1964 presidential election, hidden from much journalistic notice by the civil rights revolution, the unenthusiastic reception of the Great Society, and the rising doubts about the morality and the wisdom of the Vietnam War. The new conservatism had many origins, and many preoccupations, some of them mutually contradictory. In particular, it contained libertarian elements—especially those concerned with economic liberty and business interests, including resentment of high taxation—and on the other hand social, ethical, patriotic and religious elements. These two potentially incompatible elements were welded together, not least by the strong anticommunism of the group around William F. Buckley, Jr., at *National Review.*

The new mood was partly instrumental in the 1968 presidential election. It extended far more widely than party politics, however. It embraced skepticism, as we have seen, about the efficacy, and the justification, for government action to achieve social goals. It reflected widespread resentment among blue-collar Americans who would previously have been safe Democratic voters. The segregationist governor of Alabama, George Wallace, had astonished the political world in 1964 by his success with working-class voters in Maryland, Indiana, and Wisconsin. In 1968 he put the fear of God into both Democratic and Republican leaders. Wallace voters felt that the Johnson administration had favored African-Americans at their expense. There was a rebellion against high taxation, and in particular the "bracket creep" that was for the first time obliging working-class voters to pay property taxes. Many Americans were grossly offended by what they saw, and were coached to see, as the abandoning of traditional standards of decency in sexual behavior and patriotism. Wallace was the first to profit from such sentiments. But all these strands contributed to Richard Nixon's narrow defeat of the Democratic candidate, Hubert Humphrey, in November 1968.

When Nixon, buoyed by his and Henry Kissinger's apparently successful diplomacy with the Soviet Union and China, was overwhelmingly reelected four years later, it looked as though 1972 might be one of the occasional moments of realignment, when at intervals of a generation or so whole blocks of American voters permanently shift their allegiance.[14] In this instance, it looked as though the Republicans, under Nixon's leadership, had indeed ripped away two great chunks of the "Roosevelt coalition" that had kept the Democrats in power since 1933: southern conservatives and northern working-class Catholic voters. There were even, as 1972 turned into 1973, reports of as many as forty Democratic congressmen, most in the South but some from the North, planning to cross the aisle and become Republicans.[15]

Then came the Watergate hearings. By the early weeks of 1973, it was clear to Democratic congressmen who had already started to negotiate the terms of their entry into the Republican system that this was not a moment to become a Republican. The credibility of Richard Nixon and his administration drained slowly away until in August 1974 he chose to resign ahead of almost certain impeachment. The short-term effect was a Democratic tide in the midterm elections of that year and the election of a Democrat, Jimmy Carter, in 1976.

The conservative revolution, therefore, was postponed by some seven years, and when it came it was not a Nixon but a Reagan revolution. The interim brought two failed presidencies, those of Gerald Ford and Jimmy Carter. It brought the humiliating end of the Vietnam war and the onset of an energy crisis that shook many of the assumptions Americans had made about their country's position in the world, including assumptions about its exceptional situation. For the first time since the Great Depression, many Americans began to question whether their children would live as well as they had.

That was why people were so relieved and so grateful when Ronald Reagan assured them that it was "morning in America" again. The slogan might be vapid, but it struck a chord. A new conservative mood took hold. One theme was the intensified suspicion of government. Where in the Kennedy and Johnson era, government was seen as the fallible but necessary instrument of social progress, now an increasing proportion of Americans adopted Reagan's conviction that, as he put in his first inaugural, "in this present crisis, government is not the solution to our problem; government is the problem." In the end, even a moderately liberal Democratic president in Bill Clinton agreed that "the era of big government is over."[16]

Although Reagan was not personally either a born-again Christian or a notable exemplar of austerity in his private life, and indeed evangelical Christians came to resent how little his administration had done for them, the new Christian Right was a distinctive and powerful wing of the new conservative coalition that had brought him to power.

This in itself was new. The American constitutional tradition not only mandated a separation between church and state; it also sought to keep confessional politics at arm's length. Now, as not before, at least for many decades, American exceptionalism acquired a specifically religious tone.

The Reagan administration marked the beginning of a sharper division in public opinion than had been seen for many years. For many Democrats, Reagan's personality and politics were alike bizarre and unfamiliar. For conservatives, he was quite simply a hero, the leader who had cleansed the national stables, blown away miasmas of doubt and restored the ancient verities. In reality, Reagan's achievement was as mixed as his reputation. While in the central field of international politics, in the superpower relationship with the Soviet Union, he was highly successful, in other foreign relations, especially where he had to deal with weak countries of the so-called Third World, he blundered. His administration's conduct of the Iran-Contra affair almost led to political disaster. At home, conservatives and the corporate world welcomed his attempt to reduce the influence of government. In his brutal demolition of the air traffic controllers' strike, he administered a symbolic blow to the political power of organized labor. Yet he cannot be said to have been notably successful in reducing the importance, let alone the cost, of the federal government. His management of the economy was unsteady and of the budget incompetent.

It was his successor, George H. W. Bush, who inherited the achievements of the Reagan foreign policy. Bush managed the consequences of the collapse of communism, and especially the reunification of Germany, with great skill. When Saddam Hussein invaded Kuwait, threatening the stability of the Middle East and of the "new world order" the president was trying to promote, Bush wisely responded through the United Nations. He successfully put together a broad international coalition, including traditional allies like Britain and France, and Arab nations like Saudi Arabia, Syria, and Egypt. In this way he restored the world order with minimum damage either to the Middle East or to the reputation of the United States. In international affairs the very able team he put together were notably successful. His popularity melted away, however, as a result of the perception that he was aloof and elitist, his limited imagination in domestic politics, and widespread frustration with the economy.

His defeat brought to the White House William Jefferson Clinton, and the polarization of the American party system was now almost complete. To be a Democrat was now to be a liberal, though often a far from extreme one. To be a Republican meant to be a conservative, and often an uncompromising one. To a degree unprecedented since 1932, Clinton's election seemed to many conservatives not just a normal swing of the pendulum of party fortunes but a scandalously illegitimate interruption of the proper course of things. They had persuaded themselves that there had been a "Reagan revolution," not noticing how many of the electorate had been unconverted. To true believers in the conservative faith it now became an absolute duty to eject the usurper from the seat of power. The conservative media launched a pitiless bombardment on Clinton's policies, his friends, his morals, and his wife. No charge was too trivial or too weighty to be hurled at him with little or no supporting evidence. It was insinuated that he was guilty of murder and drug smuggling. Even more grave, he was accused of spending too much time at the hairdresser.

The 2000 presidential election was the closest since 1876. The Democratic candidate, Al Gore, carried the popular vote by more than half a million votes, but was defeated because of the vote in the electoral college. (There are those who conclude it is time to reform or abolish the electoral college.)[17] In 2004 the margin of victory for President Bush was decisive, though then, too, the electoral college system acted, as arguably it was intended by the Framers to act, to strengthen the authority of a president elected in a close contest. No doubt George W. Bush's enhanced majority owed much to the terrorist attacks in Washington and New York of September 2001. But it certainly confirmed the view—not least in the rather tight circle of true believers in the president's immediate political entourage—that the United States was now normally in the hands of a conservative ascendancy, and would remain so for the duration of a new American century.

The events in the last decade of the twentieth century set the scene for a new and invidious version of exceptionalism. In the process, what had been an idealistic and generous, if somewhat solipsistic, interpretation of the nation's character and destiny was replaced by a mood that was harder, more hubristic. The collapse of communism in Europe left the United States as "the lone superpower." A steep spike in stock market prices in the last half of the 1990s created a short-lived and illusory mood of economic triumphalism and belief in a "New Economy" that broke all the rules. Then, abruptly, the jihadists' attacks on September 11, 2001, convinced the nation, and not only the conservative half of it, that it was uniquely hated by new and insidious enemies and that it was now engaged in a prolonged "war on terror."

Each of these propositions, superficially persuasive and for a while virtually unchallenged in the media, was in fact misleading. It was, and is, perfectly true that the military power of the United States is unchallengeable. It was far less clear that this military supremacy could be effectively used to promote American values or even American interests. The nuclear weapons and missile delivery systems, the "smart" weapons and digital communication systems, the aircraft carriers and infantry divisions so lavishly provided, were not necessarily the most appropriate forces required either for the defense of the United States against the threat of terrorism or for the "projection" of American power. (This word, a favorite of the period, was in itself a somewhat euphemistic description of the American capability to destroy Beirut or Tripoli or Baghdad from the air, as one might have said that imperial Japan "projected" its power over Pearl Harbor or the power of Nazi Germany was "projected" over Guernica or London.) There was little public debate over the precise purpose for which vast sums continued to be spent on "defense," as military expenditure was classified even when, as in Iraq, its function was undeniably offensive. Instead, there was esoteric argument between those who wanted to maintain the existing force levels, accumulated more or less haphazardly in the context of the successive phases of the Cold War against communism, and the neoconservatives, who lamented that even these swollen forces would be inadequate to maintain American global supremacy through a new century. There was little understanding in either the White House or the Pentagon of the strength of weakness, or of the desperate determination of those who resented and resisted American supremacy to find new and vicious ways of punishing what they saw as an oppressor too mighty to be defeated in fair fight in the field.

The turn of the millennium was a time of faith in an American New Economy, transformed by computers, new information technology and the Internet. Though some of the key breakthroughs had not been made by Americans—the World Wide Web, for instance, was invented by an Englishman working as part of a European team in Switzerland—it was assumed that this economic wonder world was essentially American. The emphasis was not on a broad improvement of living standards (though in fact for a few years in the late 1990s the incomes of poor people did rise somewhat) but on the rise in stock market values, which disproportionately enriched a small percentage of the population at the top of the economic tree. Contrary to a mythology of universal participation in the market, no more than 60 percent of all Americans benefited at all, even indirectly through pension plans or mutual funds, and many of those held investments worth no more than the price of a secondhand car. The growth in wealth went overwhelmingly to those who were already well off before the boom, and disproportionately to those who were already rich. The more "irrationally exuberant" commentators—to borrow Alan Greenspan's felicitous term—explained excitedly that the laws of economic gravity had been repealed. The American economy, these enthusiasts predicted, with every appearance of believing their own fantasies, would soar upward indefinitely, led by stock market values no longer earthbound by any connection with earned profits. Although there were indeed encouraging aspects of the economic scene in the late 1990s, not least an appreciable upswing in productivity, after a brief siren time the spike ended.

The bubble burst. Some long-established underlying weaknesses of the American economy were again exposed. Both the public finances and the trading balance were in substantial deficit. There was a new dependence on foreign inward investment, especially from China and Japan, to make up for the low level of American savings and to support the international parity of the dollar. The American market was awash with cheap manufactured goods, especially from Asia, which boosted the real standard of living of American consumers at the expense of American manufacturing and the American balance of payments. Massive foreign holdings of dollars represented a mortgage on the future; the day might come when foreign holders, in malice or in fear, dumped their dollars. The buoyancy of the stock market owed dangerously much to financial engineering of a kind that too often laid heavy burdens on future generations, and indeed resulted in part from a generous distribution of outright fraud. Conservative commentators robustly dismissed any suggestion that the United States need take any account of the rest of the world, unless it was in the shape of an ambivalent concern with the rise of China, compacted of an exaggeration of its present economic strength and a naïve indifference to its political independence and communist ideology.

Above all, the United States, which had historically been exceptional in its self-sufficiency in raw materials and energy, was now heavily dependent on imports in both categories, and especially dependent for some 60 percent of its consumption of oil on imports from Saudi Arabia and other parts of the Middle East, Venezuela and elsewhere in Latin America, the former Soviet Union, West Africa, and other potentially unfriendly or economically unreliable regions. This was not only an economic liability in itself. It offered a permanent temptation to political and even military intervention, at least in the event of some future shortage, in areas with substantial reserves of energy. This was the more troubling because the rapid growth of developing economies, especially those of China and India, promised future competition for energy and other natural resources.

By the beginning of a new millennium, the prevailing assumptions in the United States about America's situation in the world had become substantially at odds with reality. In 2000, in an exceptionalist State of the Union message that was millennial in both meanings of the word, Bill Clinton reflected a triumphal mood. Never had the United States been more prosperous, he said (to ringing applause from the very Republicans who had just impeached him), more influential, more secure. Within months, the collapse of the stock market belied the economic premises of this mood. Less than two years later the attacks of September 11 replaced complacent foreign policy assumptions with foreboding and a puzzled preoccupation with why foreigners in general and fanatical Muslims in particular appeared to "hate us." President George W. Bush announced a "war on terror" and invaded first Afghanistan, then Iraq.

The reaction to the terrorist attacks reflected the extent to which Americans had come to misperceive their situation in the world, which was immensely powerful, but not omnipotent. There were many examples of this. A profound lack of realism about China has been mentioned. Two others in particular are worth describing in some detail: the "extreme misperception" of the amount of aid to poor countries given by the United States, and the partly mythical account that is widely held by Americans of the relationship of the United States to the state of Israel. Both fit an exceptionalist image of the role of the United States in the world that is, to say the least, substantially inflated.

Many public opinion surveys have discovered that a majority of Americans believe that the United States is the biggest, if not the only, significant giver of foreign aid. They also overestimate the proportion of the federal budget that is given by the United States as foreign aid. A survey by the University of Maryland in 1995, for example, found that respondents grossly exaggerated not only the amount of U.S. foreign aid but also the proportion it represented of the federal budget.[18]

This view obviously opens the door to a generalized resentment of foreigners, although in fact at present Americans in general are well disposed at least to those foreigners who are not actually threatening them. (For complicated reasons, due to in part to deliberate misrepresentation by the Bush administration of the French government's attitude toward Saddam Hussein, the French seem to be an exception to this benevolence.) If Americans actually believe that a substantial share of their taxes goes to foreigners, and that no one else gives much foreign aid, resentment would be natural. The median estimate in the surveys was that foreign aid amounted to 20 percent of the federal budget, and the mean estimate was even higher at 24 percent. That exaggerates the proportion of the federal budget spent on aid by a factor of more than twenty. At the same time, the U.S. population is in favor of foreign aid, and support for it has grown over recent years. So Americans are indeed generous, but they exaggerate their own generosity, especially in comparative or exceptionalist terms.

On October 10 1970, by resolution 2626, the UN general assembly set a foreign-aid goal of 1 percent of GNP for "developed" nations. This goal has subsequently been reduced to 0.7 percent. In 2006 (the most recent year for which full statistics are available) Sweden donated 1.2 percent of its GNP in foreign aid, Norway 0.89 percent, and the Netherlands 0.81 percent. Britain, France, and Germany all fell well short of the 0.7 percent goal with 0.51, 0.47, and 0.36 percent, respectively. The United States, in contrast, gave just 0.18 percent of its GNP by the same measure.[19]

These numbers need to be viewed with skepticism. For one thing, governments frequently pay substantially less than they pledge. (The failure of Italy and Canada, for example, to come up with even a fraction of the aid to Africa they promised at the G8 summit in Scotland in 2005 is notorious.) Then, of course, there is the whole argument about whether aid works. Yet both these causes for caution apply equally to United States aid and to aid promised, and given, by other nations. Again, many critics contend that the United States, by insisting on the neoliberal "reforms" of the so-called Washington Consensus, such as "structural adjustment" and privatization, may have hindered the development of poor nations as much as it has helped them.[20] All rich nations attempt to "tie" aid so as to derive some benefit, political or commercial, from it.

A number of conservative commentators in the United States, apparently annoyed by comparisons between American aid and that of other nations, have responded by pointing to what they assess as the far greater contribution of aid from U.S. private sources. Dr. Carol Adelman of the Hudson Institute, for example, has pointed out in a series of explicitly exceptionalist articles and papers that U.S. private aid greatly exceeds government aid. In 2005 Adelman and two colleagues produced a paper that estimated U.S. "total economic engagement" at $130.9 billion. They found that U.S. "private assistance" came to $62.1 billion, of which no less than $40.1 billion was "individual remittances."[21] These estimates have been criticized, however. Adelman is said to have included in her estimate of "private assistance" what is usually called "private investment." She and her colleagues certainly included in "personal aid" the very large sums remitted by foreign immigrant workers in the United States, especially those from Latin America, to families at home. It is questionable whether this represents the "generosity" of Americans, since many of the remitters are not American citizens. What is more directly relevant to American exceptionalism is that Adelman and others have repeatedly stressed that the United States is the largest giver of "private" aid but failed to note that citizens and organizations of many kinds in other nations also give large sums in private aid.

In the case of the Asian tsunami of 2004–5, for example, the U.S. government pledged $950 million, but U.S. nongovernmental organizations and private donors gave almost exactly twice as much ($1.875 billion), and U.S. corporations gave generally larger amounts than European or Japanese businesses. But the United States was not the only country where there was a massive outpouring of charitable giving. In the United Kingdom, for example, private gifts for tsunami victims came to $654 million, one-third of the U.S. total, from a country with one-fifth of the U.S. population, and private donors in Australia, Canada, Germany, and Sweden also contributed large amounts.[22]

The exact figures for private as opposed to governmental giving, and for flows to developing countries from the United States and other countries, are disputed and hard to establish. What is plain is that many Americans wrongly believe that their contribution to development aid is uniquely, or exceptionally, great. (One might add that some in the United States seem strangely keen to insist on their compatriots' exceptional virtue.) More generally, many Americans have absorbed from education or the media a view of modern history that gives disproportionate credit to the achievements of the United States in many fields. For example, the great contributions made by non-American scientists (British, émigré German, and French, among others) to the development of nuclear weapons, a principal component of American superpower status, are largely ignored in popular accounts of the history. The reasons for this are entirely understandable. But the effect has been to exaggerate an exceptionalist interpretation of an important story in twentieth-century history.

Again, recent Hollywood movies about World War II (*Saving Private Ryan,* for example) have given the impression that the defeat of Nazi Germany was essentially achieved by American arms. In reality, of course, fact, unpalatable as this is for some Americans, Hitler's Germany was defeated by a coalition of the Soviet Union, the British Empire, and the United States, with resistance movements in several European countries incurring terrible suffering for their efforts in alliance with that coalition.[23] While the part played by the United States in that coalition was important, even arguably decisive, it was not an American victory alone.[24]

A particularly significant example of this process of "exceptionalizing" international events, given the continuing crisis in the Middle East, has been the subtle, often unconscious rewriting of history that is sometimes called "the Americanization of the Holocaust."[25]

According to a version of history that came to be devoutly believed by many Americans, Christian as well as Jewish, the United States intervened in Europe in World War II at least in part in order to save a remnant of the Jewish people. After the war, in this version of history, it was the United States, and the United States essentially alone, that guaranteed the survival of the state of Israel.

This is only very approximately true. The United States did not enter World War II to save Jews but because it was attacked by the Japanese at Pearl Harbor. As a matter of historical fact it was Hitler who declared war on the United States, not the United States that declared war on Hitler. There is abundant evidence that although the Roosevelt administration in the United States, like the Churchill administration in Britain, was indeed horrified by the information that was already available about the mass murder of the Jewish people while it was happening, both countries' governments consciously decided that their highest priority was to defeat Nazi Germany, and that rescuing Europe's Jews was not practical. Their decision may seem cynical. It may have been based on incorrect information. But that was the decision.

The British government was particularly afraid that Jewish immigration to Palestine would lead to conflict with the Arab population there and so would endanger Britain's already fragile presence in the Middle East. Congress was even more reluctant than the Roosevelt administration to raise immigration quotas. Speaker Sam Rayburn warned Roosevelt that the loosening of immigration restrictions would encounter strong opposition on Capitol Hill, and Roosevelt accepted that it could not be done. There was at least one tragic instance, the case of the *Saint Louis*, where a shipload of European Jews actually reached America but was turned away. "In short," writes the historian of President Roosevelt's foreign policy, "the best means he saw for saving the Jews was through the quickest possible end to the fighting—a policy of 'rescue through victory.'"[26]

The State Department was responsible for immigration, and the senior official in charge, Breckinridge Long, who had been ambassador in Rome and was sympathetic to Mussolini's fascism, was a shameless anti-Semite. The department put up endless roadblocks to prevent Jewish immigration. After 1944, under pressure from his Treasury secretary, Henry Morgenthau, Roosevelt appointed a War Refugee Board and took the issue out of the hands of the State Department. Some actions were taken that did result in small numbers of Jews being saved. Altogether, according to the Immigration and Naturalization Service, 476,000 European refugees reached America from Europe during the Nazi period, of whom one-third, 158,000, were Jews. (In comparison, Britain, with roughly one-third of the population of the United States at the time, accepted about 60,000 Jewish refugees before the outbreak of war in 1939 made immigration impossible. Many, absurdly, were interned as "enemy aliens," albeit temporarily in decent conditions in unused rental holiday accommodations in the Isle of Man. (They created what amounted to a university there to pass the time.)

The historian of the rescue, Henry L. Feingold, concludes that "passionate commitment to save lives . . . did not exist in the Roosevelt Administration, although there were many individuals who wanted to do more." The Roosevelt administration, he states, "had no popular mandate for a more active rescue role. Public opinion was, in fact, opposed to the admission of refugees, because most Americans were not aware of what was happening."[27] It is certainly not the case that the United States entered World War II primarily or even to any substantial degree in order to save European Jews from Hitler's "Final Solution."

The Truman administration did help Israel in its earliest and most vulnerable days, but the builders of Israel understandably took their help where they could find it: from the Soviet Union, from France (the principal helper in the early phase of the Israeli nuclear weapons project), from Britain (from the Balfour Declaration to the Suez episode), and even from apartheid South Africa. It took two decades and more after 1948 before support for Israel became more important as a goal of policy in Washington than keeping the Soviet Union out of the Middle East.

The United States did help Israel with generous and growing economic and military aid, though Israel's deadly enemy, Saudi Arabia, was also a key American ally, and Egypt, a key enemy of Israel at least until 1976, also became for a time the second-largest recipient of American military aid. In terms of domestic policy in the United States, it was not until the 1970s that the alliance of Jewish and Christian supporters of Israel in the American political system made the commitment to Israel there unconditional.

This commitment did not set hard until a quarter of a century had passed after the defeat of the Nazi state.[28] The Six-Day War of 1967, and even more, the Yom Kippur War of 1973 and the Arab oil boycott, convinced many American Jews that Israel was less secure than they had assumed. Ironically, the very success of so many Jews in America and even the tolerance they encountered persuaded some Jewish leaders that the survival of the Jewish people might be at risk. It began to be said that assimilation might be a "silent Holocaust," as Jews intermarried with Gentiles, and their children lost their Jewish identity. A series of cultural events, such as the success of Anne Frank's diary in the 1950s and Leon Uris's 1958 best-seller *Exodus*, had begun to engage the sympathetic interest of the broad American public. But as Jewish leaders and intellectuals became darker in their forebodings for Israel, the Holocaust became something close to a national obsession in America.

A chain of events moved this process along. Adolf Eichmann was tried in 1961 and executed in 1962. The trial did not enter the consciousness of many Americans until the furor following the publication of Hannah Arendt's book *Eichmann in Jerusalem* in 1973. In 1975 there was anger over the way the Arab nations, newly empowered by the oil price rise, used the votes of black African countries to pass a resolution at the United Nations calling Zionism a form of racism. Senator Henry M. Jackson and his allies pressured the American government to demand freedom for Russian Jews to emigrate. The 1978 NBC miniseries *Holocaust*, seen by one hundred million Americans, helped to establish the Shoah as a unique event in American minds. At the same time Jewish leaders insisted that it was indeed unique, not to be compared with other historical atrocities such as the 1915 Armenian massacres or the slave trade.

"Since the 1970s," wrote the Chicago historian Peter Novick, "the Holocaust has come to be presented . . . as not just a Jewish memory but an American memory."[29] The institutionalization of the Holocaust became definitive with the building of the United States National Holocaust Museum in Washington in 1993, the same year in which a series of Hollywood movies about the destruction of the European Jews culminated in Steven Spielberg's *Schindler's List.* Holocaust museums were built in many other major American cities. A growing number of states mandated Holocaust teaching in schools. The Holocaust became for many Americans, Gentiles as well as Jews, a powerful parable of suffering and redemption, and one in which the United States was cast as the redeemer.

By the 1990s support for Israel in the United States was not only deeply embedded in public opinion as a whole. It was formidably well organized. Zionist organizations such as the American Israel Political Action Committee raised substantial funds for senators and congressmen, and pounced on almost any criticism of Israel, which was unfailingly put down to anti-Semitism. American support for Israel had been generous, unstinting, and based in genuine sympathy and admiration. It did, however, leave in the public mind an exaggerated image of the role the United States had played over the entire history of Israel.

At the same time there was little interest and little sympathy in the United States for the Arab nations and in particular for the Palestinians. As a consequence—quite unnoticed by most Americans, because largely unreported in American news media—fierce, if largely unjustified, resentment of the United States was building up in the Middle East.

The psychological and political impact of the terrorist attacks on the New York World Trade Center and the Pentagon evoked an entirely understandable outrage in the American public. This was not some vague feeling, to be teased out by pollsters. It was an immediate, visceral, and justified explosion of righteous anger and sorrow at the horror of the blazing infernos in New York and Washington and the massacre of almost three thousand wholly innocent people. The public services in New

York reacted with admirable courage and efficiency. This was the American people at their best.

It also evoked, however, a bizarrely inappropriate response from the administration in Washington. It was inevitable that any American government, attacked in this way, would strike back as best it could at the places from which the blows seemed to have come. Clearly one immediate target must be Afghanistan. Terrorists and jihadists from many countries had been trained in camps there, and the fact that the government of that chaotic and impoverished state was in the hands of the Taliban, fellow Islamic extremists who had provided sanctuary for Al-Qaeda, made it certain that the United States would seek to deprive the terrorists of their safe haven.

The United States was successful—at least on the surface—in securing the cooperation of the government of Pakistan. It was in the wild tribal territories of Pakistan's North-West Frontier Province, bordering Afghanistan, that many Islamic extremists and terrorists were hiding. It was relatively easy to win a quick military victory in Afghanistan, by forces supplied from bases in the Islamic republics of the former Soviet Union. The Taliban regime—Islamist, illiberal, and fiercely repressive, especially of women—which had supported Al-Qaeda, was swiftly but not permanently defeated. Both in Pakistan and in Afghanistan pro-Islamic forces—among them popular Islamic feeling, and the powerful Inter Service Intelligence agency in Pakistan—remained undeterred.

From the start the Bush administration's response was somewhat illogical. It was apparently shaped more by a wild desire to lash out in revenge than by the measured statesmanship that had generally guided American policy in the Cold War. While vast and accurate knowledge of the Middle East was available in Washington, that knowledge did not seem to guide policy. Instead, the administration listened too much to a handful of Iraqi exiles who told the Bush administration what it wanted to hear. (The British government, too, had its favorite Iraqi exiles.) The president took advice from a small inner circle who saw the tragedy of September 11 as an opportunity to make Israel more secure and spread American concepts of democracy in the Middle East. He declared war not on nations or forces or criminals but on an abstract noun, "terror."

That in itself made success almost impossible, for terror, like the poor, is always with us. The homeland both of the terrorists' chieftain, Osama bin Laden, and of most of the actual perpetrators of the New York and Washington atrocities was Saudi Arabia. Yet Saudi Arabia was influential in Washington, in part because of the president's family friendships and business connections there. It was the world's largest potential supplier of the oil the United States now needed to import. Although the Saudi government and influential individual Saudis had massively supported the spread of madrasas where the United States and the West were denounced in the most virulent terms, propaganda that had arguably contributed to the spread of anti-American passions and terrorism, Saudi Arabia continued to be treated as an ally. There was no credible evidence of Iraqi involvement in the attacks on the United States, though bogus evidence was trumped up by the Bush administration. The United Nations' painstaking attempt to find out whether Saddam Hussein did indeed have "weapons of mass destruction" was brushed aside. Influential figures around the president—almost all, except Vice President Dick Cheney, unelected—saw the terrorist attacks as an opportunity to attack Iraq. So Iraq was attacked.

Intelligence was skimpy, and apparently tailored to fit the preconceptions of this clique, including a handful of civilian officials at the top of the Pentagon and a loose coterie of neoconservative "intellectuals" with influence backstage in the White House, at the Pentagon, and in conservative media. In one of the more remarkable exercises in "inside politics" in recent history, these officials, speechwriters, publicists, and pundits saw the crisis as an opportunity to transform the Middle East into a regime of democracy and liberal capitalism by a military assault on Iraq.

Admittedly the Iraqi regime was unspeakably cruel and corrupt. But that had not deterred Washington in the past from helping Saddam Hussein's government in its bloody war against Iran, just as the United States had recruited the Taliban and even Osama bin Laden himself as allies in the earlier war against the Soviet Union in Afghanistan. (By a strange historical irony, Donald Rumsfeld, the secretary of defense in charge of the invasion of Iraq in 2003, had in an earlier incarnation been the official who visited Saddam Hussein in Baghdad to offer him American support against Iran.)

Various more or less confused motivations and preconceptions went into the disastrous decision to invade Iraq and the even more disastrous way in which the conquered country was subsequently ruled. One was a delusion that, once "liberated," Iraq would speedily develop into a pro-Western capitalist democracy, rather as Germany, Italy, and Japan had done with American help after World War II. (That ignored the obvious fact that Iraq, though a country that had made remarkable progress in some areas, such as medicine, had virtually no previous experience of democracy.) Another was a well-meant dream of knocking out a dangerous potential enemy to Israel, though replacing a Sunni dictatorship in Baghdad with a Shi'a state, necessarily closely allied to Iran, scarcely seemed the best way of helping Israel in the long term. Something perhaps was due to the president's personal animus against a dictator who had caused a world crisis in his father's time and had even attempted to assassinate the elder Bush. At any event, the motives for the invasion were both confused and delusional, and the public presentation of them was a disgraceful exercise in "spin." Tall stories—that Saddam was importing steel tubes to make nuclear centrifuges, that he had built mobile bomb laboratories, that he was importing hundreds of tons of uranium ore from Africa—were cynically trotted out as evidence; as the national security adviser, Condoleezza Rice, said, "We don't want the smoking gun to be a mushroom cloud." The best that could be said about the decision to invade Iraq, and even more about the occupation of Iraq, was what a wit said of Napoleon's kidnapping and murder of a Bourbon prince: "Worse than a crime, it was a mistake."[30]

The invasion of Iraq was of course successful. But the administration gave no thought to what would come next. It actually ignored such work as had been done in Washington to prepare for Iraq's future. (But that was in the despised State Department, the "department of nice," as conservative insiders contemptuously described it!)[31]

Stumbling mistakes were made, one after another. Too few troops were sent. The Iraqi army and police were disbanded, making anarchy inevitable, without enough American or coalition forces to restore order, let alone reconnect the electric power, provide clean water, or reopen the oil wells that were supposed to pay for the whole venture.

In Iraq and elsewhere the United States permitted outrages and a cynicism that would have been inconceivable under previous administrations: what amounted to looting by well-connected American corporations; a license to kill with impunity for private security companies; sneering contempt for the Geneva Conventions ("quaint," as the future attorney general Alberto Gonzales termed some of them) and for international law; detentions without trial for indefinite periods in Guantánamo and elsewhere; kidnappings on allied territory; torture and other grave human rights abuses; and an astonishing effort by government lawyers to redefine torture so as to permit it. It was as if the government of the United States, starting at the top, had decided that the terrorist outrages of September 11, 2001, meant that law, custom and decency had all been suspended *sine die.*

This sad story has been endlessly exposed. There is one point, however, that has not been much confronted. The overthrow of Saddam Hussein was undertaken in order to introduce democracy into the Middle East. Yet the whole operation was itself hardly a conspicuous example of American democracy in action. Policy throughout was kept to a tight circle defined not by proven competence but by ideological reliability (in an administration elected by one of the narrowest margins in history), in the White House, the Pentagon, and the uniformed military. In the memoirs of participants, now flooding into print, even some of the highest officials complain that their judgment was brusquely shoved aside. The president, in particular, made it plain that he wanted to act against Iraq irrespective of the intelligence or of disagreement from those most expert in the matter. The vice president, too, acted in the most high-handed manner. There was, until the midterm elections of 2006, more than three years after the invasion, signally little debate in Congress. Until it was obvious that things had gone very badly wrong indeed in Iraq, there was comparatively little discussion of policy or its execution in the media (except for such specialist journals as the *New York Review of Books,* contemptuously derided by the Bush administration and its drummers and trumpeters). Journalists, so reliably skeptical of executive overreaching in the Vietnam and Watergate years, seemed, with honorable exceptions, shocked into silence by 9/11.

The Bush administration had been elected in 2000 in circumstances that conferred a bare minimum of democratic legitimacy. The presidency was won by a candidate who did not carry even a plurality of the popular vote and owed his eventual victory to a decision by a Supreme Court controlled by conservative justices appointed by Republican presidents. Congress, too, was controlled by Republicans and driven by conservative Republican leaders who allowed less freedom of debate than congressional veterans could remember. The electoral system was dominated, as never before, by money and by the sometimes cynical manipulation of the news media.

In 2004 things were a little different. President Bush was returned by a popular majority, if not a large one. Republican control of the Congress was again narrow, and was to disappear in 2006. Yet the president clearly felt that he had a mandate for decisive, ideologically clear action. How much of that mandate, and that majority, came from the shock of 9/11, and from the sentiment that in such dangerous times the president must be supported unconditionally, cannot be known with certainty. In my opinion those feelings did play a significant part, though the indifferent campaign waged by the Democratic challengers no doubt contributed to the result as well.

The Bush administration's enthusiasm about converting the Islamic Middle East to the folkways of American democracy certainly contrasted ironically with the unhappy condition of American democracy at home at the time. Some, at least, of the more enthusiastic champions of bringing democracy to Iraq would have had difficulty in recognizing democracy if it had fallen on their heads. A gap seemed to have opened between the confident exceptionalist perceptions of at least a slim majority of the American voters and their chosen leaders, on the one hand, and the realities of a world in which American exceptionalism was being given an ironic twist. As we shall see, that gap, between the comfortable exceptionalist perception and the less satisfactory reality, had been growing for some time.

F•I•V•E

The Other Exceptionalism

> Notions of American exceptionalism cut us off from [a] larger understanding of ourselves and our place in the world as a nation among nations, a people among peoples. They produce an odd combination of parochialism and arrogance.
> *Thomas Bender,* A Nation Among Nations

So far, I have been examining, and questioning, the underlying assumption of American exceptionalism: that America is exceptional among nations in its general superiority, and in particular in its political and moral superiority. In the past few years, less friendly observers, in America as well as abroad, have pointed out another kind of American exceptionalism: fields in which American practice or performance seem to be exceptional in another way, by falling below international standards.

Understandably, perhaps, it was foreigners, and especially Europeans, who were the first to point out that the United States is exceptional in some less attractive ways. They observe, for example, that, though American leaders such as President George W. Bush talk as if the United States were exceptional in its commitment to freedom in the abstract, the United States is certainly exceptional among developed democratic nations in the numbers and proportion of prison inmates.

International observers, and increasingly now Americans too, have pointed out that although most Americans believe in the superiority of American health care, statistically the performance and especially the availability of health care in the United States is not impressive.

Although American incomes do remain comparatively high, especially when measured in ways that exclude services that are free or subsidized elsewhere, the distribution of income and wealth in the United States is now exceptional for its extreme and growing inequality.[1]

More generally, the practice of American politics, and the conduct of the American government, have caused many to see it as exceptional in a negative sense, both in its methods and in its outcomes. Much of the American political game today seems disconnected from policy and focused almost exclusively on who is elected, as opposed to what the winner does once in office. The American political system, once so widely admired, puzzles many foreigners, and indeed many Americans too, in its rejection of assumptions that are generally shared elsewhere—for example, in respect to global warming, international law, and respect and support for international organizations.

Some of these criticisms are more justified than others. Many apply to a particular administration rather than to the United States as a whole. Most apply only to a minority of Americans, or to some parts only of American society. What is significant, however, in terms of the argument that is being made in this book, is that over the past few years such criticisms are now increasingly heard from American critics of their own country's practice and public philosophy, as well as from foreigners. Professor Thomas Bender of New York University, from whom I have taken the epigraph for this chapter, is one such.

Another is the Princeton economist and later *New York Times* columnist Paul Krugman. In 1998 he wrote in the influential journal *Foreign Affairs* an article he called—provocatively—"America the Boastful." "Our current sense that we are on top of the world," he wrote, "is based on a huge exaggeration of the implications of a few good years here, a few bad years elsewhere. Let there be even a mild recession in the U.S., a moderate recovery in Europe and Japan, and a bounceback in emerging Asia, and all this talk of the return of American dominance will start to sound very silly indeed." He went further. "Future historians," he predicted, "will not record that the 21st century belonged to the United States."[2]

In 2003 the dean of the Yale law school, Harold Hongju Koh, a law professor of great distinction who is the son of a South Korea ambassador to the United States, who also worked in the Justice Department in the Reagan administration and as an assistant secretary of state in the Clinton administration, wrote an article in the *Stanford Law Review* that was subsequently published as a chapter in a book with the title *America's Jekyll-and-Hyde Exceptionalism.*[3] Dr. Koh's article is a careful analysis of what he sees as a split personality in American attitudes to human rights, especially in the international arena.[4]

Many other influential American intellectuals have begun to examine the dark side of American exceptionalism. In some cases they question the whole idea that the United States is morally exceptional among nations. However, such questioning remains shocking to the American majority and is angrily denounced by the small but still influential sect of neoconservatives.

We have seen that Alexis de Tocqueville was struck above all by the degree of equality in early-nineteenth-century America, and how much things have changed in that regard. He was also impressed by the leniency of American criminal justice. "Whereas the English," he wrote, "seem to want to preserve carefully the bloody traces of the Middle Ages in their penal legislation, the Americans have almost made the death penalty disappear from their codes." A recent American historian has reported that other European visitors in the United States in the past were "astonished" by the existence of movements in the United States to abolish the death penalty. Until the middle 1960s, American practice in this respect was similar to that of other developed democracies. While most states, as well as the federal government, kept capital punishment on the books—as did most of Europe, Canada, and most Australian states—in America, as elsewhere, the punishment was rarely inflicted.

Beginning in the 1970s, that changed sharply. England and Wales stopped applying the death penalty for murder in 1965 and abolished it permanently in 1969. Canada abolished it for murder in 1976, Spain in 1978, France in 1981, Australia in 1984, and Ireland in 1990. By 1994 capital punishment had been abolished for all crimes in the whole of Western Europe.[5] In the United States in 1972, although homicide rates had roughly doubled over the previous ten years, the Supreme Court, in *Furman v. Georgia*, temporarily held capital punishment to be unconstitutional. The fact that the death penalty was disproportionately inflicted on nonwhite convicts played a part in that judgment.[6]

Four years later, however, in *Gregg v. Georgia*, and in a subsequent set of cases, the Court changed its mind. It held that capital punishment was not in itself the "cruel and unusual punishment" forbidden by the Constitution. Since then the number of executions first rose abruptly and has recently fallen somewhat. By 2000 there were 3,593 prisoners under sentence of death, 1,990 of them white and 1,535 black, in the federal prison system and in thirty-seven states. In that year, 85 prisoners were executed, 49 of them white, 35 black, and one Native American. Executions took place overwhelmingly in the former states of the Confederacy and in border states, forty of them in Texas alone. The number of executions has fallen in the last few years. In 2006, 53 prisoners, all men, were executed in fourteen states, all but one by lethal injection: 24 in Texas; 5 in Ohio; 4 each in Florida, North Carolina, Oklahoma, and Virginia. Thirty-two of them were white and 21 were black. In recent years there has been an increasing number of criticisms of and attacks on capital punishment.

The United States, however, still finds itself in embarrassingly exceptional company: the countries that executed the most criminals in 2007 were China, Saudi Arabia, Pakistan, Iraq, and Iran—and the United States. It is arguably in even worse company with the other countries who execute prisoners who were under eighteen when their crimes were committed: China, the Democratic Republic of Congo, Iran, Nigeria, Pakistan, Saudi Arabia, Sudan, and Yemen.[7]

In other respects, too, the American criminal justice system is exceptional. The number of people in prison as a proportion of the population is the highest in the world. More than 2.1 million Americans are in local, state, or federal prisons. In 2001, 686 Americans out of every 100,000 were in prison. Only Russia held a higher proportion of its citizens in prison (739). That compares with 139 per 100,000 in Britain (which has risen to 148, an unprecedentedly high number, giving great concern), 102 in Canada, 96 in Germany, 85 in France, and lower figures in the rest of Western Europe.[8]

The racial imbalance in prisons as a whole is even greater than on death row: 40 percent of all prisoners are African-American and another 31 percent Hispanic. One in nine African-American males aged between twenty and thirty-four is either a prisoner or a former prisoner or is on probation.[9]

Perhaps the most strikingly exceptional area in the field of crime and punishment is gun crime and the availability of guns in the United States. In Western Europe gun ownership is quite widespread because hunting is popular. But ownership of guns is closely regulated, and it is particularly hard to own handguns, let alone automatic weapons. In Britain, where landowning has been confined to a relatively small proportion of the population for centuries and hunting (or "shooting," in the British usage) is largely the sport of large landowners, their friends, and paying visitors, gun ownership has long been tightly controlled. It has been even more strictly limited as a result of a number of incidents in which deranged individuals went on the rampage and shot multiple victims.[10]

In Britain, the possession of handguns, usually illegal, is associated in the press and in the public mind with professional criminals and street gangs, especially from the Caribbean. In the United States, on the contrary, gun ownership is associated with a mystique of freedom. It is held to be sanctified by the Second Amendment to the Constitution, which states, "A well-regulated Militia, being necessary to the security of a free State, the right of the People to keep and bear Arms, shall not be infringed." Argument has raged over whether that text means that the right to bear arms is so associated with the militia that citizens should own guns only if they are militia members. The widest interpretation of all citizens' right to bear arms, and almost every imaginable kind of arms, is ferociously defended by the National Rifle Association, one of the most powerful political lobbies in the land, with almost three million members and formidable clout on Capitol Hill.

The NRA presents the right to bear arms as one of the most precious of the attributes of American freedom. It is contrasted with the slavish condition of citizens in other democracies where guns are regulated. In recent years, especially after the assassination attempt on President Reagan in March 1981 by John Hinckley, which severely wounded the presidential press secretary James Brady, there has been a countervailing antigun lobby in the United States. It was able to pass the "Brady bill" in 1993, restricting some access to guns. But it is politically outgunned by the NRA.

The NRA's framing of the issue has been highly influential—so much so that, when incidents have occurred, as at Columbine High School in Colorado in April 1999 or at Virginia Tech in April 2007, of precisely the kind that led to tightening of the gun laws in Britain, many in America argued that it would have been better if more students and teachers had been armed so that they could shoot back.

With some political courage, the Clinton administration did pass legislation in 1994 increasing the regulation of gun purchase and banning assault rifles and other semiautomatic weapons. But the National Rifle Association was able to persuade a Republican-controlled Congress to reverse these measures. The legislation expired in 2004. As of the time of writing, not only is there little effective regulation of gun ownership in many states, but there is hardly any discussion of tighter regulation, and Democrats are wooing the support of the NRA. It is of course entirely possible that public attitudes toward gun ownership will change. For now, the contrast between the United States and other developed democracies in this respect, as with regard to capital punishment and to incarceration, could hardly be sharper.

In the cases of both capital punishment and gun ownership, American practice, however exceptional, is stoutly defended with many arguments. The most interesting of these, for our purpose, stand the issue on its head. It is that American support for capital punishment and resistance to gun regulation, so far from being examples of "negative exceptionalism," really provide evidence of positive exceptionalism in that they result from the greater "democracy" of the American political system. Thus it is argued that public opinion in Europe was strongly in favor of retaining capital punishment, but "elites" frustrated the will of the majority. Similarly, the gun lobby argues that those who would take away an American's constitutional right to "keep and bear arms" are an unrepresentative elite that ignores the democratic will.

Throughout the nineteenth century American society was seen, in Europe just as much as in the United States itself, as exceptional in its equality. Millions of Europeans gambled their own lives on that faith, and if for many immigrants life in America, in the phrase of Langston Hughes, "ain't been no crystal stair," yet for the majority it was a bet that paid off. The American Dream was a reality, not just in the sense that for many the Dream did come true, but in the arguably more important sense that millions believed they could aspire to a more prosperous and juster life in America. Not every immigrant became a millionaire, far from it. But most felt that they had been given a fair chance in a society that respected the rule of law and the principle of social equality.

In the last third of the twentieth century, that began to change. The source of immigration shifted. Now the "huddled masses" came not in the main from Europe, but primarily from Central America and the Caribbean, and secondly from East and South Asia. For migrants from those societies, American prosperity still offered a "golden door" of opportunity. But equality, except in the purely social sense, was no longer on offer. Perhaps it never had been. To be sure, there were no legacies of feudalism, no unspoken snobberies to surmount, if only you could scratch together the money. But statistically America was no longer exceptionally equal. Or, to put the matter in a different way, the claim to exceptionalism had changed from the equality of condition observed by Tocqueville to an equality of opportunity to become exceptionally rich.

Every two years since 1996, Cornell University Press has published a study of "The State of Working America" by a group of economists at the Economic Policy Institute in Washington. Like its predecessors, the latest study includes a set of international comparisons based on statistics covering the world's twenty or so most successful countries, members of the Organization for Economic Cooperation and Development (OECD): the United States, Canada, Japan, Australia, New Zealand, and the countries of Western Europe.[11]

The latest study concedes that "the more market-driven U.S. economic model is often deemed superior to European economic models," and this is often supported by the bald assertion that the United States is the richest country in the world. This is true, the compilers concede, if it is taken to mean that the United States is the richest single country. But the aggregate size of the European Union's economy is now greater than that of the United States, and there are predictions that China, too, will overtake the United States in the next few decades, though the per capita wealth of the populations of Eastern Europe and of China still lag far below American levels. The Working America study concedes that, while "in per capita terms the United States is quite wealthy," a comparative analysis "must take into consideration a broader set of criteria." If comparative incomes are measured in terms of "purchasing power parity," the United States is second in per capita terms, with an average income of $39,728, after Norway's $41,804, while eleven other countries (Australia, Austria, Belgium, Canada, Denmark, Finland, Ireland, the Netherlands, Sweden, Switzerland, and the United Kingdom) have average earnings over $30,000. If the comparison is made in terms of market exchange rates, the Japanese also had higher incomes than Americans ($42,146), but this is largely to be attributed to the way the parity of the Japanese yen was boosted by speculative currency movements. The authors of the study point out that many Europeans and Canadians view their social protections as "factors that raise their living standards." In most developed countries workers enjoy more leisure, and while there is no statutory minimum vacation time in the United States, Canada, and Australia, in the other OECD countries this varies between four and five weeks a year.

Unemployment is substantially higher in some European countries than in the United States: in France and Germany it was 9.6 percent and 9.5 percent, respectively, in 2004, and in Spain as high as 10.9 percent. Several other countries, however, had lower unemployment rates than the United States (5.5 percent), including New Zealand, Switzerland, Ireland, the Netherlands, the United Kingdom, Japan, Austria, and Denmark. Definitions of unemployment, however, and therefore unemployment statistics, are notoriously contentious and subject to manipulation by government and others.

One main determinant of an economy's standard of living, says the EPI, is productivity, measured by the gross domestic product (GDP) per hour worked. For long after World War II, American productivity was the standard others tried to match. By 2004, however, several European countries had either caught up with or surpassed American productivity growth. If the American level is equated to 100, productivity in Norway was 125, in Belgium 113, in France 107, in Ireland 104, and in the Netherlands 100. If the rate of growth of productivity is measured over the whole of the years 2000 to 2005, the United States does best, just ahead of the United Kingdom. But as the EPI team puts it, "the work force responsible for this high level of productivity has not been able to enjoy the fruits of their very productive labor. . . . Earnings have been stagnant for the majority of workers throughout this cycle."

The most striking aspect of American incomes today—whatever may have been the case in Alexis de Tocqueville's day—is not equality but inequality. American incomes are the most unequal in the world. The closest parallels, moreover, are to be found in those countries, like the United Kingdom and Australia, that have most nearly followed the American economic model. Economists commonly use two measures of household income inequality. The first is the Gini coefficient. If equality is perfect, the Gini coefficient will be zero; the less equal the society, the higher the Gini coefficient. In both 1989 and 2000 the United States had the highest Gini coefficient of any OECD country. The second measure is the ratio between the income of a household in the 90th percentile—that is, a household whose income is in the top 10 percent—and the income of a household in the 10th percentile, or in the lowest ten percent. Again, the ratio was highest for the United States and lowest for Norway and Finland. A graph in the EPI book for 2006 shows that in comparison with both France and the United Kingdom, in statistics dating back to 1913, the share of national income going to the top one-tenth of one percent followed closely parallel paths—until quite recently. Then, in the 1980s, the share of the very richest shot ahead in all three countries, but most dramatically in the United States. While the richest one-tenth of one percent took about 2 percent of the family income in France and Britain, in the United States this same cohort of the very rich took more than 7 percent in 1998 and almost as much in 2003.

By all statistical measures, therefore, the United States, in terms of income and wealth, is the most unequal country in the world. While the average income in the United States is still almost the highest of any country (with only Norway higher by one measure, and Norway and Japan by another), the gap between wealth and poverty is higher than anywhere else, and is growing steadily greater.

Many Americans assume that inequality of incomes is somehow a beneficial consequence of the way the economic system in the United States rewards enterprise. They contrast what they see as their open society with the supposedly closed societies of Europe and Japan. Yet the reality is that a very high proportion of the highest incomes in the United States goes to those whose families are already highly prosperous. The surprising conclusion seems to be that, given the high cost of elite education, far higher than in any comparable developed country, and given, too, the high cost of health care, the United States—so far from being a land of unparalleled opportunity—is on its way to becoming a class society. Reviewing a group of books about American education, for example, the well-known political scientist Andrew Hacker reported that all the authors warned that "social barriers in the U.S. are higher and economic inequality is more pronounced than at any time in recent memory. All three books also frame this issue by asserting or implying that lines between classes are hardening."[12]

In this environment, the owners of capital, corporate executives, and expensively educated professionals are pulling away, in terms of income, wealth, and standard of living, not just from the poor but from the majority of Americans. Moreover, if average incomes in America are only slightly higher than in twenty other countries, and those American incomes are exceptionally unequally divided, it follows that the gap between the income of most Americans and that of the populations of other developed countries is even narrower than would appear from overall statistics, and indeed may not exist at all. Take away the very rich, and Americans may be little better off than Frenchmen or Swedes.

This is not some trivial debating point. It challenges a traditionally central proposition of American exceptionalism, the idea that the United States was uniquely a land of equality and opportunity.

No idea has been more proudly cherished by Americans for as long a time than the belief in the superiority of American medicine. It was, for Americans, a proverbial matter. They ate better—they were sure—they were healthier, they lived longer, and you could always tell an American by the shining quality of his teeth. If they did fall ill, it was taken for granted, then American doctors would cure them with the technological virtuosity of American surgery, American wonder drugs, and the su-

perbly antiseptic magic of American hospitals. A well-known medical critic, Dr. Jack Geiger of SUNY, told me in a 1973 interview that in the Kennedy years many Americans thought "it was only a matter of time before the brilliant, dedicated doctors discovered a cure for death."[13]

For some, this was almost literally true. Europeans, unlike Americans, wrote the critic Leslie Fiedler, not satirically, after a visit to Italy in 1952, "found it impossible to reject the reality of death."[14] This, surely, is a disturbing early example of the hubris common in the 1950s in the circles that would soon become neoconservative. One can only comment, in a trope of that time, "I've heard of optimism, but this is ridiculous!"

To this day, many Americans continue to believe, in spite of statistical evidence to the contrary, that their health care is the finest in the world. Their confidence has recently been shaken. But they have been convinced, by patient and skillful campaigns of public relations over several generations, not only that the skill and practice of American medicine are superior, but that the system, the essentially commercial fee-for-service system, as modified by the insurance industry and health-maintenance organizations, is intrinsically more efficient. They have been taught that any form of universal health insurance or health care provision (often tendentiously described as "socialized medicine") is necessarily inferior.

Facts are against them.

It is true that, at its best, American medicine is indeed very skillful, innovative, and effective. Nowhere else, not even in the wealthiest countries of Western Europe or in Japan, has so much capital investment been devoted to heroic therapies for the most deadly diseases—especially, as has been pointed out by feminists, among others, for the diseases commonest among middle-aged white men, namely heart disease, cancer, and stroke.[15]

While the best private American health care is certainly excellent by any standards, one problem is access. American health care is prohibitively—and exceptionally—expensive. Health spending per capita in 1998 was $4,178 in the United States. The next three countries in health spending were Switzerland, Norway, and Germany, with $2,800, $2,425, and $2,424 per head, respectively.[16]

While most Americans are covered by some form of insurance, or are members of health-maintenance programs of one kind or another, more than 15 percent of the population, or some forty-six million people, are not covered at all. Moreover, many who do have some insurance are not by any means covered for all the contingencies that might occur. The growth of "managed care," too, means that both health insurance companies and health-maintenance organizations exert pressure on care, limiting, for example, periods of hospitalization or the supply of drugs.

How does one judge the overall success of a nation's health care system? The single most important measure, surely, is life expectancy. According to the World Health Organization, in terms of "disability-linked life-expectancy," the United States came twenty-fourth out of the twenty-five high-income countries in the OECD.[17]

Nor is this some arbitrary measure. Out of the 192 nations and territories listed in order in the *United Nations World Fact Book*, the United States ranks forty-eighth in life expectancy. If you limit yourself to sovereign states, then the United States is twenty-ninth. The category of human beings in the world with the longest life expectancy as of 2006 were Japanese women, who could expect to live to well past 88. The Swedes and the Swiss could count on more than 81 years of life, the Italians and the French just under eighty years. The British, in twenty-fifth place, had a life expectancy of more than 78 years, six months, as against Americans, who just surpassed the Cubans, 77.85 years' life expectancy to 77.23. In many respects Cuba, a poor country made poorer by American boycotts, has health care as good as, or better than, the average in America.

The second-most important overall statistical measure of a health care system's success, most would agree, is the level of child mortality. In the United States, as of 2006, eight children out of every thousand died before the age of five. Thirty-three countries or territories in the world do better than that.[18] In Denmark, Norway, and Singapore only four children out of every thousand die before age five, and Sweden, the world champion in this, as in so many other indexes of well-being, loses just three out of a thousand.

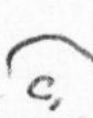

Ever since the Truman administration first proposed health care reform, powerful interests have supported relentless and often disingenuous ideological attacks on the sort of universal health care provision that all developed countries except the United States have provided for generations. (Famously, President Eisenhower was persuaded that Sweden suffered from an epidemic of suicide, which many Americans have continued to believe ever since. The fact is that the suicide rate in Sweden is slightly higher than in the United States, but lower than in many other countries and far from the highest in the world.) More recently, the insurance industry paid for the devastatingly effective and shamefully disingenuous "Harry and Louise" television campaign against the health care reforms proposed by a commission led by Hillary Clinton in the 1990s.

As Jonathan Cohn argued in the *New Republic* online in 2007, it is not even true that the United States leads in the availability of medical technology against every country that has universal provision: Japan, for example, has more CT scanners and MRIs per capita than does the United States.[19]

In any case, technology is not the only test of good medicine. Many European countries provide patients with more face time with physicians and longer hospital stays when needed. Cohn points out that defenders of American medicine love to confuse the argument by generalizing about "Europe," diluting the higher standards of Scandinavia and Western Europe with the generally poorer performance of countries in Eastern Europe only recently freed from Soviet standards of health care. "It's difficult to make an ironclad case that any one system is better than another," Cohn concedes. "But the fact that countries with universal health care routinely outperform the United States on many fronts—and that, overall, their citizens end up healthier—ought to be enough, at least, to discredit the argument that universal care leads to worse care."[20]

Health care, in short, is a classic instance of negative exceptionalism. What is troubling is that, in a field where by most relevant measures U.S. performance is mediocre, so many Americans believe that it is superlative. However, this may soon change. Only 40 percent of Americans are satisfied with the health care delivery system, and politicians are slowly beginning to make health care a high priority.

A less obvious, but still comparable, area is education. Until the late twentieth century, American public education was the envy of the world.

This was true both of secondary schools and of universities. Gradually the excellence of big-city school systems was damaged, first by social and racial turmoil, and then by financial stringency. Where once the majority of middle-class and professional parents in cities like New York and Chicago were happy to send their children to the excellent public school systems there, by the end of the twentieth century that was no longer the case. A high proportion of those parents who could afford to do so either sent their children to fee-paying schools or moved to suburbs with well-funded local school systems. So in Chicago, though more than 40 percent of the city's population is "white non-Hispanic," 91 percent of the children in the public schools are African-American or Hispanic. In New York City the public schools are 85 percent "minority," while in the District of Columbia, although the population is only 56 percent minority, the public schools are 93 percent so.[21]

For whatever reasons, the learning performance of American school pupils has fallen behind international standards, in spite of the Bush administration's intention that no child should be "left behind." Since 2000 the Organization for Economic Cooperation and Development, set up largely on American initiative after World War II precisely to help bring other countries up to American standards of development, has measured educational performance in a survey called PISA (Program for International Student Assessment). The country that performed best overall in the last tests to be published, in 2003, was Finland, whose students placed second in mathematics and first in both reading literacy and science. Hong Kong, South Korea, Norway, Canada, and Australia also did well. Overall, the United States placed twenty-fourth out of twenty-nine.[22] The methodology is careful, and the results are taken seriously by governments. Detailed results are less significant than the overall negative conclusion. So far from being exceptionally good, American high school education appears to have fallen far behind the best international standards, especially in science and mathematics.

In higher education, the damage done by state cost cutting has been concealed by the highly publicized performance of a couple of dozen schools, mostly private ones with large endowments.[23] From time to time, lists are published pronouncing that a high proportion of the "best" universities in the world are made up of these highly endowed private American universities: Harvard, Yale, Princeton, Stanford, and a few more. Although such universities place great emphasis in their publicity on the number of scholarships they give to bright students who would otherwise not be able to attend, it is also true that a substantial proportion (perhaps around 15 percent) of their students are "legacy" students—that is, the children of alumni or donors—and these applicants have a much higher chance of being admitted than equally qualified nonprivileged applicants. There is much emphasis on the availability of scholarships, but a high proportion of scholarships, too, go to bright, well-taught children from prosperous families and well-funded suburban high schools. Where once the great state universities were generally accounted to give as good an education, and in general to do as much worthwhile research, as the highly endowed private universities, a gap has begun to open there too, as a result of cuts in state budgets, in favor of private wealth as opposed to public provision.

One possible explanation for the surprisingly unexceptional performance of the United States in various measurable international comparisons may be precisely the truly exceptional and apparently rapidly

growing inequality in American society documented above. This inequality, and specifically the growing gap between the very rich and the rest of the population, is no accident. It is the result of a number of outcomes from the working of the political system, and in particular of tax policy and public finance.

Inequality is a consequence of changed attitudes: of a more conservative economic climate, of public acceptance of the claims made on behalf of the deserts of entrepreneurs and managers as compared with other kinds of workers, and of a decline in the idea that democratic government is a beneficent force in society. Those changed attitudes, in turn, are the consequence of determined, intellectually ruthless, and well-financed conservative propaganda, promoting and justifying tax and

other policies and practices that favor the rich and especially the "super-rich."

The way politicians have systematically favored the rich in general, and especially those in a position to lobby for special interests and to raise money for political campaigns, has been spelled out in many books and studies, both academic and popular.[24] This must raise questions about the quality of American democracy. In spite of the partial success American conservatives have had in attempting to spread their doctrines abroad, this is certainly a clear example of what I have called negative exceptionalism.

One of the clearest accounts of what has happened is that of Paul Krugman, the *New York Times* columnist, written in 2002.[25] The trends he described then have not yet been reversed. For one thing, while average salaries in America have risen with painful slowness—from $32,522 in 1970 to $35,864 in 1999, a 10 percent increase over twenty-nine years—the average pay packet for chief executive officers rose from $1.3 million to $37.5 million in that span. According to the Congressional Budget Office, while the after-tax incomes of families near the middle of the income distribution went up 10 percent from 1979 to 1997, the after-tax incomes of the highest-paid 1 percent of families rose by 157 percent. Moreover, most of the gains made by the top 10 percent actually went to the top 1 percent. Indeed, the pyramid was even steeper than that. Sixty percent of the increased income of the top 1 percent went to the top one-tenth of that one percent, which in 1999 meant those earning more than $790,000. The trend has intensified in the subsequent years.

Krugman's overall point is that income distribution in the United States has reverted to the pattern familiar in the Gilded Age and as late as the early 1920s. The broad, relatively equal advance of all classes of Americans, characteristic of the New Deal and the immediate post–World War II years, should be seen, he argues, not as the norm but as an aberration from an established pattern of great inequality in American incomes. The relative equality and shared prosperity of the postwar suburbs in which Krugman grew up, when America was a middle-class society, were, he acknowledged ruefully, "another country."

"According to Thomas Piketty and Emmanuel Saez," Krugman wrote, citing two well-known income statisticians, "in 1970 the top 0.01 percent of taxpayers had 0.7 percent of total income—that is, they earned 'only' 70 times as much as the average, not enough to buy or maintain a mega-residence. But in 1998 the top 0.01 percent received more than 3 percent of all income. That meant that the 13,000 richest families in America had almost as much income as the 20 million poorest households; those 13,000 families had incomes 300 times that of average families."

Some of this change to a less equal society, no doubt, comes from subtle but pervasive alterations in the values and assumptions of Americans. But one should not underestimate the influence of the way the political system actually works. There is broad agreement among observers of American politics, both academic experts and thoughtful participants in the way the game is played in Washington, that two of the most significant changes over the past thirty years have been, on the one hand, declining public participation, and, on the other, the increase in the influence of money.

Although from time to time there are tender shoots of hope that the trend toward public apathy might be reversed, for example by the Internet or by new and less elitist methods of fund-raising, so far there has been no significant or lasting reversal. The trend in voter turnout seems to continue to fall, except in the immediate aftermath of September 11. In the 1960 presidential election, it was 63 percent. In 1972 it was 55 percent. By 1996 it was under 50 percent. It recovered slightly in 2000, perhaps because of the prospect of a change in party control of the White House. In 2004, no doubt as a consequence of the fear and outrage caused by the September 11 atrocities, it was almost 57 percent, or as high as at any time since 1968. It remains to be seen whether this increase will be maintained in 2008. These figures are exceptionally low by international comparative standards.

The role of money continues to expand. The 2008 presidential election was the most expensive ever. The money spent on federal elections, it has been pointed out, is no more than would be needed to give every man, woman, and child in the United States a deep pan pizza with limited toppings.[26] Certainly the United States can afford to spend two or three billion dollars every four years. That is not the point. What it cannot afford to do is to select members of the legislature to any great extent in accordance with their ability to persuade wealthy individuals or organized lobbies to hand over large sums in order to buy preferential access.

In the early-twenty-first-century news media nothing has been more striking than the way politics is now reported almost exclusively in terms of money. One presidential candidate after another is written off as hopeless because he or she has been unable to raise as much money as the others in the field. (This was true even of Senator John McCain before he became the Republican nominee.) Candidates are taken seriously in proportion as they have been able to accumulate large "war chests." What is true at the presidential level is increasingly true too at the level of statewide races, at least in states with one or more major media markets. The biggest single cause, of course, is the politicians' dependence on television advertising and the rising cost of that commodity.

The cost of presidential elections rose dramatically because some twenty-seven states decided to hold primary elections (or equivalent caucuses) by mid-February 2008. Future candidates must therefore be ready to pay for television advertising at the very outset of election year, in many states, some of them with several major television markets. Moreover, the most expensive phase of the campaign, in terms of TV spending, has lengthened, from the two months from Labor Day to polling day, to some eight months.

It is no surprise, then, that elected politicians are increasingly drawn from wealthy backgrounds. Some men with great private fortunes (Michael Bloomberg, Jon Corzine, Steve Forbes, Ross Perot, Mitt Romney) have even been able to finance political campaigns substantially with their own money. (In the closing stages of the preconvention campaign, Senator Clinton lent more than $10 million of her personal fortune, which with her husband's amounts to more than $100 million, to subsidize her campaign funds.) Some of these are self-made men. Others inherited capital. Others again are more or less transparently dependent on interest groups. Many, perhaps most, members of the House of Representatives, faced with reelection every two years, spend an inordinate part of their time on the Rolodex treadmill. In Washington they must ceaselessly call donors. When they visit their districts, they have little time for hearing about, let alone responding to, the problems or aspirations of the general body of their constituents. They must focus on the wealthiest and those with most political "clout." Clout, of course, means money, and the political access and influence it buys. Even President Bush, never short of financial backing, often speaks in his travels only to all-ticket groups of financial donors from which other mere citizens are excluded.

Money talks in other ways, too. Private interests, from the most high minded to the most sordid, can and do influence the political system through paid lobbyists. Recent reports have revealed not only the exponential growth in the number and turnover of lobbyists in Washington and in major state capitals but also the excesses of a scandalous minority among them. The respectable end of the lobbying industry was portrayed in telling detail by the *Washington Post*'s 2007 "Citizen K Street" series.[27] It described how the firm of Cassidy and Associates, using a network of contacts including corporate business, defense contractors, universities, and senior elected officials and their professional staff, worked with whoever had the power. When the Democrats controlled Capitol Hill, it seemed like a Democratic firm: Gerald Cassidy got his start from George McGovern, of all politicians. When the Republicans took over, the firm was remodeled as one that worked just as fruitfully with Republicans. The Cassidy firm is only one of hundreds of lobbying firms in Washington, and something similar has begun to develop in major state capitals such as Albany, Austin, and Sacramento.

The seedier side of the business has been graphically revealed by the activities of Jack Abramoff, intimate of the inner circle of the Bush administration, who is now serving a prison sentence for corrupt activities. He is a longtime associate, from their days working for College Republicans, of Ralph Reed of the Christian Coalition, Grover Norquist of Americans for Tax Reform, and (until his resignation in late summer 2007) the president's most trusted counselor, Karl Rove.[28] Where Cassidy and his associates could promote the legitimate interests of General Dynamics, Boeing Corporation, or Boston University, Abramoff could use Native American casinos that employed him as their lobbyist as piggy banks to buy influence in Washington by taking greedy or naïve legislators to fancy restaurants or Scottish golf courses.[29]

Both stories support the gloomy forebodings of Kevin Phillips, once the prophet of an emerging Republican majority, now turned Cassandra. In a book published in 2002, Phillips castigated with Old Testament fervor the failure of the unsuccessful presidential candidates of both parties in the year 2000 (Senator John McCain of Arizona and former senator Bill Bradley of New Jersey) to connect "tainted government, corrupted politics, corporate venality and the unprecedented two-decade build-up of wealth itself." "The shared top-bracket status of speculators, corporate raiders, $100,000-soft money political donors, insider traders, chainsaw-wielding corporate CEOs and Washington mega-lobbyists," he said, "never became a talking point." Phillips drew attention to the steady rise of unelected players in the political game, including judges, political staffers, consultants, and central bankers. In his closing paragraph he made explicit the connection between the influence of money and the threat to American exceptionalism:

> As the twenty-first century gets under way, the imbalance of wealth and democracy in the United States is unsustainable. . . . Market theology and unelected leadership have been displacing politics and elections. Either democracy must be renewed, with politics brought back to life, or wealth is likely to cement a new and less democratic regime—plutocracy by some other name. Over the coming decades, American exceptionalism may face its greatest test simply in convincing the American people to continue to believe in its comfort and reassurance.[30]

One of the proudest boasts of American exceptionalists, and one of the propositions that has most endeared the United States to its admirers in Europe and elsewhere, is the idea that it is not only an exceptionally equal society but also a "classless" one. That claim has always been somewhat dubious. Even at the time of the American Revolution, there were not only substantial inequalities but also political conflicts between wealthy classes on the one hand—Boston and Salem merchants, New York and Philadelphia bankers, planters in Virginia and the Carolinas—and the "workies," landless laborers, recent immigrants, and frontier debtors on the other. By the late nineteenth and early twentieth centuries, these class divisions had set almost as hard as in Europe. Two factors kept them from erupting into the bitter class conflicts of Europe: first, these divisions were not sanctified either by law or by acknowledged practice; and second, the widespread belief—call it the American Dream—prevailed that any man or woman who worked hard, saved money, and took such opportunities as came along could hope to "get ahead." And this belief was made credible by the fact that many, includ-

ing many immigrants, did indeed rise from unprivileged backgrounds to success and wealth.

Since the 1970s that Dream has been called into question. Many, perhaps most, Americans still believe in it. There are still heart-warming success stories. In the past few years African-Americans, long exceptionally excluded, have succeeded financially in many fields and risen to the highest offices in the land. Senator Obama has shown that a black man or even a black woman could now aspire, many other things being equal, to be president. Many Americans, once stony in their resistance to black achievement, are now genuinely proud of the success of a Barack Obama, a Colin Powell, or a Condoleezza Rice. Others are grudging toward African-American achievement. If you look not at individual stories of brilliant success but at the statistical evidence, it is still not easy to escape from poverty. It is less easy than it was. And, most surprising, it is less easy than in most other developed countries.

So the hard numbers suggest. The poverty rate in the United States in 2000 stood at 17 percent. That was measured by the standard methodology, which counts as poor those receiving less than half the median income. By that test the poverty rate in America was the highest of seventeen OECD countries. The rate of child poverty, at 21.9 percent, was also the highest. The poverty rate before "taxes and transfers"—that is, welfare and benefit payments—was slightly higher in two other countries, France and New Zealand, where it was just under 28 percent, against 26.6 percent in the United States. But after transfers the rate fell to 16.3 percent for New Zealand children and 7.5 percent in France. In other words, social policy in those countries had succeeded in drastically reducing the impact of child poverty—much more so than in the United States. The Economic Policy Institute points out that this is not due to a shortage of resources. The United States has a higher per capita income than either France or New Zealand. Rather, it was the result of deliberate political choice. There is positive correlation between low child poverty and high social expenditure. No doubt many Americans have been convinced that taxation and government intervention are bad in themselves. But there is a sad way of putting this. The United States is exceptional in its unwillingness to pay to take children out of poverty.

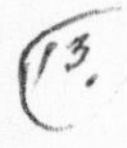

Something, it seems, did go wrong in the 1970s. In large part, this was a matter of harder, less generous behavior on the part of management, rationalized and justified by a rejection of social democratic beliefs and their replacement with neoliberal faith in the automatically benevolent operation of "the market." But there was also a democratic deficit, a failure of democracy.

I have noted the growing influence of money within the political system, and that it has gone step by step with a decline in voter participation. The power of corporate business and of the lobbyists who represent business interests has grown. The power of trade unions, and of groups representing citizens, consumers, or minorities, while still far from negligible, has weakened. This is too obvious to require elaboration. Indeed, those who defend the dominance of corporate wealth do not feel the need to defend it; they see it as good for the country.

What is less openly acknowledged is that in certain respects the Constitution itself has been abused. This is in part the result of the unrestrained ferocity of political conflict. The modern conservative movement set out in the 1970s with the fixed ideas that its demonized enemies, the liberals, had perverted the constitutional system, politicized the institutions of the federal government, monopolized its patronage, and abused its powers.

There is a paradox here. For the polarization of politics, and the violence of the political struggle, happened at a time when the ideological difference between the parties was not too wide to be bridged by debate. It was far narrower than it had been, for example, in the 1930s, or in the 1900s. Forced by the new politics of fund-raising to buy television advertising to appeal to the wealthier groups in society and—comparatively speaking—to ignore poorer strata of the electorate, the two parties came to resemble each other ideologically, culturally, and sociologically.

By the 1990s foreign observers often remarked that the political game in the United States was played between two conservative parties, one admittedly even more conservative than the other. Of course, that ignores very real differences between the Republican and Democratic parties in terms of their values, their style, the groups of voters they attract, and the details of their policies. But it is true that the Democratic Party, at least from 1980 until 2006, was deeply shaken by the loss of major swaths of its traditional support, and in particular by the defection of many former southern Democrats and many of the unionized working-class voters, the "Reagan Democrats." Under this pressure, the Democrats steadily yielded ideological ground. President Clinton, in the name of what was obscurely called "triangulation," went much farther than previous Democratic leaders in the direction of embracing Ronald Reagan's insistence that government was part of the problem, not part of the solution. Few Democrats, least of all at election time or when they were looking for financial contributions, emphasized profound policy differences, whether in relation to taxation, the organization of health care, or welfare.

Republicans believed that there had been a "Reagan Revolution," that under the Reagan administration the national party system had been permanently realigned. They saw as irreversible the splitting off from the Roosevelt coalition of northern workers and southern conservatives. They were therefore shocked when Bill Clinton defeated George H. W. Bush for the presidency in 1992. They cried foul. A new, angry tone of outraged legitimacy underlay the ferocity of the partisan attacks on President Clinton. By 2000 the political system was sharply polarized between conservatives and liberals, "red" and "blue" states. Although the substantive differences between the parties were less sharp than at many past periods, the rhetoric of partisan debate was more violent than for many long decades. After the so-called "Borking" of a Republican nominee to the Court, Robert H. Bork, in 1987, Senate hearings to confirm presidential appointments to the Supreme Court and on occasion to other offices, which had once proceeded with some restraint, became bouts of partisan all-in wrestling, with no holds barred.

The presidential election of 2000 was not only the closest in history since 1876. In many ways it was the least edifying. Neither the media nor the legal profession distinguished itself. In the end George W. Bush was elected by a single vote, that of the Justice of the Supreme Court, a Republican appointee, who cast the deciding vote in *Bush v. Gore.*[31]

The outcome of the 2000 election trod close to the fundamental constitutional principle of the separation of powers. A presidential election, a supreme moment in the life of the executive branch, was decided by the judiciary. As a consequence, the constitutionality of the electoral college, a fundamental component of the constitutional system, has been called into question.

In other ways, too, since then, the separation of powers has been if not breached, at least threatened. Since the events of September 11, 2001, President Bush has claimed numerous powers by virtue of his status as commander in chief. On important issues, not least those connected with the Iraq War, the president has—at least in the opinion of his numerous political opponents—defied the authority of the Congress. He has taken much farther than any of his predecessors the custom of issuing explanations of how he proposes to interpret legislation. In effect, it is claimed by his opponents, this amounts to announcing his intention of disobeying statutes.

Nor is it only in the executive branch that many see serious departures from constitutional propriety. Since the congressional victories of 1994, the Republican leadership is charged with systematically limiting the discussion of legislation in committees, and with limiting floor debate. In the Senate, both parties have greatly increased the use of filibusters, or the threat of filibusters, called "holds." The use of "earmarks" has—it is complained—dramatically increased the amount of "pork barrel" legislation by which members of Congress curry favor with special interests and raise funding for their own reelection. These are intensely political and partisan matters. The least that can be said is that the integrity of the Constitution has been called into question as never since the middle of the nineteenth century.

The government of the United States, under both a Democratic and a Republican president, has, more than ever since the collapse of communism, acted on the assumption that it is the duty and destiny of the United States to spread the American version of democracy to as much of the world as possible. This aspiration, implicit in the "neo-Wilsonian" speeches of the Clinton administration as much as in the Project for a New American Century embraced by many conservatives influential in the George W. Bush administration, is predicated on American exceptionalism. It is hard not to interpret the statements of the second Bush administration as tantamount to proposing that the United States must spread American democracy, at gunpoint if necessary, because of the unique virtues of the American constitutional system. Explicitly, the George W. Bush administration declared that it would invade Iraq in order to bring democracy to the Middle East.

But what if the practice of American politics, so far from being a model for all to emulate, a beacon to guide the world, does not deserve to be exported? What if the theory of American democracy, as exemplified in the way the Constitution works in practice, has been corrupted by political and financial interests, ideological intolerance, or a combination of the two? What if, contrary to patriotic rhetoric, American democracy is exceptional not only in its virtues but also in certain of its defects? Given the power and influence the United States exerts in the world, culturally and economically as well as militarily, there could be few more troubling questions.

For at least six decades, and arguably since the United States became involved in the quarrels of Europe in World War I, the United States has been almost universally accepted as the ultimate guarantor of the decency and the viability of the international system. Of course there have always been many—among them Germans in 1917, Germans again and Japanese from 1941 to 1945, Russians and Chinese in the 1950s to the 1980s, some Muslims today—who fiercely rejected that proposition. Nor has the actual conduct of the United States always been even generally approved. The decision to reject the League of Nations in 1919, the dropping of two atomic bombs on Japan in 1945, the Vietnam War: these are only three of the most prominent instances of American conduct that were widely criticized even by America's friends.

The point I am making is different. It is that, over most of the twentieth century, whatever people in other nations felt about the United States in relation to specific issues, America was widely regarded as the one nation with the strength and—crucially—the trustworthiness to keep the international system on the rails. That is why few dissented from the proposition that the United States was, as Secretary of State Madeleine Albright felicitously put it, the "one indispensable nation." Other countries had great contributions to make. But the United States set the standard, and was widely accepted as doing so. In spite of occasional specific backsliding, the international consensus was that America could generally be relied on to work with other nations to help other countries to fight poverty, even when that meant subjecting American interests to competition; to obey norms of behavior; to keep the peace; and to stand for the common decencies of international behavior.

Slowly, reluctantly, the United States was persuaded to join a coalition to resist the pretensions of German militarism in 1917 and again in 1941. With little hesitation, Americans sided with the peoples of colonial territories and sometimes helped them to win their independence. With wisdom and restraint, the United States built up the military power to contain Soviet Communism. Even after the fall of communism, the administration of George Bush senior played a crucial part in brokering the transition from Soviet empire, and when Saddam Hussein threatened the integrity of the international system by invading Kuwait, the forty-first president organized a broad international coalition to vindicate the international system in a cooperative way. The Clinton administration, too, accepted an obligation to help when the European powers failed to prevent war and atrocity in the former Yugoslavia. The United States seemed to be playing the leading role in creating a new, cooperative international system, led by American power but recognizing the interests and respecting the dignity of others.

Then—it is a leitmotif of the last third of the twentieth century—something went wrong. Over decades, at least since the 1970s, impatience and resentment of others grew in the United States. The international institutions that the United States itself had created, out of characteristically American ideals of progress and cooperation, not least the United Nations, became unpopular with many Americans. Some of their unpopularity was no doubt justified by instances of sloth, incompetence, and even corruption. But in some circles the wildest slanders found credence. The collapse of Soviet countervailing power left the United States, as the unceasing mantra put it, "the lone superpower." No one noticed that no other country, not even China, however keen to push its economic and political interest, showed any great interest in becoming a "superpower," that the very concept looked to many in the rest of the world like a pompous relic of nineteenth-century nationalism.

So over the dozen years between 11/9—the fall of the Berlin Wall—and 9/11, the United States drifted in the direction of a new and dangerous mood of international exceptionalism. Its values tested by the terrorist atrocities in 2001, the United States government lashed out. In the process it seemed ready to jettison long-cherished principles. Human rights, which the United States had done so much to promote, no longer seemed so precious. The American government adopted "exemptionalism" in many international transactions; it exempted itself from standards it wanted to impose on others. In some instances—in permitting humiliation, abuse, and torture of prisoners at Abu Ghraib and elsewhere in Iraq, in locking away "enemy combatants" outside normal legal guarantees in a colonial enclave at Guantánamo, in the odious practice of "extraordinary rendition" (a euphemism for kidnapping unindicted persons on suspicion of collusion in terrorism and sending them for secret torture in foreign prisons), in lawless conduct in conquered territory in Iraq and Afghanistan, the United States government seemed to have crossed a whole series of lines. It was, it seemed, not merely falling short of its own high standards in respect to human rights and the rule of law. It was shamefully delinquent. Suddenly, in the first decade of the twenty-first century, the United States was in danger of losing that precious, almost universal reputation for trustworthiness.

The point that I am making, I must repeat, is not that the United States is exceptionally bad, either in the performance of American society or in the conduct of the American government. On the contrary, America remains one of the most successful, if not *the* most successful, societies on earth in many respects. Moreover, it remains a home to freedom, including the freedom to criticize American institutions. Most of the evidence from which I have constructed this chapter of negative exceptionalism, after all, comes from freely available American sources. The point is simply that, thanks to the wrong turnings taken in recent years, it can no longer be maintained, without argument, that America is proudly exceptional. In so many fields where Americans long believed, often justifiably, that their society was both exceptionally successful and exceptionally virtuous, it is now just one great, but imperfect, country among others.

S•I•X

The Corruption of the Best

Corruptio optimi pessimum: The corruption of the best is the worst.

Ancient Latin proverb

In this essay I have criticized American exceptionalism, sometimes sharply, on several different grounds. I first argued that the history of the United States ought to be seen as only one part of a broader history, not as the teleological preparation of a present and future perfection; as history, that is, and not as patriotic commemoration.

That history has not exclusively been the product of Puritan religion or the frontier, or any other purely American influences. On the contrary, it has been shaped by vast international historical processes, from the expansion of Europe and the African slave trade, through the Reformation and the Enlightenment, the global competition between the European powers, especially Britain and France, and the industrial revolution. America's development was greatly affected by two world wars, the Depression of the 1930s, and the Cold War. It has continued in the context of the rise of a global economy, first in the early years of the twentieth century and then, after the interruptions of the "short twentieth century," in the past few decades.[1]

Of course there were events and processes that were specific to the United States. They included mass immigration, the frontier, slavery, and the minting of an American political ideology. Their part in shaping the modern nation should never be underestimated. Yet nor should they be exaggerated at the expense of the wider processes that affected the world as a whole. Indeed, the first three of those four cardinal factors in American history also affected the development of many other nations. Historians, in other words, should not cherry-pick what was unique in the American experience and ignore its historical context. And there is an important reason for this. If Americans are brought up in their education, and encouraged by their leaders, to believe that they are a unique and special people, that will affect the way they behave toward the rest of the world, over which they now have so much influence and so much power.

I have suggested that in the early decades after the Revolution, in part as a result of developments in the colonial period, American society truly was more exceptional than it has subsequently become. That exceptionalism consisted in a relatively greater achievement of both freedom and equality, at least for white males, than was to be found elsewhere. The development of freedom and equality in America was always, however, more limited, more constrained, and more under attack than patriotic myth would sometimes have us believe.

After the Civil War, I have maintained, at the very time when the myth of the unique democratic influence of the frontier was coming into existence, America was in many ways becoming less exceptional. That was in part because the United States was beginning to experience the consequences of the industrial revolution, of unregulated capitalism, and of urbanization, in the same way that these forces were already affecting the British Isles and western and central Europe. In some respects, no doubt, the United States had greater resources for resisting or deflecting those dangerous consequences. But by the 1880s, to contrast a Europe enslaved by poverty with a land of opportunity inhabited by "people of plenty" was historically inaccurate. After the abolition of slavery, in fact, American politics were more and more about the "social question": about poverty, inequality, injustice—exactly the matters that were concerning writers, social reformers, and political leaders in Europe. On the one hand, the period brought the development, for the first time on American soil, of what was called in Europe a "proletariat." On the other, in what Mark Twain called the Gilded Age, America bred, on a far larger scale than ever before, a class of plutocrats whose wealth gave them social and political power. So far from being the mother of capitalism, as is sometimes suggested, the United States, though always a capitalist country, came later than several European countries to fully developed industrial capitalism.

America was also becoming less exceptional in reality (though not necessarily less exceptionalist in rhetoric) precisely because—largely unnoticed or at least unappreciated in the United States—Europe, too, was going through an Age of Liberalism. Mid-nineteenth-century Europe was the world of John Stuart Mill and William Ewart Gladstone. Greater freedom, equality, and democracy were aspired to, and—albeit imperfectly—achieved. This was admittedly more painful in Europe, because of the strength of established powers, vested interests, and traditions. But then it was not that easy in America, either. You could say that America was becoming less exceptional because Europeans, or many of them, were adopting American values. But those values had in any case long been European values too for most Europeans.

Many of the historical realities that had once made Europe appear so different from America were disappearing or at least were under attack in late-nineteenth-century and early-twentieth-century Europe. Absolute monarchy had been displaced by constitutional monarchy in Britain, Holland, and Scandinavia. The power of aristocracy was being crippled, not least by the effects of imported American foodstuffs on agricultural rents. Empire was dividing the politics of the imperial powers from 1900 on, the time of the Boer War, and by the second decade of the twentieth century two of the three major political parties in Britain, the Liberals and Labour, were already committed to decolonization in the long term. Americans, and especially American conservatives, have a high opinion of Winston Churchill. British people remember that in the 1930s he was one of the rather few British politicians who strenuously opposed independence for India.

In the twentieth century, America was exceptional not so much for a commitment to democratic ideals but for two other reasons. For one thing, the United States became exceptionally rich, partly because of its natural and human resources, but also because, unlike its European rivals, it was not devastated and impoverished but was enriched by two world wars. At first, and especially in the generation immediately after World War II, that wealth was widely and generously spread. Inequality declined sharply in America during and immediately after World War II. But the "glorious thirty years" after 1945 were a time of rapidly increasing prosperity, far more widely distributed than ever before, in Western Europe and in Japan as well. Workers in automobile plants in Britain and Germany, France and Italy, like auto workers in the United States, were improving their standard of living, buying their own homes, seeing their children go to college, helped by powerful trade unions. More recently, in America and in Europe, economic growth has been disproportionately appropriated by the very rich, both by those who have inherited and by those who have earned their good fortune for themselves. But the differences in the standard of living between America and the rest of the developed world are now differences of degree, not, as they had been before the 1960s, differences of kind. Once, American incomes were something Europeans could only dream of. Now, in Western Europe at least, it is a question of whether the American average income is reached next year or the year after.

In the 1930s and 1940s the United States also escaped the political disaster of fascism, and indeed played an important, though not (as exceptionalists sometimes imply) the only, role in destroying fascist and Nazi rule. The fact that fascism never seriously threatened the American political system (or, for that matter, the political systems in Britain, the British dominions, or Scandinavia) reflects the strength of the democratic tradition and the political skill of President Roosevelt, as well as the robust common sense of most Americans. Yet even in America some fascist tendencies and quasi-fascist movements appeared.[2]

Untouched by foreign invasion, the American economy boomed in both world wars, at the very time when America's rivals were in their greatest difficulties. The United States "did well" out of the two world wars. After 1945 it was natural for American exceptionalism to be seen in large measure as the consequence of exceptional economic success and military power, not to mention the Faustian power of nuclear weapons and the ability to deliver them almost everywhere at will. So in the 1950s the current version of exceptionalism was a new blend of the moral exceptionalism of Roosevelt's fight for the Four Freedoms and pride in economic recovery, material progress, and military power. A good example is the book by David Potter, *People of Plenty.*[3] "In every aspect of economic welfare," Potter wrote, "the national differentials between the United States and other countries are immense." The United States, he said, had 7 percent of the world's population and 42 percent of the world's income. The equivalent figures today show that the U.S. gross national product is $13.2 trillion out of a world GNP of $48 trillion, or about 27 percent (slightly less than the European Union's share of $14.5 trillion), and the U.S. population, though much larger at about 300 million, is only 4.5 percent of the world's estimated population of 6.6 billion people, a lower proportion than fifty years earlier.[4] The average American in 1949, Potter stated, consumed 3,186 calories, "unquestionably the highest nutritional standard in the world." Half a century later, few would equate calorie consumption with nutritional standards. Moreover, Potter claimed, the high American standard of living was the result much less of natural resources than of the "economic efficiency of all kinds of Americans." The phrase now evokes a gentle smile. Potter's book, like many works of the 1950s, was explicitly devoted to disproving "zany" Marxist or socialist ideas. Many similar books written in the 1950s—for example, works by Max Lerner or Daniel Boorstin—were predicated on similar assumptions of incomparable American material superiority in areas where today the American advantage is comparatively slight and sometimes depends on what precise method of comparison is used.

In recent decades this second, material exceptionalism, now less clear, has helped to breed or to strengthen a third, missionary exceptionalism. This is the belief that it is the destiny, some say the God-given destiny, of the United States to spread the benefits of its democratic system and of its specific version of capitalism to as many other countries as possible. This view is not wholly new. Seeds of it can be seen in early Protestant religion. It played a part in the patriotic rhetoric of the new Republic, in the confidence of the champions of Manifest Destiny that theirs was an "empire of liberty," and in the belief system of many American leaders, including especially Woodrow Wilson but also, in different ways, Theodore Roosevelt, Franklin D. Roosevelt, Harry Truman, and John F. Kennedy.

One specific new element in the American belief system, from the last quarter of the twentieth century, was the elevation of American capitalism, alongside American freedom and American democracy, in the pantheon of American exceptionalism. Of course, America has been the home of capitalism from the start, though not its only home. There was a fascinating episode in the earliest years of the Pilgrims' struggle to survive in Plymouth Colony, described in William Bradford's classic account. At first the Pilgrims intended to hold all land and wealth in common. But when the young colony was desperately worried about the shortage of food, the governor, Bradford, "with the advice of the chiefest among them," assigned land as property to each family. This experience, Bradford comments, "may well evince the vanity of that conceit of Plato's and other ancients applauded by some of later times; that the taking away of property and bringing in community [meaning communism or at least common ownership] into a commonwealth would make them happy and flourishing, *as if they were wiser than God.*"[5]

Although ideas of communal ownership of property were to be found in the sixteenth and seventeenth century—for example, among the Anabaptists in sixteenth-century Westphalia, Moravia, and Bohemia and the seventeenth-century Levellers and Diggers in England—capitalism was closely associated with Protestantism, in Holland and Germany as well as in Britain and New England, as has been argued by great modern historians, including Max Weber and R.H. Tawney.[6] If modern capitalism was largely developed in Holland and Britain in the sixteenth and seventeenth centuries, and carried across the Atlantic by Protestant colonists, capitalism itself is as old as civilization. Its fundamental ideas, such as the idea of investing in the hope of future profit, are as old as agriculture, and the part played by markets in setting prices can be traced back at least as far as the earliest towns in the Near East. It is true that at certain times and in certain places—for example, in the ancient river valley civilizations, when economic behavior and prices were regulated by royal authority, and in the European Middle Ages, when usury was prohibited by the church—capitalism was subordinated to temporal or spiritual authority. But capitalism existed long before the United States of America.

Economic historians distinguish a series of successive phases in the development of capitalism, for example, petty capitalism, mercantile capitalism, industrial capitalism, and finance capitalism. None of these can be said to have developed exclusively or even mainly in the United States. It is true, however, that in the twentieth century many European societies reacted to economic crisis by adopting one or another version of socialism. Even in the United States, from 1933 to the 1970s, the federal government embraced a form of social democracy, though control of enterprise was exercised not mainly by state ownership but by state regulation. In Western Europe, as well as in the former British dominions and in Latin America, though various "socialist" devices, including public ownership, were more widespread than in the United States, the economic system was still one variant or another of capitalism, more or less regulated. (Sometimes it was described as a "mixed economy.") It is possible therefore to speak of the United States as having led the way in the propagation of neoliberal ideas in the late twentieth century, but misleading to suggest that capitalism as such is in any way an American invention.

In the past thirty years or so, however, and especially after the presidency of Ronald Reagan, an exceptionalist philosophy has been more confidently enunciated and more openly accepted as the basis for American foreign policy. This missionary spirit has come in two variants. One is the gentler and more consensual version, as preached and practiced by the Clinton administration. Its leaders acknowledged that they were followers of Woodrow Wilson, and that they inherited his desire to bring the benefits of American democracy to the world. But they wanted to do so, as far as possible, only to the extent that others wanted those benefits. They were keen that America should be the leader. But they interpreted that to mean that others were eager to be led. They wanted to act out their beliefs, so far as possible, with the agreement of as many other nations as possible. This, too, had been the instinct, or at least the practice, of the previous Republican administration of George H. W. Bush.

At least as long ago as the debates in the early Cold War years over the National Security Act, and over NSC-68 and the sharp consequent increases in defense budgets, there had been those, the "hawks," who were impatient of restraint.[7] They saw the nation as being virtually at war with communism. They resented the occasional reluctance of allies to endorse American interests or to go along with American initiatives. They called for maximum military readiness and brushed aside those who warned of the dangers of transforming America into a "garrison state" or a "national security state." Surprisingly, perhaps, it was not when the danger of communism was at its height, but when it had to all intents and purposes disappeared in the early 1990s, that the partisans of aggressive, unilateral missionary policies finally triumphed.

In Chapter 4, I have argued, as many others have now done, that these policies have been disastrous, not only for the damage they have inflicted on the domestic American economy or even for America's reputation in the world, but also for any realistic prospect of achieving their own goals. There can be little doubt that the prospects of spreading American ideals of democracy have weakened, not improved, especially in the Middle East, since the invasion of Iraq in 2003. Survey data from late 2007 suggest that roughly two-thirds to three-quarters of the world's population disapprove of the American invasion and occupation of Iraq. The prospects of American democracy would be seriously damaged by an attack on Iran or even by a nod and a wink to an Israeli attack on Iran. Nor has the prosperity of the United States been enhanced by the new aggressive foreign policy. An America on bad terms with its suppliers of energy, raw materials, cheap manufactured goods, migrants, and credit is not going to be a stronger America, especially if its finite resources have been dissipated in incompetently planned military adventures. Finally, the domestic regime that accompanies conservative foreign policy seems unlikely to strengthen the society in the long term. An America, for example, in which the richest 1 percent were piling up ever greater fortunes, and chief executives of corporations earned many hundreds of times more than their average employee, while half the population could not afford to buy a home or go to the doctor, would not be a stronger America, however spectacular the fortunes accumulated by a few.

A number of questions must, however, be answered if my argument is to hold together: Is it only Americans who believe in American exceptionalism? How much have the recent mistakes in foreign policy been a consequence of the spread of exceptionalist ideas? Is there, then, any truth at all, or has there been no merit, in exceptionalism? What are the consequences of Americans' belief in their own exceptionalism for their relations with the rest of the world?

Is it only Americans who believe in American exceptionalism?

Since the American Revolution, and indeed since colonial times, many Europeans have indeed been tempted by American exceptionalism. That is why so many of the key texts of the exceptionalist litany were spoken or written by Europeans. John Winthrop was an Englishman. Crèvecoeur was a Frenchman who had been naturalized as an Englishman. Tom Paine was an Englishman who brought his very English hatred of despotism with him to America.

The myth of America, the dream of an "empty" country where land was all but free, where there was no landlord, no bishop and no king, was in itself a European myth. Native Americans did not think of America as empty. John Donne, the sensual metaphysician, compared his mistress's body to "my America! my Newfoundland!" To this day some Europeans, and perhaps especially those who have been left behind in the headlong enrichment of the old continent over the last fifty years, still imagine America as Eldorado, a mythical land of equal opportunity, easy money, and low-hanging fruit. A standby of Britain's tabloid newspapers is the recurrent story of some family that could not get a high-technology treatment for a sick child in England, and, thanks to the generosity of some American individual or charity, has been miraculously cured in an American clinic. Sometimes it really does happen, though poor families in Britain might not be well advised to trade their admittedly imperfect national health service for an uninsured life in America.

A telling point, however, is that over the past half-century, admiration for America has changed from being part of the value system of the European Left to being a trait of the Right. Senator Daniel Patrick Moynihan once said to me that the United States has "a fifth column in every country on earth." I asked whether he meant the CIA. No, he replied, "I mean the lower middle class." Professor Max Beloff once told a conference in my presence that the last parliamentary debate in Britain where the Conservative Party voted against an American policy and the Labour Party voted for it was the vote on the American loan to Britain in 1947.

The terms of the proposition are sufficiently vague that it may not be literally provable. But the general point is true nonetheless. Before 1945 it was first the Liberal Party in Britain, then the Labour Party, that admired and wanted to imitate the United States. One of the early neoconservatives told me that the only three friends who had keys to his New York apartment were three leading members of the British Labour Party. Since World War II, British Conservatives, even before Margaret Thatcher, have hailed the United States as a model of capitalist enterprise, low taxes, social conservatism, law and order (and capital punishment), and anticommunist fervor. Labour, until it was captured by Tony Blair with his concept of "New Labour," was wary of what were seen as trigger-happy American nuclear policies, unregulated American capitalism and union-bashing, and perceived indifference to Third World poverty.

I am not saying either of these attitudes, or stereotypes, was either just or well informed. I am simply asserting what I believe is incontrovertible, that in the past fifty years, America has crossed over from being seen as the guarantor of progress to being the champion of the status quo, or—as the French categorize it—from leading the party of movement to heading the party of order. It was in the ranks of Old Labour that Tony Blair first aroused resentment for being too close to a Republican American administration. The same would be true in every Western European country. Alongside Blair, the chief European governments allied with the U.S. invasion of Iraq were the conservatives, Silvio Berlusconi in Italy and José Maria Aznar in Spain. Even in what former secretary of defense Donald Rumsfeld was pleased to call "New Europe"—that is, in the former Communist Europe—a similar alignment seems to be taking place. In Eastern Europe it is conservatives like Vaclav Klaus, not the leaders of the anti-Soviet struggle like Vaclav Havel, who are Washington's natural allies. Of course, for a Republican administration, that may seem both natural and healthy. But a Democratic administration might do well to ask whether it is good that the United States, once the champion of democracy and progress, is now seen as the defender of corporate capitalism and social conservatism.

Of course many people, all around the world, still look up to what they see as distinctively American ideals of justice and democracy, just as many believe, and not without reason, that their material condition would be improved if they were able to migrate to the United States. It is also true that there are few governments in the world that do not seek the best possible relations with Washington, and those that do not are by no means the most admirable or even reputable. At the same time it is my impression, and it would be hard to prove or disprove this by survey data, that two less flattering propositions are also true. While American culture has perhaps never been more influential worldwide, admiration for American political ideas, and political support for America—it seems plain—are at a lower level than they were a dozen years ago, or indeed for many decades. They may also be lower than most Americans imagine.[8]

There is another dimension to this. Since the end of communism, and indeed for many years before that, it has suited Europeans and especially Western European governments to rely on Americans to spend more on defense than they did. In some cases, this was because European governments, notably in France, did not really believe that the danger of Soviet military attack was as great as successive governments in Washington insisted. In other cases, Europeans simply preferred to spend their money on infrastructure, or education, or social security. Whatever the different subjective rationalizations, objectively Europeans between the 1950s and the 1990s came to accept that the United States was, and could be counted on to remain, exceptional in its willingness to maintain a hugely expensive defense establishment. Ostensibly this was intended to defend Europe and other allies against communist encroachment, but—as many Europeans saw it—in reality its purpose was to uphold the supremacy of American power.

How much have the recent mistakes in foreign policy been a consequence of the spread of exceptionalist ideas?

On the face of it, to lay the invasion and occupation of Iraq, and the general deterioration of American relations with those who used to be its allies, at the door of the exceptionalist tradition might seem excessive, even preposterous. After all, there has always been an exceptionalist strand in American patriotism, and it has not always, or even often, translated into military aggression. Many, no doubt most, Americans have always believed that their historic good fortune entailed high responsibilities.

It seems from all evidence to have been a profound assumption in the United States since the Revolution, sometimes expressed, sometimes not directly spoken, that people all over the world would be happier if they could get rid of their current governments and be ruled by the American Constitution and the "empire of liberty." On his way to the Paris peace conference, President Wilson explained to the bright young men of his Inquiry team that he alone among the world leaders was the democratic choice of his people. David Lloyd George and Georges Clemenceau, leaders of Britain and France, respectively, had just been reconfirmed in power by huge majorities (about four to one in each case) in their parliaments, and Wilson's party had just lost control of Congress in the midterm elections. None of that could penetrate Wilson's exceptionalist prejudice.[9]

Only occasionally, however, in specific places and on limited occasions, has a practical opportunity of acting on that general assumption presented itself. In the early nineteenth century, to be sure, administrations in Washington had four opportunities to annex territories on a vast scale. In three of the four cases (as we have seen), this was a direct consequence of events in Europe. Napoleon's difficulties in Saint Domingue, as the French called Haiti, persuaded that shrewdest of traders to dispose of the Louisiana Purchase. The collapse of the Spanish monarchy made it possible for John Quincy Adams to acquire the two Floridas by treaty, albeit in a negotiation in which the pressure and the military threat of American settlers made American expansion inevitable. The movement of land-hungry Anglo settlers into Mexico's remotest northern province, Tejas, set the scene for the Mexican War and the imperial provinces acquired under the treaty of Guadalupe Hidalgo. Finally, the Oregon Territory was acquired from Britain without war because London could not have defended it and had no urgent motive for doing so. No doubt, as Tom Paine pointed out in *Common Sense*, there was "something very absurd in supposing a continent to be perpetually governed by an island." But it has been equally absurd, or at least mythical, to maintain that the continental United States sprang into existence spontaneously, by natural law or manifest destiny, rather than as a result of some determined statesmanship. From time to time in the nineteenth century, as we have seen, Americans hankered after Canada, Cuba, and many parts of the Caribbean and Central America. But no opportunities for bringing the benefits of American life to substantial other territories arose until the very end of the century, when the United States was able to acquire Hawaii, Puerto Rico, the Philippines, and, in effect, Cuba. Woodrow Wilson had, as he repeatedly stated, to the irritation of many Europeans, no territorial ambitions after World War I. But in Wilson's plan, the United States had an even prouder ambition: to determine the territorial boundaries and political arrangements of all other nations.

In the aftermath of the Second World War, the United States was able to influence the departure of the somewhat discredited monarchy in Italy, and to play a decisive part in the establishment of democratic governments more or less modeled on American patterns in Germany and Japan. Those constitutional arrangements have lasted well on the whole. Indeed, the parts of both the German and the Japanese constitutions that have been most challenged have been those that prohibited military adventures; and it has been Washington that has been most frustrated by the unwillingness of Germans and Japanese to join in its wars.

Between the late 1940s and the 1990s, however, there was little appetite in Washington for state making. Thanks to the Cold War, the United States was not much tempted to export its constitutional arrangements, still less to bring yet more territory into the empire of liberty.

With the end of the Cold War, the situation was different. The United States was no longer confronted and blocked by a rival superpower, armed with nuclear weapons, and supported by a "socialist camp." Once again, an opportunity had arisen to follow whatever instincts an administration in Washington might have. The instincts of the first Bush administration were to work with as many allies as could be persuaded to share American policies. The clever and tactful way in which the Bush team took advantage of the dissolution of Soviet power to allow the Western *Bundesrepublik* in effect to take over the Eastern *Deutsche Demokratische Republik* without seriously alarming either the Russian leadership, the French, the British, or anyone else, is a model of multilateral diplomacy. The assembly of a coalition, including Britain, France, and Japan as well as Arab nations, to repel Saddam Hussein from Kuwait was an equally impressive operation in the tradition of post-1945 American collective leadership.

Yet throughout the 1990s the movement that was to succeed in imposing the disastrous, unilateral policies of the second Bush administration was gathering momentum. This is not the place to retell the story of how that movement, itself a coalition of originally disparate conservative groupings, was put together, or the circumstances, after 9/11, in which it was able to triumph over all policy criticism and bureaucratic opposition. There are, however, two curious aspects of that story that are not widely understood.

The first is that there was an almost seamless transition from those who supported more vigorous policies to confront and challenge the Soviet Union to those who stood for a similarly forward strategy toward Arab nationalism or Muslim fanatics. The only logical connection would seem to be that in both contexts men like Dick Cheney and Donald Rumsfeld, as well as intellectuals like William Kristol, Robert Kagan, and various academics, national security officials, and members of the policy community, shared a conviction that whenever thwarted, and by whomsoever, the United States must assert itself more vigorously. They agreed that it should cast aside the caution and moderation of the mainstream Cold War style of the "foreign policy Establishment." In his celebrated and highly popular 1993 thesis of a coming "clash of civilizations," Samuel Huntington seemed almost to be looking for an enemy strong enough to justify increased American preparedness.[10] The only credible antagonist he could come up with was surely implausible: an alliance between China and Islam.

There is another curious aspect to the tone of the new conservative, or neoconservative, foreign policy. Its exponents might occasionally be truculent. But it was not triumphalist, let alone optimistic. On the contrary, the case was stated in terms of reversing a perceived decline in American power and the need for reviving the willingness to assert it. At the heart of this new conservative foreign policy was fear that one enemy or another would take advantage of the United States unless American leaders stood to arms.

Given the overwhelming military advantage enjoyed by the United States, it is reasonable to look for unstated motives for this Spenglerian tone. Several candidates suggest themselves. It may simply reflect the foreboding beliefs of that guru of neoconservatives in general and the Kristol family in particular, Leo Strauss. Perhaps the real concern was over the survival not of the invincible United States but of its vulnerable ally Israel, threatened by Muslim states with far larger and rapidly growing populations. A third is that the Project for a New American Century reflected the past as much as the future, in that it essentially transferred to new enemies the fear, and the more aggressive policies, inherited from the anti-Soviet Team B and Committee on the Present Danger of the 1970s.

A psychological explanation for the new mood could be that the second generation of neoconservatives and their older Republican allies had inherited the pessimistic worldview of the first neoconservative generation. One of them, Nathan Glazer, had powerfully described how liberals like himself, of the World War II generation, had been dismayed by the "increasing radicalization, increasing vituperation, increasing disaffection with the country and its institutions" of the New Left.[11] They had seen the structures of university and intellectual life that were dear to them threatened by "an invasion of centaurs," as Theodore Roszak called the counterculture of the 1960s, conjuring an image from "the pediment of the Temple of Zeus at Olympia. . . . It recalls what must always be a fearful experience in the life of any civilization: the experience of radical cultural disjuncture, the clash of irreconcilable conceptions of life."[12] It takes a certain stretch of the imagination to see the signatories of the Project for a New American Century, the sponsors of Guantánamo Bay, and the defenders of "waterboarding" as the guardians of civilization. Yet that, no doubt, is how they see themselves.

As the George W. Bush administration prepared in secret to invade Iraq, its leading personalities, Dick Cheney, Donald Rumsfeld, and Paul Wolfowitz, in particular, as well as the president himself, united to give the impression that the decision was taken as a consequence of the terrorist attacks of 9/11.

That was not, however, the whole truth. From the very first days of his administration, well before 9/11, George Bush showed an interest in attacking Iraq. There have been graphic descriptions in the memoirs already published of this apparent obsession. Richard Clarke, for example, who had been in charge of the Counterterrorism Security Group under President Clinton and in the new administration, was surprised when, as early as the evening of September 12, 2001, George W. Bush was already insistent that Iraq might have been involved in the previous day's attacks. "See if Saddam did this," Clarke recalled the president saying. "See if he's linked in any way."[13] Yet Bush had been preoccupied with the danger from Iraq long before 9/11. In 2004 a *Wall Street Journal* reporter, Ron Suskind, published a book heavily dependent on the recollections of President George W. Bush's first treasury secretary, Paul O'Neill. As early as January 30, 2001, at his first National Security Council meeting, Bush turned to Condoleezza Rice in what O'Neill said "several observers understood was a scripted exchange" and asked, "What's on the agenda?" She replied, "How Iraq is destabilizing the region, Mr. President." At which, on cue, the director of Central Intelligence, George Tenet, produced a grainy aerial photograph of a factory. It might be, he said, "a plant that produces either chemical or biological materials for weapons manufacture." Already, in the first weeks of the Bush presidency, O'Neill realized that the talk within the administration's inner circle was not about the why, but about the how and the how quickly.[14] By 2004, when Suskind's book came out, O'Neill was interviewed for CBS's *60 Minutes* by Lesley Stahl. "From the very beginning", he said, "there was a conviction that Saddam Hussein was a bad person and that he needed to go."[15]

That strategic aim had a long history, dating back even before the presidency of Ronald Reagan. There seemed (as I remarked above) no logical connection between an aggressive attitude toward the Soviet Union and a similar stance toward Islamic jihadism or toward Saddam Hussein's secular Iraq. There was, however, a historical connection. It can be traced to the school of thought that feared that American policy had been too soft in its search for détente with the Soviet Union. It was under the Carter regime, later caricatured by conservatives as indifferent to the dangers of communism, that a middle-level official, the deputy assistant secretary of defense for regional planning, one Paul Wolfowitz, was first asked by the defense secretary, Harold Brown, to look at areas outside Europe where American interests might be challenged and American forces might be required to respond.[16]

Wolfowitz was influenced by Geoffrey Kemp, later a White House official under Ronald Reagan but at the time a professor at Tufts University in suburban Boston, and he hired a recent Berkeley Ph.D. named Dennis Ross, later to become one of the most skillful of American diplomats in the Middle East, to work with him. Together they produced a document called the Limited Contingency Study. It focused on the danger that the Soviet Union might seize the Middle Eastern oil fields, a contingency so far from being limited that Wolfowitz's study judged that if the Soviet Union got Persian Gulf oil, it would "probably destroy NATO and the U.S.-Japanese alliance without recourse to war by the Soviets." Wolfowitz was fascinated by the importance of Middle Eastern oil and therefore by Iraq. But his interest began before Saddam Hussein had even fully consolidated his power in Baghdad, let alone before he used chemical weapons on the Kurds and then on the Iranians.

It is revealing that there really was a continuity, in conservative circles, between fear of Soviet influence in the Middle Eastern oil fields and fear of Saddam's influence there. And of course—however often this is denied—conservative concern over Iraq was originally not about the cruelty or the undemocratic nature of Saddam's regime, not about the danger of his acquiring "weapons of mass destruction," certainly not about Iraq's role as a base for terrorism. Historically and primarily, whatever else American interest in the Middle East may have been about, it has always also been about oil.

Oil was important. So was the wholly admirable commitment to support and defend Israel. But those concerns had been present for many years. By the 1990s the background to the growing obsession with Iraq among neoconservatives was exceptionalist sentiment. Neither Saddam Hussein nor any other foreign leader must stand against the high historic mission of the United States to bring democracy to the Middle East.

This was the view of the neoconservative coterie. It was equally the view of those, including the president's brother Jeb, Dick Cheney, and Donald Rumsfeld, who joined the neoconservatives in signing the Project for a New American Century. It was also emphatically the personal credo of the president himself.

"George W. Bush believes in U.S. exceptionalism," wrote David L. Phillips, the State Department official chosen to head plans for postwar Iraq, plans that were brushed aside by Rumsfeld's Pentagon. "Bush embraces the use of U.S. diplomatic, economic, and military might to build a better world and to promote global freedom." Condoleezza Rice, too, Phillips added, "extolled the purity of America's mission: 'We may be the only great power in history,' she said, 'that prefers greatness to power and justice to glory.'"[17] That is a naïvely exceptionalist reading of history. All great powers have sought "greatness," and most have identified justice with their own interests.

President Bush has struck the pure exceptionalist vein again and again in his speeches. More than most, he has added his own religious color to the exceptionalist rhetoric, never more clearly than in his speech accepting the Republican nomination at the 2004 convention: "Like generations before us," he cried in his peroration, "we have a calling from beyond the stars to stand for freedom. This is the everlasting dream of America, and tonight, in this place, that dream is renewed. Now we go forward, grateful for our freedom, faithful to our cause, and confident in the future of the greatest nation on earth."

A calling from beyond the stars! The phrase recalls the quip of the Victorian radical member of Parliament, Henry Labouchère, about another evangelical Christian in politics, the prime minister, William Gladstone. He didn't mind the prime minister's having the fifth ace up his sleeve, Labouchère said, he just objected to his saying that the Almighty had put it there.

Is there, then, any truth at all, or has there been no merit, in exceptionalism?

That is not my thesis.

American exceptionalism has inspired the political dreams and ambitions of men and women across the political spectrum. Both Martin Luther King and George Wallace, it has been said, were American exceptionalists. That may go too far. Wallace was more an Alabamian or a southern exceptionalist. Yet certainly two such different groups of influential Americans as the group of African-American lawyers at the Howard University Law School, led by Thurgood Marshall, who developed the case for reversing *Plessy v. Ferguson* and abolishing segregation, and the circle around William F. Buckley at the magazine *National Review,* who made conservatism respectable again in the same years, would have agreed on one thing, if on nothing else: their political dreams were about fulfilling specifically American beliefs as they interpreted them. Woodrow Wilson and Henry Cabot Lodge, bitter rivals with incompatible concepts of America's destiny in the world, were alike American exceptionalists.

The Founding Fathers shared a belief in the special quality and the mission of the new nation they were bringing to birth. Tom Paine expressed it in the biting contempt he invited the citizens of his new country to feel for the government of his old one. James Madison, in the thirty-ninth of the Federalist papers, argued that only a republican form of government "would be reconcilable with the genius of the people of America; with the fundamental principles of the revolution; or with that honorable determination, which animates every votary of freedom, to rest all our political experiments on the capacity of mankind for self-government."[18] He then proceeded to argue that although it had been claimed that some governments in Europe were republican, such as Holland or Venice, or Poland or even Britain itself, in truth only America deserved the name.

Thomas Jefferson, for all his sympathy with the spirit of revolution in France, never doubted that America would be the teacher of liberty to the nations of Europe. In the following generation, as we have seen, such different men as John Quincy Adams, Noah Webster, and Horace Mann acted on the assumption that American life already surpassed the life of Europe in political justice, and would unfailingly soon outstrip all other nations in the arts of civilization. Abraham Lincoln was an eloquent exceptionalist, and so was his secretary of state, William Henry Seward. Both Franklin Roosevelt and Lyndon Johnson were driven by a determination that the United States would set a new example, whether it was called a New Deal or a Great Society.

This is true also of American popular culture. The popular music of the 1920s, 1930s, and 1940s has endowed the nation and the world with its rich treasury of "standards," many of them as explicitly patriotic as Irving Berlin's beloved "God Bless America." The classic movies of Hollywood, also largely created, as producers or directors, by first- or second-generation immigrants, many of them Jewish, and also popular far beyond America's shores, have as a constant, uplifting theme the "only in America" saga of immigrant success. American exceptionalism is less pervasive, though not wholly absent, in classic fiction, but it (or various strands of nationalism) has been a powerful factor in the appeal of many of the great best-sellers, from Mark Twain to Tim LaHaye by way of Ayn Rand and Tom Clancy.

From the beginning, one legitimate and positive component of American national pride has been the idea that the United States had unique qualities as a society and a special destiny as a nation. That conviction has been a powerful motivating incentive. It has caused Americans on the whole to set themselves high standards, especially in their public life. If they sometimes supposed that their standards were higher than anyone else's, that may not have been altogether a bad thing. If it set an example for other nations to emulate, so much the better.

At different times in the past, exceptionalism has admittedly taken the objectionable shape of a pompous and intolerant "Americanism," or even "100 percent Americanism." This was the stuff of blowhard Fourth of July oratory in every generation. It took the form of the odious prejudices of nineteenth-century Nativists and of the second Klan of the 1920s, with its bigoted hatred of Catholics and Jews as well as African-Americans.

This was the soil in which the Red-baiting and witch-hunting of the 1950s grew. One of my students recently showed me a strip cartoon booklet circulated to schools in 1950 by the service organization Lions International. It recited a propaganda version of "history" in which cavemen, ancient Egyptians, and Spartans were portrayed as slaves. It contrasted the Spartans, directly compared to Russians, with the freedom-loving Athenians, though of course there was slavery in Athens as well as in Sparta. Americans were portrayed as uniquely brave soldiers for freedom, explicitly contrasted with British "socialism." As this cockamamie version of world history went on, to be told to the children, it was made clear that Americans were in danger of being enslaved . . . by taxation.

There is no means of telling how widespread such propaganda about American history was in the early Cold War years. It was certainly not far to seek. Nor perhaps should it be taken too seriously. Some of George Bush's admirers at the 2004 convention carried posters asking how they were to shoot liberals if their guns were taken from them, but everyone knew that that was only a joke in bad taste, not the portent of an American fascism.

The American exceptionalism I am describing is quite different from such coarse prejudice. It has been on the whole a tradition that stresses the superiority of America and Americans, not the inferiority of anyone else. That may be irritating to those of us who are not Americans, but it is generously meant. George W. Bush may not have taken the trouble to find out whether the people of Iraq were pleased to have him impose his conception of democracy on them, but at least it was liberty, not slavery, that he thought he was offering.

The corruption of the best, says the old Latin tag, is the worst. My thesis is not that American exceptionalist thought is intrinsically corrupting or that it was destructive in the past, but that what has been essentially a liberating set of beliefs has been corrupted over the past thirty years or so by hubris and self-interest into what is now a dangerous basis for national policy and for the international system.

Even in the times when its overall thrust was beneficent, the exceptionalist narrative of American history left out half the story. The history of the migration to America, I have suggested, could not be understood in isolation from the conditions and the political and religious beliefs of Europe at the time, certainly not by simply contrasting an American commitment to "liberty" with the presumably servile cultures of everyone else. The religious faith of New England was not antithetical to European Christianity; it was one variant of the Protestant faith shared by Ulstermen and Swedes, Afrikaners and Prussians. The impulses that pushed Europeans to migrate to the United States were not wholly different from the motives of those who settled in Canada, or Australia, or the Argentine, or from those of the Russians who broke the black soils of the Ukraine, or even of the settlers from all over Europe who mined the gold and diamonds of South Africa.

Even in the twentieth century, at least the first two-thirds of it, if the American experience was more fortunate than that of other countries, still life in the United States was always influenced and conditioned by what was happening everywhere else. The United States was hardly untouched by the breakdown of the European diplomatic system in 1914 and of the world economic system in 1929, by the invention of the internal combustion engine in Germany in the 1890s or of radio by an Italian working in England, or by the work of nuclear physicists in Cambridge or Berlin in the 1920s.

The point would not need to be labored, were it not that in the political rhetoric of American conservatives since the last quarter of the twentieth century, exceptionalism has nourished a new and less passive version of isolationism, a deeply unrealistic and false appreciation of America's relationship with the rest of the world.

This new, more aggressive, unilateral attitude toward the outside world from the middle 1970s on was no doubt part of a general reaction against the perceived failures and betrayals of "liberal" thinking in the 1960s. As many on the left of the American political spectrum came to see the Vietnam War as a disastrous failure, others reacted by yearning for renewed national strength. As some came to believe it was wrong to fight it, others only wished it had been won. Much of the appeal of the Reagan administration came from Ronald Reagan's ability to present himself as restoring national strength, self-respect and reputation. Reagan loved to strike patriotic notes, and his listeners loved it when he did. He constantly and naturally used exceptionalist language in his speeches.

In a much-cherished speech to the first Conservative Political Action conference, sponsored by the Conservative Political Union in January 1974, Reagan nailed his exceptionalist theses to the mast. "I have always believed," he said, "that there was some divine plan that placed this great continent between two oceans to be sought out by those who were possessed of an abiding love of freedom and a special kind of courage." He ended his intensely emotional patriotic speech with these words: "We cannot escape our destiny, nor should we try to do so. The leadership of the free world was thrust upon us two centuries ago in that little hall of Philadelphia. In the days following World War II, when the economic strength and power of America was all that stood between the world and the return to the dark ages, Pope Pius XII said, 'The American people have a great genius for splendid and unselfish actions. Into the hands of America God has placed the destinies of an afflicted mankind.'"

This wholehearted, red-blooded patriotism was a crucial element in Reagan's political message. His admiring but shrewd biographer Lou Cannon understood that "Reagan's picture of a golden, patriotic past was filtered through the dark, distorting lens of Vietnam." Many Americans, Cannon pointed out, "shared Reagan's innocent conviction that they were the good guys in a world no longer appreciative of goodness," that many in the 1980s "longed for the days when the American flag was an honored emblem and 'Yanks' were the envy of the earth." If Reagan knew that he was punching political buttons, he was anything but a cynic. He passionately believed his own traditional patriotic rhetoric, but his pride in America was tempered by realism and not disfigured by any love of war.

The Reagan legacy, however, was a powerful talisman for the younger conservatives who saw his presidency as a liberation and a holy cause. Not all of them shared his realism or his distaste for sending young men to fight in wars that could not be won. "Let us tell those who fought [in Vietnam]," ran one of his applause lines in his unsuccessful 1976 primary campaign, "that we will never again ask young men to fight and possibly die in a war that our government is afraid to win." It was a clever formulation of a position that could appeal both to those who thought it was wrong to ask young men to die, and to those who thought it wrong to be "afraid to win."

Reagan's presidency was succeeded by the administration of George H. W. Bush. He and his chief advisers on foreign policy, men like James Baker, Brent Scowcroft, Robert Zoellick, and their ilk, were even more realistic and cautious than Reagan, and their record in foreign affairs was all the more successful for it. But when the elder Bush was defeated by Bill Clinton, another spirit, more troubled and less humble, was coming to dominate the Republican ranks.

No doubt the exceptionalist view of foreign policy is related to the general ascendancy of the new conservatism. Many strands of national thought and feeling contributed to it. We have touched on many of them. There was pride at restored national self-confidence, teamed with fear of national decline. There was disappointment and anger at European allies, fed by malicious reporting and liberated by the disappearance, with the end of the Cold War, of the need to restrain irritation. There was a renewed sense of America's power to shape the world according to American ideals, strangely mixed with a fear of new forces that America might not be able to control: China, Islam, India, a Europe that refused to disappear as a competitor, however much the conservative pundits predicted that the muezzin would soon be heard in Notre Dame de Paris.[19]

One factor of incalculable importance in this new mood was the growing influence of unelected ideologues. Conservatives had long complained that liberals dominated the intellectual life of the United States. It was true that liberal thinking, liberal ideals, and liberal prejudices were dominant in the great metropolitan newspapers, in the television networks before the coming of cable, satellite, and Rupert Murdoch, in book publishing, news magazines, and above all in the great graduate schools that contributed so much to the marketplace of ideas. It was one of the projects of the original neoconservatives to contest this liberal ascendancy by creating conservative institutions to challenge it. And this they did with considerable success. Conservative foundations—Coors, John M. Olin, and many others, and especially the Hoover Institute at Stanford University, the Heritage Foundation on Capitol Hill in Washington, and above all the American Enterprise Institute downtown—supported a new breed of conservative intellectuals in a style to which they were glad to become accustomed. Unanimity was not exacted. But a degree of ideological homogeneity was enforced through the carrot, rather than the stick. The administration of grants, fellowships, stipends, and publication contracts gradually created an Establishment of the Right.

Since the term—and the social type—*intelligentsia* originated under czarist oppression in the mid-nineteenth century, it had been a characteristic of the *intelligent*, the individual member of the new class, to speak truth, or at least criticism, to power. Now, almost for the first time, a new intelligentsia of the Right came to power and to considerable prosperity.

Their sharpest barbs were directed at the powerless. Their shibboleths were loyalty to corporate America, demonization of elected government, a libertarianism that focused especially on the abolition of taxes, indifference to the poor, and often a professed contempt for idealism. By these new centaurs, sensitivity to the feelings of ethnic and sexual minorities, and even of women, were too often derided as "political correctness." A class of persons expensively educated mainly at private schools and private universities, remunerated by private foundations, and whose work consisted largely in defending the interests of private wealth tried, and to a startling extent succeeded, to represent itself as the defenders of the working poor against the rapacious rule of effete, moneyed liberals.

It was from this new class—to use a phrase with which they liked to label their opponents—that a new, harder spirit spread over much of public life in America. It was from the conservative think tanks, factories of self-congratulatory delusion, that a number of erroneous or at best half-true dogmas poured forth. These were especially influential in the world of foreign policy. A series of little-challenged, though dubious, exceptionalist beliefs took root.

There was the illusion that the collapse of communism had been caused by the stern admonitions of Ronald Reagan. There was a hubristic myth about the autarkic character of the American economy. Complacent predictions of the collapse of the European economy, in particular, gave much pleasure, as the euro and even the pound appreciated against the dollar. The industrialization of China and its accumulation of vast financial reserves through rapid export-led growth was seen as a triumph for American capitalism, when in reality it constituted the most dangerous threat to it. A related fantasy was the idea that Chinese Communism, seduced by the fleshpots of capitalism, was inexorably doomed to be replaced by political democracy. As the experts in American research institutes looked out at the world, they faltered between fatuous optimism about the prospects for democracy in states (Chile, Uganda, or some of the former communist dictatorships of Central Asia) whose leaders had gone along with the imposed privatizations of the Washington Consensus, and sniping resentment of impeccably capitalist and democratic nations (Germany, Canada, France) that had dared to claim independence of American tutelage. Instinctively, they sided with a military dictatorship in Pakistan against Indian democracy, and with authoritarian governments everywhere.

In short, the millennium election of 2000, scarcely the most shining example of American democracy in action, brought to power men and a few women who had acquired influence and earned power not by long service in public or elected office but essentially as courtiers. This group brings to mind the "prosopography" of Sir Lewis Namier, who analyzed British politicians in the reign of George III in terms of a network of families, friendships, rivalries, and private interests.[20] As an example, of the twenty-seven individuals who were either the initiators of or signatories of the Project for a New American Century, the inner circle of the new foreign policy elite, more than half were graduates of, or faculty at, just three elite universities: eight of Harvard, four of Yale, and three of Princeton. If one adds Columbia, Cornell, and the University of Chicago, double-counting appears. Paul Wolfowitz, for example, was educated at Cornell, Chicago, and Yale. All but seven of the twenty-seven were educated in one of those six institutions.

Some of the connections, however, are far more interesting, in Namierite terms, than that. One network, for example, consists of the pupils, protégés, and colleagues of Paul Wolfowitz. They include Eliot A. Cohen, Francis Fukuyama, Fred C. Iklé, Zalmay Kalilzad, and Peter Rodman. Iklé, in a world of scholars and operatives funded by foundations, is a champion; he has had connections to the Center for Strategic and International Studies, RAND, the Hudson Institute, and of course the American Enterprise Institute.

Important family connections appear, like those of the Grenvilles and the Pitts in the world Namier studied. Neoconservatives not only support family values. Theirs is a family business. Midge Decter is the wife of Norman Podhoretz and the mother-in-law of Elliott Abrams, who was a colleague of the Catholic philosopher George Weigel at Abrams's Center for the Study of Ethics and Public Policy, a center founded after he had been convicted of, and through political influence pardoned for, unethical behavior. Jeb Bush, of course, is the brother of George W. Bush and the son of former president George H. W. Bush. Donald Kagan, the Yale classical historian, is the father of Frederick Kagan, a leading neoconservative expert on military affairs. William Kristol, the principal impresario of the Project, and also editor of the *Weekly Standard,* the neoconservative journal funded by Rupert Murdoch's News Corporation, is the son of Irving Kristol, the most influential of the older generation of neoconservatives and a prime mover at the American Enterprise Institute. Paul Wolfowitz was a pupil of Allan Bloom, Leo Strauss, and Albert Wohlstetter, all major prophets of the neoconservative sect. He was for seven years the head of the Johns Hopkins School of Advanced International Studies in Washington, with which Eliot A. Cohen, Francis Fukuyama, Frank Gaffney, and Peter W. Rodman, all among the signatories, were at one time or another associated. Another circle closes there.

By no means are all of the signatories are close friends, nor do they all agree about everything. Saint-Simon, the immortal memoirist of Versailles, taught us that there is nothing more ferocious than the feuds within courts. Frank Gaffney, for example, has had a particularly shrill disagreement with George W. Bush's influential economic adviser Grover Norquist, who once went so far as to refer to Gaffney as a "sick little bigot."

Nevertheless, even this cursory account of the personnel of the Project for a New American Century suggests the extent to which its signatories are part of an interlocking directorate, supported by foundation funding and recruited through networks of personal contact and cronyism, albeit generally at a respectable level of intellectual ability. The very last word that comes to mind to describe the instincts or the operating style of this influential, even powerful, coterie, however, is the word *democracy*—the regime they say they want to impose, willy-nilly, on the world.

What are the consequences of Americans' belief in their own exceptionalism for their relations with the rest of the world?

For more than two centuries Americans have been motivated to set themselves the highest public standards, both in the conduct of their own affairs and in their dealings with the rest of the world, by a national ideology. The essentials of that system of belief concerned such values as liberty, the political sovereignty of the people, equality before the law, and the paramount rule of constitutional law. From the beginning, that national ideology contained both exceptionalist and universalist elements. "The cause of America," said Tom Paine, "is in a great measure the cause of all mankind." The victory of the Union, said Abraham Lincoln, was "the last, best hope of earth." The emancipation of the slaves, he meant, would guarantee the freedom of all Americans. So the United States would be an example to the world. Some Americans in the nineteenth century believed that the "empire of liberty" would inevitably "overspread" at least the whole of North America and perhaps Central America and the Caribbean, and even the whole of the Americas as far as

Tierra del Fuego. But public holiday rhetoric aside, there was no idea then that the United States either could or should bring freedom to the entire world. To this day, even the most messianic neo-Wilsonians have allowed their universalist ambitions to be checked by realism. It is one thing to invade Grenada, Lebanon, or at a stretch Iraq. No one is speaking of bringing democracy, by shock and awe, to nations with millions of soldiers and nuclear weapons, such as Russia, India, or China.

It was not until the twentieth century that this combination of exceptionalism with at least a theoretical universalism—a belief, that is, that the United States has a special destiny to bring freedom to the Americas, brought to bear on the idea that the United States could be an example of freedom to the world—began to take on the characteristics of a program.

The collapse of the European diplomatic system in 1914 was largely unexpected. If we look for any one cause, most historians would now identify it in the fear of the German generals and admirals that Russia was industrializing so fast that it would soon be too strong to be defeated. This was the thesis advanced in 1961 by Fritz Fischer, and it has been generally, though not universally, accepted.[21] The reciprocal fear and the folly it engendered in the European nations, and the way they destroyed each other's strength, presented the United States with the historic opportunity to become the greatest power on earth. Woodrow Wilson understood that opportunity and set about grasping it, until he was unhorsed by his own miscalculation of the political support, or lack of it, for his League of Nations.

The First World War set off a series of causally linked cataclysms, most of which enhanced that opportunity. Six great empires—Germany, Russia, Austria-Hungary, the Ottoman Empire, France, and Britain—either imploded or were seriously weakened. Of the combatants, only Japan and the United States emerged stronger in either economic or military terms. Not all the consequences of this transformation of the geopolitical order became plain until the end of the Second World War in 1945. What was clear by then was that the first war had triggered a chain reaction. War led to revolution. Revolution led to economic disruption, which led to the rise of fascism. Fascism in turn made a second war inevitable.

There were, however, also implications and consequences in the world of ideas. The Russian Revolution led to an angry division between communism (that is, the autocratic Leninist Marxism of the Bolshevik revolution) and the various forms of democratic socialism or social democracy that had previously been increasing in appeal and influence. The collapse of the Ottoman Empire and the weakening of Britain and France, not to mention the successes of Japan against China in 1895, Russia in 1905, and, temporarily, against the United States and Britain in 1941–42, shattered the prestige of the imperial powers and belief in the invincibility of the white race. By 1945 European imperialism was utterly discredited, even very largely in the metropolitan countries themselves. China, the Indian subcontinent, Indonesia, and Africa thrilled with the dream of independence. The Middle East, although stirring with political passions, was less successful in achieving political autonomy, while the countries of Russia's "near abroad" were held hostage to Soviet ideology and paranoia. All these events cemented American strength. They also confirmed America's inescapable involvement in a world from which it neither could be, nor wanted to be, isolated.

The United States, after 1945, found itself in a strange and apparently uniquely privileged position. It was a world power, which in the course of the Cold War accumulated interests and assets worldwide. It was also a power whose own ideology, rooted in the anticolonial American Revolution, seemed—and not only to Americans—free from any imputation of colonial self-interest.

In the 1920s the United States had largely, though by no means totally, withdrawn from the political affairs of the world, and especially from the politics of Europe, while individual Americans continued to act vigorously as investors and entrepreneurs. The financial and economic collapse of 1929 made active American involvement in world politics inevitable. As Franklin Roosevelt understood, it would not be possible to keep the United States aloof from the angry new politics resulting from economic crisis and the ambitions of those, especially in Germany, Japan, and Italy, who sought to save their own people from the general misery by domestic tyranny and foreign war. While few Americans understood Roosevelt's fears, they were shared by a small, unelected foreign policy establishment, largely recruited from international bankers and their lawyers.

Roosevelt therefore did what he could to prepare the United States for war. When it came, thanks to an almost unparalleled act of folly on the part of the Japanese government, the United States was ultimately triumphant. Roosevelt found himself, in the last months of his life, like Woodrow Wilson for a few months in 1918–19, in a position almost to dictate the shape of the postwar world. The priorities he set included the final destruction of the colonial empires, the democratic development of China, and the creation of a set of international institutions based on democratic values, international cooperation, and respect for the sovereignty of "Westphalian" states, sovereign for better and worse over their own people. In effect Roosevelt envisioned a world of nation states, cooperating in international institutions, with the United States as moral leader, ideological guide, political arbiter and banker of last resort.

Roosevelt died before his grand design could be more than sketched. Before it could be achieved, two enormous events intervened. The first was an act over which the United States government did have control, the arrival of atomic weapons. Besides their impact on international relations, especially with the Soviet Union, they enormously increased the power of the executive branch within the American constitutional system. The second was an even more complicated event: the outbreak of the Cold War.

For a full generation after 1945 American foreign policy was guided by the perceptions and the values of wise and essentially temperate, though in many respects very different, men. At the apex of the system men like Harry Truman and Dean Acheson, and later Dwight Eisenhower, John Kennedy, and Lyndon Johnson, even Richard Nixon and Henry Kissinger, persevered according to their very different lights with the strategy of the foreign policy establishment. This was a middle way between isolation and aggression, usually described in terms of George Kennan's influential concept of containment. From 1945 until the middle 1970s most senior officials and influential policy makers, under Republican as well as Democratic administrations, shared a commitment to that strategy. Congress steadily lost control over foreign policy. Decisions (partly because of the secrecy demanded by Cold War nuclear rivalry and intelligence wars) came more and more to be concentrated in the White House. Most congressional leaders, in any case, shared the essential tenets of that containment philosophy. The rhetoric, for example of President Kennedy's stirring inaugural speech, might be exceptionalist. But the practice was internationalist and cooperative.

In the 1970s, for several reasons, that changed. Gradually American policy began to move from containment to détente—that is, from a stern confrontation of the communist powers to an effort to reach accommodation with them. The United States lost the Vietnam War. (There are still those who seek to deny that, but the world has understood what happened.) The commitment to the security of Israel, and the new dependence of the United States and its allies on imported oil, made the Middle East a new and bitter source of geopolitical vulnerability. The revival of the economies, first of Europe, then of Japan and Korea, and finally the economic development of China, in part as a result of the Nixon-Kissinger diplomatic opening to Beijing, ended the unassailed dominance the U.S. economy had enjoyed for a few years after 1945. As a reaction to the domestic upheavals of the 1960s, and especially to the aftermath of the civil rights movement, a darker, less optimistic mood suffused American public life.

By the end of the 1970s the country was thirsty for the breezy optimism of Ronald Reagan, and for a more aggressive assertion of national interest and exceptionalist ideology. Largely unperceived at first, the balance of arguments within a national security establishment, now largely free from congressional or other democratic regulation or even scrutiny, had shifted. A new tone was dominant. To personalize the debate—appropriate enough when it was held largely out of the public eye on the premises of private foundations—the arguments were lost by the partisans of George Kennan and won by the followers of Paul Nitze. The search for détente gave way to harder, more suspicious attitudes, at first to the communist adversary, and then to America's allies as well. Already in the Reagan years, though the president personally searched for agreement with the Soviet Union, intellectual fashion had moved to the Right.

The fall of communism was brought about largely by the failures of the communist system itself, and specifically by the decision of leaders like Mikhail Gorbachev throughout the Soviet sphere of influence that the only way to save something of the communist system in which they had been brought up was to embrace radical change. The neoconservatives were fascinated by the idea—they called it a law—of unintended consequences. One such consequence of the fall of communism was that the United States no longer needed—or so its leaders thought—to concern itself with the sensitivities of its allies. Another was that many in the allied nations in Europe concluded that they no longer needed American military aid against Soviet invasion. As democracy returned peacefully in one form or another to Russia, to Poland, Hungary, and what was still Czechoslovakia, one former communist state went in a different direction.

The former republic of Yugoslavia had seemed to be freeing itself from Soviet tyranny. Now it became the scene of civil war, ethnic cleansing, and massacre. The major powers of Western Europe were half-hearted at best in their response. The lesson they taught to impatient, even contemptuous, observers in Washington, was that the Europeans were hopeless. They had neither the means nor the will to defend civilized values in what appeared from across the Atlantic to be their own backyard, but seemed to them—to borrow Neville Chamberlain's phrase of evil augury at the time of the Munich crisis of 1938—"a far away country of which we know little."

The George H. W. Bush administration of 1989–92 was perhaps the last hurrah of the Atlantic alliance as it had been understood since the time of Dean Acheson: an association of mutually respectful nations, committed to defend at least a minimum of common values, with the United States as a leader freely and (with occasional exceptions!) gratefully accepted as such by weaker but still considerable allies.

The Clinton administration was still multilateral, at least in style. But it was committed, in a series of speeches by its ranking foreign policy officials, to exceptionalist principles—they called them "neo-Wilsonian"—including the idea that it was the high duty and destiny of the United States to spread democracy, willy-nilly, to the world. By the end of the Clinton years, transatlantic and other rifts—for example, with Mexico, Canada, Japan, and China—were already apparent.

They were, however, as nothing compared to the gulf that began to appear between the United States and virtually all other nations after the inauguration of George W. Bush. To be sure, President Bush did make efforts to have good relations with at least some allies. Personally, however, he seemed neither well-informed about, nor particularly well-disposed to, foreigners unless they accepted his highly ideological world view. Part of that view appeared to be the assumption that the spread of democracy meant the imposition of American dogmas, wishes, and interests. This was not only or even mainly a personal matter, however. The new president was surrounded by men and women who gave the impression that they had a sacred mission to cleanse the Augean stables of the filth of liberalism, and would stop at nothing to carry out their historic task.

From the start, understandably, a number of irritant issues arose. Some were more apparent than real, like the refusal of the United States to take part in an international criminal court, seemingly because the United States government could not accept the possibility that Americans might fall under such a court's jurisdiction. The issue was only apparent, because such concessions were made that there was never any likelihood of that occurring. On several other matters, the new administration seemed intent on showing how impatient it was with what its members saw as mere sentimentality and "do-gooding." Perhaps the most serious irritant was the American attitude to the Kyoto Protocol and more broadly to climate change. Again, to be sure, there was little or no possibility that the United States would enter wholeheartedly into what the international community, with something approaching unanimity, proposed. Indeed, those proposals were largely symbolic. What was disastrous was the widespread perception that the president of the United States was in denial about the reality of climate change as a result of human activity, and, worse, that he was little better than the uncritical captive of an industrial oil and gas lobby.

The Clinton administration handed on to its successor a multiple agenda of international problems that needed to be tackled as a matter of urgency. There is anecdotal evidence that the new president personally dismissed most of these concerns and insisted that the one item that dominated his personal agenda was the overthrow of Saddam Hussein.[22] Certainly from the earliest days of the new administration "regime change" in Iraq was one of the highest priorities of the administration's inner circle.

Then came the terrorist plot of September 11, 2001. That was not only the supreme test of the administration's competence. It was an event that revealed its true values. To the Bush circle, "9/11" was not only tragedy, outrage, a national insult to be avenged. It was also an opportunity. It justified extreme measures, including the invasion of Iraq, whether or not allies could be found to join the venture.

Underlying the whole story was a fabric of assumptions that were indeed predicated on a new, aggressive interpretation of the exceptionalist creed. The United States, it was said, would act as it saw fit. It neither needed nor wanted international agreement, approval, or cooperation. Those in the world who dissented in any way from the wrath to come were, by administration officials, not to mention their loyal journalists, ignored, or insulted, or derided.

So long as the world was threatened by dictators, first by fascist dictators, then by communists, the world was happy to accept American leadership. It helped that for decades that leadership was exerted in a spirit of generosity and comity. In those days, many around the world who were not Americans found it easy to share the ideals of the traditional American exceptionalist creed, among them freedom, democracy, and popular sovereignty. But in those days, such ideals were not presented in bluntly exceptionalist terms. Now the common ideals of what had come to be known as "the free world" were claimed as the private property of Americans.

To the world, however, freedom cannot mean military occupation. Democracy cannot mean a world's political decisions made behind closed doors in Washington. Popular sovereignty, as an ideal for the world, cannot be reduced to the wishes of the electorate in one country, still less to the instincts of an elite "within the Beltway" that seemed increasingly isolated from the rest of America. Prosperity, for the world, cannot mean the monopoly of the planet's resources by a few hundred corporations and a handful of financial enterprises.

Nothing is more passionately to be hoped for than that the American government will once again hold before it the values that inspired Jefferson and Madison, Lincoln and Roosevelt. Nothing is more heartily to be wished than that the American people should once again see itself, not as a master race whose primacy is owed to the shock and awe inspired by terrifying weaponry, but once again, freely and generously, as first among equals.

Such a change in the face America shows to the world will not come, of course, until Americans have shown once again, as they have so often done in the past, that they will not allow their generous instincts and sound values to be travestied by charlatans and bullies. Until American democracy girds itself to recapture the political system and reasserts its healthiest instincts, the United States is not likely to recapture the admiration and affection the American people earned by their achievements over the first two centuries of their national history.

A good start would be to tone down the boasting.

Unfortunately, the consequences of the Iraq disaster will not be limited to the foreign relations of the United States. What a nation does in the world reflects what it is and what it has become, at home as well as abroad. The ancient Greeks believed that *hubris*—overweening pride and self-conceit—led inevitably to *nemesis,* divine punishment, and ultimately to *ate,* utter destruction.

The great Athenian historian Thucydides gives as an example the experience of his beloved Athenians.[23] In 416 B.C. Athens, planning an ill-fated expedition against Sicily, sent an expeditionary force against Melos, an island originally settled by Athens's archenemy, Sparta. It was seen as strategically vital to remove the danger that Melos could serve as a base for Spartan operations against the Athenians' lines of communication with Sicily.

In the part of his history that has come to be known as the Melian dialogue, Thucydides gives an account of the arguments the Athenians used to persuade the Melians to surrender. They are not pretty. The text has become a classic in the academic study of international relations. As a result Thucydides has been hailed as the progenitor of the "Realist" school in that discipline. Certainly his account of the arguments used by his countrymen makes them out to be hard-nosed and cynical. It is not so clear what the historian himself thought of them. "The powerful," he makes the Athenian envoys tell the men of Melos, "exact what they can. The weak put up with what they must." Again, when the Melians ask why they cannot be allowed to remain friends, and not allies of either side in the war, the Athenians answer: "No. Your hostility does not hurt us as much as your friendship. For in the eyes of our subjects that would be a proof of our weakness, whereas your hatred is proof of our power."

Thus brutally offered the choice between war and slavery, the Melians decided to fight. They did the best they could. Twice they sallied out and raided the Athenian siege lines. In 415 the Athenians came back with stronger forces. In the end, weakened by treachery, the Melians surrendered. The Athenians simply slaughtered all the grown men and took the women and children away into slavery, leaving an Athenian garrison to secure the island.

Thucydides does not say explicitly what he feels about this episode. Posterity, however, has been clear about one thing. Melos marked the moment when Athens, the birthplace of democracy and its glorious champion against Persian imperialism in the days of Thucydides' grandparents, abandoned its principles and replaced them with the arrogant pursuit of power and self-interest. The disaster of the Sicilian expedition, which condemned thousands of Athenian prisoners to the salt mines, was not a direct consequence. Still, at Melos, Athens practiced the policy of "shock and awe." And Athenian democracy never did fully recover.

The point at which the principles of American democracy are reduced to mere boasting and bullying, justified by a cynical "realism," is the point at which the practice of American democracy, at home as well as abroad, is in mortal danger. It is also the point at which the best of the exceptionalism in the American tradition has been corrupted into the worst. We can only hope that mortal danger will be avoided.

Notes

Preface

1. A number of distinguished historians have recently reinterpreted American history in a way that acknowledges its aggressive or expansionist dimension. See, for example, Robert Kagan, *Dangerous Nation* (New York: Knopf, 2006), and Walter Nugent, *Habits of Empire: A History of American Expansion* (New York: Knopf, 2008).

2. Wilson ceaselessly denounced the "old diplomacy" whereby the Powers swapped provinces without concern for the feelings of their inhabitants. Yet in Paris he consigned the German-speaking inhabitants of the Tyrol to Italy, where they and their descendants have simmered with resentment ever since. And that is only one example of his double standards.

ONE A City Set upon a Hill

1. John Winthrop, sermon, "A Modell of Christian Charity," 1630, text in Collections of the Massachusetts Historical Society (Boston, 1838), 3rd ser., 7: 31–48. Incidentally, this text (erroneously) states that the sermon was given "on the Atlantic Ocean."

2. Andrew Delbanco, *The Puritan Ordeal* (Cambridge: Harvard University Press, 1991), 72.

3. Francis J. Bremer, *John Winthrop: America's Forgotten Founding Father* (Oxford: Oxford University Press, 2003).

4. Ronald Reagan, speech to Conservative Political Action Conference, 1974.

5. Bremer, *John Winthrop,* 368.

6. J. Hector St. John de Crèvecoeur, *Letters from an American Farmer* (New York: E. P. Dutton, 1957); Robert, baron de Crèvecoeur, *Vie de Hector St. John de Crèvecoeur* (Paris, 1883).

7. William Bradford, *Of Plymouth Plantation,* ed. Samuel Eliot Morison (New York: Modern Library, 1967), 75–76.

8. Nathaniel Philbrick, *Mayflower: A Story of Courage, Community, and War* (New York: Viking, 2006), 352; see also George A. Lipsky, *John Quincy Adams: His Theory and Ideas* (New York: Crowell, 1950), 93, citing John Quincy Adams, *An Oration delivered at Plymouth, December 22 1802 at the anniversary commemoration of the First Landing of Our Ancestors at that Place* (Boston: Richardson, Lord, and Holbrook, 1831). What Adams actually said, in a speech in Congress in 1802, was hedged with qualifications that make his remark more defensible than it is in the abbreviated form in which it is usually cited. It was, he said, "the first example in modern times of a social compact or system of government instituted by voluntary agreement conformable to the laws of nature, by men of equal rights and about to establish their community in a new country." Even so there must be hundreds of other agreements with as good a claim to have inspired the U.S. Constitution.

9. Perry Miller, *Errand into the Wilderness* (Cambridge: Harvard University Press, 1956), 11.

10. Bercovitz's unusual first name comes from the names of the Italian-American anarchists Sacco and Vanzetti, executed in 1927. Fifty years later they were declared not guilty by Governor Michael Dukakis of Massachusetts. A parallel is the name of the (very conservative) dean of the Yale Law School, Eugene Victor Debs Rostow, named by socialist parents for the head of the American Socialist Party.

11. Max Lerner, *American Civilization: Life and Thought in the United States Today* (London: Jonathan Cape, 1957), 63.

12. David Potter, *People of Plenty* (Chicago: University of Chicago Press, 1954).

13. Frederick Jackson Turner, *The Frontier in American History* (New York: Henry Holt, 1921), 266.

14. For example, Patricia Nelson Limerick, *The Legacy of Conquest: The Unbroken Past of the American West* (New York: Norton, 1987).

15. Gary Marks and Seymour Martin Lipset, *It Didn't Happen Here: Why Socialism Failed in the United States* (New York: Norton, 2000).

16. Alexis de Tocqueville, *Democracy in America,* trans. Gerald E. Bevan (London: Penguin, 2003), 662–71; Victoria Glendinning, *Trollope* (London: Hutchinson, 1992), 319.

17. Walter Prescott Webb, *The Great Frontier* (Austin: University of Texas Press, 1951), 7.

18. Robert Kagan, *Dangerous Nation* (New York: Knopf, 220): "The British prime minister, Lord Aberdeen, had offered the Texas government support against Mexico in return for the abolition of slavery." British abolitionists supported Mexico in its independence struggle, buying Mexican bonds and financing the creation of a Mexican navy.

19. The proportion of American exports accounted for by agricultural products was 75 percent in the 1860s, 79 percent in the 1870s, 76 percent in the 1880s, and still more than 70 percent in the 1890s.

20. Wilson refused the U.S. government's guarantee of a massive loan sought by the British government from the House of Morgan. Wilson's Treasury secretary, William Gibbs McAdoo, also intervened to stop Britain and France from selling American securities for gold, to their disadvantage.

21. See Godfrey Hodgson, *Woodrow Wilson's Right Hand: The Life of Colonel Edward M. House* (New Haven: Yale University Press, 2006), 122, 131.

22. "Soft power" comes from the title of a book by the Harvard professor and official in the Clinton administration, Joseph S. Nye, Jr., *Soft Power: The Means to Success in World Politics* (New York: Public Affairs, 2004).

23. Richard Hofstadter, "Without Feudalism," review of Louis Hartz, *The Liberal Tradition in America: An Interpretation of American Political Thought Since the Revolution, New York Times,* February 27, 1955.

24. Though not naval: the U.S. Navy was the second-largest after World War I and equal to Britain's between the two world wars.

25. In a 2004 interview with *Time* magazine, Bush agreed that some people thought of him as a sheriff. In 2000 Prime Minister John Howard of Australia said his country was America's "deputy sheriff for South-East Asia." In 2003 President Bush denied that he thought of Australia in that way, saying rather that he thought of Australia as a sheriff. That provoked an angry response from the prime minister of Malaysia and others in Asia.

TWO Myth and Reality in the Birth of a Nation

1. Gordon S. Wood, *The Radicalism of the American Revolution* (New York: Random House, 1993), 7–8.

2. Howard Zinn, *A People's History of the United States* (New York: HarperCollins, 2001), 59.

3. Lord Mansfield concluded that there was no legal backing for slavery in England. He is often misquoted as saying "The air of England is too pure for a slave to breathe." Those words were used by Somerset's counsel, citing a 1569 case. Two points should be made: while full chattel slavery did not exist in English law, and certainly not for Englishmen, black servants were often legally held in "near slavery," not wholly free but more protected than under colonial law and practice. Second, Mansfield was consciously avoiding pronouncing on colonial law because of the danger of further infuriating the American slaveowners.

4. Edward Countryman, *The American Revolution* (London: I. B. Tauris, 1985), 239.

5. This incidentally contradicts Gordon Wood's view, that "far from remaining monarchical, hierarchy-ridden subjects on the margin of civilization, Americans had become, almost *overnight,* the most liberal, the most democratic, the most commercially minded, and the most modern people in the world"; Wood, *Radicalism,* 6–7; emphasis added.

6. Bernard Bailyn, *The Ideological Origins of the American Revolution* (Cambridge: Harvard University Press, 1992), 1, quoting a letter from John Adams to Thomas Jefferson in 1815. In 1818 Adams wrote in similar but slightly different terms to Hezekiah Niles, "The revolution was effected before the war commenced. The Revolution was in the minds and hearts of the people"; quoted ibid., 160.

7. Roughly one-half of English subjects in 1776 lived in Great Britain, one-quarter in Ireland.

8. This phrase is difficult to track down to any specific place in Gladstone's writings. It was quoted, in a slightly different form, by James M. Beck in 1922 lectures at Lincoln's Inn on "The Constitution of the United States," subsequently published as James M. Beck, *The Constitution of the United States* (London: Hodder and Stoughton, 1922).

9. The point was made by Madison (as Publius), in *Federalist,* no. 39, *The Federalist Papers* (Cutchogue, N.Y.: Buccaneer, 1992), 190.

10. There were attempts to provide universal education in Scotland since the Reformation. By 1696 primary schools were universal and there was statutory provision to support them, though they were not wholly free.

11. Noah Webster, *An Examination into the Leading Principles of the Federal Constitution . . . by a Citizen of America,* cited in Bernard Bailyn, *Ideological Origins,* 373.

12. The text of Cushman's sermon, "The Sin and Danger of Self Love," of December 1621, on the text from Corinthians 10, "Let no man seek his own, but every man another's wealth," is published in several Web sites, including by Caleb Johnson at http://members.aol.com/Calebj/sermon.html. It is discussed in David S. Lovejoy, "Plain Englishmen at Plymouth," *New England Quarterly* 63 (1990): 232–48.

13. Alexis de Tocqueville, *Democracy in America* (London: Penguin, 2003), 201, 228.

14. See K. Theodore Hoppen, *The Mid-Victorian Generation, 1846–1886,* vol. 3 of *The New Oxford History of England* (Oxford: Oxford University Press, 1998).

15. Alexander Keyssar, *The Right to Vote: The Contested History of Democracy in the United States* (New York: Basic, 2000).

16. Ibid., 53. Some women did vote in colonial America; ibid., 6.

17. Keyssar, *Right to Vote,* 68.

18. Ibid., xxiii.

19. Seymour Martin Lipset and Gary Marks, *It Didn't Happen Here: Why Socialism Failed in the United States* (New York: Norton, 2000), 15, 292. The earlier book was Seymour Martin Lipset, *American Exceptionalism: A Two-Edged Sword* (New York: Norton, 1996).

20. Quoted in Sean Wilentz, *The Rise of American Democracy: Jefferson to Lincoln* (New York: Norton, 2005), 398.

21. Quoted ibid., 482.

22. Zinn, *People's History,* 212.

23. Ibid., 214–16.

24. Wilentz, "Against Exceptionalism: Class Consciousness and the American Labor Movement, 1790–1920," *International Labor and Working Class History,* no. 26 (Fall 1984): 1–24. An interesting part of Wilentz's thesis is that, while it is true that American labor politics were not predominantly socialist, neither were working-class politics in Europe at the time. In Britain the Labour Party's relationship with socialism has always been complicated and ambivalent.

25. Lawrence A. Cremin, *American Education: The National Experience, 1783–1876* (New York: Harper, 1980), 103.

26. Lyman Beecher, *A Plea for the West* (Cincinnati: Truman and Smith, 1835), 11, cited ibid., 37.

27. Cremin, *American Education,* 269.

28. Graham Robb, *The Discovery of France* (London: Macmillan Picador, 2007), 322.

29. John Roach, "Education and Public Opinion," in *The New Cambridge Modern History, vol. 9, War and Peace in an Age of Upheaval,* ed. C. W. Crawley (Cambridge: Cambridge University Press, 1995), 193–97.

30. Linda S. Hudson, *Mistress of Manifest Destiny: A Biography of Jane McManus Storm Cazneau, 1807–1878* (Austin: Texas State Historical Association, 2001). See also Frederick Merk, *Manifest Destiny and Mission* (New York: Vintage, 1963).

31. This is well described in Walter Nugent, *Habits of Empire: A History of American Expansion* (New York: Knopf, 2008), 3–40.

32. Samuel Eliot Morison and Henry Steele Commager, *The Growth of the American Republic* (New York: Oxford University Press, 1962), 1: 356.

33. Robert Kagan, *Dangerous Nation* (New York: Knopf, 2006), 116–19.

34. Quoted ibid., 104.

35. Henry Steele Commager, *Documents of American History,* 7th ed. (New York: Appleton-Century-Crofts, 1963), 235.

36. Frank Thistlethwaite, "The United States and the Old World, 1794–1828," in *The New Cambridge Modern History,* 9: 596.

37. Russia, too, was showing some interest in expanding across the Bering Straits into North America.

38. Merk, *Manifest Destiny and Mission,* 20–21.

39. Americans took as a *casus belli* the crossing of the Rio Grande by Mexican forces. But the territory between the Rio Grande and the Nueces was disputed, and the Mexicans believed it to be their own.

40. Speech by John C. Calhoun on his resolutions in reference to the war with Mexico, January 4, 1848. The text varies slightly in contemporary versions. In what appears to be the best version the full passage reads: "Nor have we ever incorporated into the Union any but the Caucasian race. To incorporate Mexico would be the first departure of the kind; for more than half of its population are pure Indians, and by far the larger portion of the residue mixed blood. I protest against the incorporation of such a people. Ours is the government of the white man." Quoted in John Caldwell Calhoun, *The Works of John C. Calhoun,* ed. Richard Kenner Crallé (New York: Appleton, 1874), 4: 410.

41. Samuel Johnson, "Taxation No Tyranny" (1775), *Yale Edition of the Works of Samuel Johnson,* vol. 10, ed. Donal J. Greene (New Haven: Yale University Press, 1977), 454.

THREE From Civil War to Cold War

1. The thesis was first presented at a special meeting of the American Historical Association at the Columbia Exposition on July 13, 1893, in Chicago, and was published later that year, first in *Proceedings of the State Historical Society of Wisconsin,* then in the *Annual Report of the American Historical Association.* It has been subsequently reprinted many times, and was incorporated into a book, *The Frontier in American History* (New York: Henry Holt, 1921).

2. See, for example, Carl E. Sollberg, *The Prairies and the Pampas: Agrarian Policy*

in Canada and Argentina, 1880–1930 (Stanford: Stanford University Press, 1987); Morris W. Wills, "Sequential Frontiers: The California and Victorian Experience, 1850–1900," Ph. D. diss., University of Sussex, Brighton; Robin W. Winks, *The Myth of the American Frontier: Its Relevance to America, Canada, and Australia* (Leicester: Leicester University Press, 1971).

3. I have rounded the figures given in a careful estimate in the Wikipedia online encyclopedia: http://en.wikipedia.org/wiki/World_War_I_casualties and http://en.wikipedia.org/wiki/World_War_II_casualties.

4. In 1926 "Detroit" (including some Canadian plants owned by U.S. manufacturers) produced 4.4 million automobiles, while the four major manufacturing countries in Europe—Britain, France, Germany, and Italy—produced 549,000.

5. As the clever hopes expire
Of a low dishonest decade:
Waves of anger and fear
Circulate over the bright
And darkened lands of the earth.

W. H. Auden, "September 1, 1939," in *Another Time* (New York: Random House, 1940). Later Auden came to "loathe" the poem, he told a friend, especially the last two stanzas, which include the famous line "We must love one another or die." The poet tried to change it to "We must love one another and die." He often refused permission for the poem to be included in anthologies, and referred to it as "trash."

6. I am thinking, for example, of the Authorized Version of the thirteenth chapter of Paul's first epistle to the Corinthians, or the testament of Mr. Valiant-for-Truth in *The Pilgrim's Progress.* The passage in 1 Corinthians 13 begins, "Though I speak with the tongues of men and of angels, and have not charity, I am become as sounding brass, or a tinkling cymbal . . . " and ends "And now abideth faith, hope, charity, these three; but the greatest of these is charity." In Bunyan, I mean the passage beginning "My Sword I give to him that shall succeed me in my Pilgrimage, and my Courage and Skill to him that can get it. My Marks and Scars I carry with me, to be a witness for me that I have fought his Battles who now will be my Rewarder" and ends "So he passed over, and all the Trumpets sounded for him on the other side."

7. William Dean Howells, *Impressions and Experiences* (New York: Harper, 1915), 127–49 (rpt. of 1896 *Harper's* article).

8. J. H. Mackay, *The Anarchists: A Picture of Civilization at the Close of the Nineteenth Century,* trans. George Schumm (Boston: Tucker, 1891).

9. Alfred R. Wallace, *The Malay Archipelago* (Whitefish, Mont.: Kessinger, 1869), available in a 2004 reprint.

10. Matthew Arnold, "Dover Beach," in *Collected Poems* (Oxford: Oxford University Press, 1950).

11. This section of this chapter was much influenced by the impressive study by James T. Kloppenberg, *Uncertain Victory: Social Democracy and Progressivism in European and American Thought, 1870–1920* (New York: Oxford University Press, 1986).

12. Hayek, of course, insisted that he was no conservative but a liberal, in the Manchester sense. See the postscript to F. A. Hayek, *The Constitution of Liberty* (Chicago: University of Chicago Press, 1960), "Why I Am Not a Conservative."

13. In 1905 Jaurès merged the Socialist Party into the *Section Française de l'Internationale Socialiste* (SFIO).

14. Kloppenberg, *Uncertain Victory*, 411.

15. Ibid.

16. On the crisis of Europe on the eve of World War I, see, in a vast literature, George Dangerfield, *The Strange Death of Liberal England* (London: Constable, 1936).

17. See Jonathan Fenby, *Alliance: The Inside Story of How Roosevelt, Stalin, and Churchill Won One War and Began Another* (New York: Simon and Schuster, 2006).

18. See, for example, Michael J. Hogan, *A Cross of Iron: Harry S. Truman and the Origins of the National Security State, 1945 to 1954* (Cambridge: Cambridge University Press, 1998); John Lewis Gaddis, *The Cold War: A New History* (New York: Penguin, 2005); Robert Beisner, *Dean Acheson: A Life in the Cold War* (New York: Oxford University Press, 2006).

19. Tony Judt, *Postwar: A History of Europe Since 1945* (London: Penguin, 2006); Vernon A. Walters, *Silent Missions* (Garden City, N.Y.: Doubleday, 1978); Frédéric Charpier, *La CIA en France* (Paris: Le Seuil, 2008); Roberto Faenza and Marco Fini, *Gli Americani in Italia* (Milan: Feltrinelli, 1976); Ted Morgan, *A Covert Life: Jay Lovestone, Communist, Anti-Communist, and Spymaster* (New York: Random House, 1999); Frances Stonor Saunders, *The Cultural Cold War: The CIA and the World of Arts and Letters* (London: New Press, 2000).

20. Hanson W. Baldwin, *The Price of Power* (New York: Harper, 1948), 146–148, quoted in Aaron L. Friedberg, "Why Didn't the United States Become a Garrison State?" *International Security* 16 (Spring 1992): 109–42, and in Hogan, *Cross of Iron*, 1.

21. See Allen Weinstein, *Perjury: The Hiss-Chambers Case* (New York: Random House, 1997).

22. See Andrew Levison, *The Working Class Majority* (New York: Coward, McCann, Geoghegan, 1974). The myth that, as the neoconservative publicist Ben Wattenberg put it, "the massive majority of the population of the nation is now in the middle class" was achieved by (1) excluding all "service workers," such as janitors, guards, policemen, firemen, and other typical working-class types; (2) including in the "white collar" category more than six million male clerical and sales workers, most of them much less well paid than industrial workers; and (3) counting more than twelve million women clerical and sales workers, including typists and sales clerks, as "white collar"!

23. Dean Acheson, *Present at the Creation* (New York: Norton, reissued 1987), 219. The only reference to Armageddon in the Bible is in the sixteenth verse of the sixteenth chapter of the book of Revelation. There is no reference there to a final battle, which is an accretion of ancient Christian tradition. Seven angels are pouring out the wrath of God from seven bowls. The sixth bowl was poured out upon the river Euphrates. Out of the mouth of a monstrous dragon there come forth spirits "to gather them together unto the war of the great day of God, the Almighty. And they gathered them together into the

place which is called in Hebrew Har-Magedon." This means the hill of Megiddo, a place where many battles have been fought over the centuries, and where the Roman army mustered in A.D. 67 to attack Jerusalem.

24. Harold U. Faulkner, Tyler Kempner, and Victor E. Pitkin, *U.S.A.: An American History for the Upper Grades* (New York: McGraw-Hill, 1948).

25. "Concluding Statement: The Course of American History," in Wesley Marsh Gewehr, *The United States: A History of a Democracy* (New York: McGraw Hill, 1960), 626–38.

26. Lawrence Mishel, Jared Bernstein, and John Schmitt, *The State of Working America, 2000–2001* (Ithaca, N.Y.: Cornell University Press), for Economic Policy Institute, 2001, 371–406.

27. Daniel J. Boorstin and Brooks Mather Kelley, with Ruth Frankel Boorstin, *A History of the United States* (Lexington, Mass.: Ginn, 1981).

FOUR From Liberal Consensus to Conservative Ascendancy

1. Lionel Trilling, *The Liberal Imagination* (New York: Viking, 1950), preface.

2. Louis Harris poll, January 18, 2006, "Party affiliation" table.

3. Harris Interactive, "Party Affiliation and Political Philosophy Show Little Change, According to National Harris Poll," http://www.harrisinteractive.com/harris_poll/index.asp?PID=548.

4. Ibid.

5. Ibid.

6. Norman Ornstein, Andrew Kohut, and Larry McCarthy, "The People, the Press, and Politics: The Times Mirror Study of the American Electorate," September 30, 1987, http://people-press.org/reports/pdf/19870930.pdf.

7. "The People, the Press & Politics: The New Political Landscape," September 21, 1994, http://people-press.org/reports/pdf/19940921.pdf.

8. The following passage is in part a restatement of an argument I made in Godfrey Hodgson, *The World Turned Right Side Up* (Boston: Houghton Mifflin, 1996), 287–305.

9. Thomas Frank, *One Market Under God: Extreme Capitalism, Market Populism, and the End of Economic Democracy* (New York: Doubleday, 2000).

10. U.S. Department of Commerce, Bureau of Labor Statistics, "From the Editor's Desk," *Monthly Labor Review*, January 2007.

11. Lawrence Mishel, Jared Bernstein, and John Schmitt, *The State of Working America, 1998–9* (Ithaca, N.Y.: Economic Policy Institute, ILR Press, 1999), 65.

12. In 1973 a Nashville writer, John Egerton, wrote *The Americanization of Dixie: The Southernization of America* (New York: Harper's Magazine Press, 1974). In 1906, Peter Applebome, the *New York Times* correspondent in Atlanta, wrote *Dixie Rising: How the South Is Shaping American Values, Politics, and Culture* (New York: Times Books, 1996). See also Michael Lind, *Made in Texas: George Bush and the Southern Takeover of American Politics* (New York: Basic, 2003).

13. Roderick J. Harrison and Daniel Weinberg, "Racial and Ethnic Segregation: 1990," U.S. Bureau of the Census, March 13, 2001.

14. I say "apparently successful diplomacy" first because Nixon and Kissinger presented among the results of their diplomatic coup that democracy was on the march in China and that American business would conquer the Chinese market, whereas in fact nearly forty years later, China remains a Communist tyranny, and it is Chinese business that has triumphed in the American market rather than the other way round. See Margaret Macmillan, *Nixon and Mao: The Week That Changed the World* (New York: Random House, 2007).

15. This was described to me in some detail by one of the instigators, Paul Weyrich, a veteran conservative operator.

16. President William J. Clinton, State of the Union message, January 23, 1996, *The Public Papers of the Presidents of the United States: William J. Clinton,* book 1 (Washington D.C.: Office of the Federal Register, National Archives and Records, 1997).

17. Including Senator Dianne Feinstein, former Democratic presidential nominee Michael Dukakis, former senator Birch Bayh, his son Senator Evan Bayh, and the columnist E. J. Dionne, among many others.

18. University of Maryland Program on International Public Attitudes, "Americans on Foreign Aid and World Hunger: A Study of U.S. Public Attitudes," http://65.109.167.118/pipa/pdf/feb01/ForeignAid_Feb01_rpt.pdf, February 2, 2001.

19. UN resolution at http://daccessdds.un.org/doc/RESOLUTION/GEN/NR0/348/91/IMG/NR034891.pdf?OpenElement; aid statistics at http://stats.oecd.org/wbos/Index.aspx?DatasetCode=ODA_DONOR.

20. Criticism of the Washington Consensus can be found in Anup Shah, www.globalissues.org; Jeffrey D. Sachs, "The Development Challenge," *Foreign Affairs,* March–April 2005, and *The End of Poverty* (London: Penguin, 2005); and Daniel W. Drezner, *U.S. Trade Strategy: Free versus Fair* (New York: Council on Foreign Relations, distributed by Brookings Institution Press, 2006).

21. See Carol Adelman, "American Generosity in Foreign Giving," *American Outlook,* December 1, 2000; Carol Adelman, "The Privatization of Foreign Aid," *Foreign Affairs,* November–December 2003; Carol Adelman, Jeremiah Norris, and Jean Weicher, "America's Total Economic Engagement with the Developing World: Rethinking the Uses and Nature of Foreign Aid," *Hudson Institute* press release, June 29, 2005.

22. "U.S. Nearly Triples Tsunami Aid Pledge, to $950 Million," *New York Times,* February 10, 2005; "U.S. Private Sector Tsunami Relief Donations Top $1 Billion," Environmental News Services, February 28, 2005; "Tsunami Aid: Who's Giving What," BBC News, http://news.bbc.co.uk/2/hi/asia-pacific/4145259.stm, January 27, 2005.

23. I recall with amusement the astonishment and outrage with which I was greeted by a "scholar" from the American Enterprise Institute when I pointed out in a radio discussion that the Soviet Union had played some role in the defeat of Nazi Germany.

24. The achievements, and the sufferings, of the resistance movements have recently been colorfully brought before American readers in the novels of Alan Furst.

25. This is the title of a collection of essays, Hilene Flanzbaum, ed., *The Americanization of the Holocaust* (Baltimore: Johns Hopkins University Press, 1999).

26. Robert Dallek, *Franklin Roosevelt and American Foreign Policy, 1932–1945* (New York: Oxford University Press, 1979), 448; see also Henry L. Feingold, *The Politics of Res-*

cue: The Roosevelt Administration and the Holocaust, 1938–1945 (New Brunswick, N.J.: Rutgers University Press, 1970).

27. Feingold, *Politics of Rescue*, 295, 304.

28. This account owes much to the careful narrative in Peter Novick, *The Holocaust in American Life* (Boston: Houghton Mifflin, 1999).

29. Ibid., 207.

30. The witticism, often attributed to Talleyrand, was in fact said by Boulay de la Meurthe, principal author of the legal Code Napoléon.

31. This phrase was attributed to Douglas Feith, undersecretary of defense in the George W. Bush administration; see Bob Woodward, *State of Denial: Bush at War, Part III* (New York: Simon and Schuster, 2006), 108, 129.

FIVE The Other Exceptionalism

1. Recently Americans have usually made comparisons in terms of Purchasing Power Parity (PPP). This measure (originally used by international organizations to compare the incomes of developing nations) tends to favor the United States, where a substantial proportion of income is spent on items, such as health care or health insurance, which are either free or much less expensive in other countries. The older measure, based on the foreign exchange market, favors those other countries. It is somewhat ironic that American conservatives, in particular, should favor a measure in this instance that is derived not from the market but from the practice of those international institutions they so much dislike.

2. Paul Krugman, "America the Boastful," *Foreign Affairs*, May–June 1998.

3. Harold Hongju Koh, "On American Exceptionalism," *Stanford Law Review* 55 (2003), reprinted in *American Exceptionalism and Human Rights*, ed. Michael Ignatieff (Princeton: Princeton University Press, 2005), 111–43.

4. See, inter alia, the other articles in the Ignatieff collection.

5. Carol S. Steiker, "Capital Punishment," in Ignatieff, *American Exceptionalism and Human Rights*, 57, 59. Steiker goes on to warn us against shallow interpretations of these facts.

6. Amnesty International USA, "30th Anniversary of Gregg vs. Georgia: The Beginning of the Modern Era of America's Death Penalty," 2006, http://www.amnestyusa.org/abolish/greggvgeorgia/.

7. "Capital Punishment," Wikipedia, www.en.wikipedia.org/wiki/Capital_punishment.

8. UK Home Office World Prison Survey, 4th ed., undated, www.homeoffice.gov.uk/rds/pdfs2/r188.

9. *Washington Post*, February 29, 2008. Pew Center on the States, "One in 100: Behind Bars in America 2008," 2008, http://www.pewcenteronthestates.org/uploadedFiles/One%20in%20100.pdf, 6.

10. In 1987 one Michael Ryan, a local man who lived with his mother, armed with an AK-47 assault rifle and a Beretta handgun, killed sixteen people and wounded fifteen for no clear reason in Hungerford, a small, prosperous southern English country town. In

1996 Thomas Hamilton, a scoutmaster suspected of pedophile conduct, took two 9mm Browning pistols and two Smith and Wesson .357 caliber revolvers into a primary school in Dunblane, a small town in central Scotland, and killed fifteen children and one teacher. It seems that he blamed police inquiries into his sexual conduct for the failure of his business. Shortly afterward in Tasmania, Australia, Martin Bryant killed thirty-five people in a copycat rampage said to have been "inspired" by the Dunblane massacre. Both the Hungerford and the Dunblane incidents led, after excited press campaigns, to tightening of British gun laws.

11. Lawrence Mishel, Jared Bernstein, and Sylvia Allegretto, *The State of Working America, 2006–2007* (Ithaca, N.Y.: Cornell University Press, 2007).

12. Andrew Hacker, "The Rich and Everyone Else," *New York Review of Books,* May 25, 2006. This is also the thesis of my own book, Godfrey Hodgson, *More Equal Than Others* (Princeton: Princeton University Press, 2004).

13. Interview with Dr. Jack Geiger, 1973, cited in Godfrey Hodgson, *America in Our Time* (Garden City, N.Y.: Doubleday, 1976), 464.

14. Leslie Fiedler, "Our Country and Our Culture," *Partisan Review* symposium, 1952, pub. in Leslie A. Fiedler, *The Collected Essays of Leslie Fiedler,* vol. 2 (New York: Stein and Day, 1971).

15. Stephen P. Strickland, *Politics, Science, and Dread Disease* (Cambridge: Harvard University Press, 1972).

16. OECD figures quoted in "The U.S. Health Care System: Best in the World, or Just the Most Expensive?" *Bureau of Labor Education,* University of Maine, 2001, http://dll.umaine.edu/ble/U.S.%20HCweb.pdf.

17. Ibid.

18. UNICEF, "At a Glance: United States of America," 2008, http://www.unicef.org/infobycountry/usa_statistics.html.

19. Cohn, a senior editor at the *New Republic,* is the author of *Sick: The United States Health Care Crisis and the People Who Pay the Price* (New York: HarperCollins, 2007).

20. David Cohn, "Health Care Like the Europeans Do It," *New Republic,* April 10, 2007.

21. Institute of Educational Science, National Center for Education Statistics, "Status and Trends in the Education of Racial and Ethnic Minorities," http://nces.ed.gov/pubs2007/minoritytrends/tables/table_7_3.asp; "Racial Breakdown of Schools," *Washington Post,* January 22, 2008, http://www.washingtonpost.com/wp-dyn/content/graphic/2008/01/22/GR2012200060.html.

22. A new PISA survey was carried out in 2006 and published in early 2007. However, only the results for science have been published in full. Among the findings are that the United States ranks twenty-first of twenty-seven countries in terms of high school completion, and in terms of college graduates has slipped from second in 1995 to fourteenth in 2005. Americans aged twenty-five to thirty-four are roughly half as likely to have science degrees as their contemporaries in Australia, Finland, France, or Korea. www.oecd.pisa.

23. See Andrew Delbanco, "Scandals of Higher Education," *New York Review of*

Books, May 31, 2007; Andrew Hacker, "The Rich and Everyone Else," *New York Review of Books,* May 25, 2006; Jerome Karabel, *The Chosen: The Hidden History of Admissions at Harvard, Yale, and Princeton* (Boston: Houghton Mifflin, 2007).

24. For example, Jeffrey H. Birnbaum, *The Money Men: The Real Story of Fund-Raising's Influence on Political Power in America* (New York: Crown, 2000); Elizabeth Drew, *The Corruption of American Politics* (New York: Overlook, 1999); Stephen Wayne, *The Road to the White House,* 7th ed. (New York: Thomson/Wadsworth, 2004).

25. Paul Krugman, "For Richer," *New York Times Magazine,* October 20, 2002.

26. Wayne, *Road to the White House,* 304.

27. Robert G. Kaiser, "Citizen K Street," *Washington Post,* March 4 and following, 2007.

28. All four were among the organizers of College Republicans in Massachusetts in 1980. They have remained close associates ever since, at least until Abramoff's activities were revealed.

29. One of the odder (unintended!) consequences of the federal system is that Native American tribes, designated since the nineteenth century as in effect wards of the federal government, are immune from state regulation. Tribes have prospered greatly by exploiting this immunity.

30. Kevin Phillips, *Wealth and Democracy* (New York: Broadway, 2002), 408, 422.

31. Chief Justice William Rehnquist and Justices Kennedy, Souter, Scalia, and Thomas, all Republican appointees, all voted that a recount of Florida's vote was unconstitutional, thereby assuring Bush's election.

SIX The Corruption of the Best

1. The phrase "the short twentieth century" was coined by the British historian Eric Hobsbawm to refer to the seventy-five years from the onset of the First World War in 1914 to the fall of the Berlin Wall and the collapse of the Communist states of Eastern Europe beginning in 1989.

2. Most historians accept that there were similarities between European fascism and the beliefs and aims of, for example, Huey Long, Father Coughlin, the Liberty League, and the wealthy individuals and representatives of corporate America who approached Marine Major General Smedley D. Butler to lead the bonus marchers to prevent the inauguration of President Franklin Roosevelt. This was alleged by General Butler and others in testimony to an executive session of the McCormack-Dickstein committee on Un-American Activities in 1934.

3. David Potter, *People of Plenty: Economic Abundance and American Character* (Chicago: University of Chicago Press, 1954).

4. "Population Growth Rate," World Bank Group, 2001, http://www.worldbank.org/depweb/english/modules/social/pgr/; "World POPClock Projection," U.S. Census Bureau, 2008, http://www.census.gov/ipc/www/popclockworld.html.

5. William Bradford, *Of Plymouth Plantation,* ed. Samuel Eliot Morison (New York: Modern Library, 1967), 120–21. The reference to Plato may be to the criticism of the

Greek philosopher in Jean Bodin, *De Republica,* a book which is mentioned in the inventory of Bradford's estate: Plato "understood not that by making all things thus common, a Commonweal must needs perish; for nothing can be public, where nothing is private."

6. Max Weber, *The Protestant Ethic and the Spirit of Capitalism,* trans. Talcott Parsons (1904; London: Allen and Unwin, 1976); R. H. Tawney, *Religion and the Rise of Capitalism* (London: Murray, 1926). Weber also wrote an essay on *The Protestant Sects and the Rise of Capitalism.*

7. See, in particular, Michael J. Hogan, *A Cross of Iron: Harry S. Truman and the Origins of the National Security State, 1945–1954* (Cambridge: Cambridge University Press, 1998). The political distinction between "hawks" and "doves" dates from an article by the columnists Stewart Alsop and Charles Bartlett in the *Saturday Evening Post,* December 8, 1962, about the Cuban missile crisis.

8. The most recent survey data of which I am aware, by the Pew Center, dates from 2006. Seventeen thousand people were interviewed in fifteen countries. Admiration for the United States had fallen, for example, from 83 percent to 56 percent in Britain, from 78 to 37 percent in Germany, and from 62 to 37 percent in France. U.S. popularity had held up only in Russia and India. It had fallen from 75 to 30 percent in Indonesia, from 77 to 63 percent in Japan, and from 52 to 12 percent in Turkey.

9. See Arthur Walworth, *America's Moment: 1918—American Diplomacy at the End of World War I* (New York: Norton, 1977), 131.

10. Samuel Huntington, "The Coming Clash of Civilizations," *Foreign Affairs,* Summer 1993, later published in book form as *The Clash of Civilizations* (New York: Simon and Schuster, 1996).

11. Nathan Glazer, "On Being Deradicalized," *Commentary,* October 1970, pp. 74–80.

12. Theodore Roszak, *The Making of a Counter-Culture* (Garden City, N.Y.: Doubleday Anchor, 1969).

13. Richard A. Clarke, *Against All Enemies: Inside America's War on Terror* (New York: Simon and Schuster, 2004), 32. Saddam had attempted to organize the assassination of President George H. W. Bush in 1993.

14. Ron Suskind, *The Price of Loyalty: George W. Bush, the White House, and the Education of Paul O'Neill* (New York: Simon and Schuster, 2004), 96.

15. Paul O'Neill, interview by Lesley Stahl, *60 Minutes,* January 11, 2004, http://www.cbsnews.com/stories/2004/01/09/60minutes/main592330.shtml.

16. James Mann, *Rise of the Vulcans* (New York: Viking, 2004), 79–83.

17. David L. Phillips, *Losing Iraq: Inside the Postwar Reconstruction Fiasco* (New York: Westview, 2005), 13–14.

18. Publius (James Madison), *Federalist* no. 39, *The Federalist Papers* (Cutchogue, N.Y.: Buccaneer, 1992), 189.

19. This particular flight of malicious fancy comes from a 2007 review by Martin Peretz, the publisher of the *New Republic,* of a book by Walter Laqueur. But it has become a staple of right-wing commentary in the United States to predict that Europe will have a Muslim majority population, presumably before the United States has a Hispanic majority.

20. *Prosopography,* a term Namier derived from military intelligence, is the study of orders of battle, and therefore of the makeup and interrelationships of an elite.

21. Fritz Fischer, *Germany's Aims in the First World War* (New York: Norton, 1967).

22. I have heard from two quite distinct but authoritative sources that on the very day of the inauguration the outgoing President Clinton gave his incoming successor a list of international priorities, and that President Bush insisted that none was as important as the destruction of the Saddam Hussein regime in Iraq.

23. Thucydides, *History of the Peloponnesian War* (1921; Cambridge: Harvard University Press, 1977), book V, 34–116, 3: 155–79.

Index

Aberdeen, Lord, 57, 192*n*18
Abramoff, Jack, 146, 202*n*28
Abrams, Elliott, 180
Acheson, Dean, 84, 89, 93, 184
Adams, Henry, 78
Adams, John: and education, 46; on the Revolution, 32–33, 36, 193*n*6; and westward expansion, 51
Adams, John Quincy: claim to Texas renounced, 57; exceptionalist beliefs, 173; Florida acquired, 166; on the Mayflower Compact, 4–6, 192*n*8; and the Monroe Doctrine, 55–56
Addams, Jane, 79
Adelman, Carol, 117–18
affirmative action, 106, 108
Afghanistan, 123, 124, 154. *See also* war on terror
African-Americans: and education, 141; equality of opportunity, 12, 148; in prison, 131, 132; white resentment of, 106, 108, 109. *See also* slavery
Alamán, Lucas, 58
Alaska, 59
Albright, Madeleine, 152
Alger, Horatio, 48
Al-Qaeda, 123. *See also* September 11 terror attacks (9/11); terrorism
America as a Civilization (Lerner), 8
American Dream, 95, 134, 147–48. *See also* class divisions; equality
American exceptionalism: American Revolution and, 19, 27–28, 30–31, 61, 193*n*5 (*see also* freedom [liberty]); changing character of, 11–13, 99–100, 158–59, 163–64; Civil War and, 69; during the Cold War, 25–26, 91–98, 174 (*see also* Cold War); consequences, 181–89; conservatism and present-day exceptionalism, 113–15, 117–18, 167–72, 176–81, 185–88 (*see also* conservatism; neoconservatism); Constitution and, 13, 19; corruption of, xiii–xv, 10, 161–62, 167–72, 174–81, 185–90; criticisms of, 128–30; dangers of, xii–xvii, 16, 156, 162; defined, 174–75; eighteenth to mid-nineteenth century, 28, 34–37, 42, 48–50, 60–61, 156, 173; as incomplete picture, 175; interna-

American exceptionalism (*continued*) tional events exceptionalized, 116–22, 199*n*23; late nineteenth to early twentieth century, 62, 68, 73, 156–58, 173; late twentieth to early twenty-first century, xiii–xv, 99–100, 113–14, 127, 137–38, 151–54, 158–62, 165–73, 177–81, 185–89 (*see also* Iraq War [2003–present]); need for change, 188–90; negative exceptionalism, 128–29; nobility of ideals, xvi; outsiders' changing views, 163–65; overview, 10–16, 27–28, 172–74; in popular culture, 173–74; religious overtones, 93–94, 99, 111, 187; truths within, 14; and the World Wars, xiv, 22–24, 26 (*see also* World War I; World War II). See also *specific topics*

Americanism, 10, 174. *See also* American exceptionalism

American Revolution: and the belief in American exceptionalism, 19, 27–28, 30–31, 61, 193*n*5 (*see also* freedom [liberty], ideology of); college text on, 95–96; and the distribution of political power, 30, 36–37; European origins, 9, 19, 61, 96; historical significance, 30–37, 193*nn*5–6; and the ideology of republicanism, 35–36; and the meaning of liberty, 12–13; the Other during, 93; radical artisans and, 44; as revolution of the mind, 32–34, 36, 193*n*6

American Studies, 7

Arbella sermon. *See* "A Model of Christian Charity" (Winthrop's *Arbella* sermon)

Argentina, 65, 68

Armageddon, 93, 197–98*n*23

Arnold, Matthew, 77

Asia, 85–86, 114–15, 118. *See also* Vietnam War; *and specific countries*

Athens, 35, 174, 189–90

Atlantic Charter, 23

atomic bomb, 84, 118, 152, 184. *See also* nuclear weapons

Auden, W. H., 69, 196*n*5

Australia: capital punishment, 130; economic depression, 68; education, 141; exploration and colonization, 63, 64, 65; gun crimes, 201*n*10; per capita income, 135; as sheriff, 193*n*25; tsunami relief, 118; women's rights, 37

Austria, 37, 135

authoritarian regimes, U.S. support for, 25, 179

Aznar, José Maria, 164

Bailyn, Bernard, 32–33, 36

Baker, James, 177

Baker, Ray Stannard, 72

Bakke case, 108

Baldwin, Hanson W., 89

Balkan wars, 27, 153, 186

Beach, Moses Yale, 58

Beecher, Lyman, 48

Belgium, 22, 135

Beloff, Max, 163

Bender, Thomas, 128, 129

Benton, Thomas Hart, 39

Bercovitz, SacVan, 7, 192*n*10

Berlin airlift, 85

Berlusconi, Silvio, 164

Bernstein, Eduard, 79–80

biblical scholarship, 77

bigotry, 174

bin Laden, Osama, 124. *See also* terrorism

Bismark, Otto von, 78

Blair, Tony, 164

Bloom, Allen, 180

Boorstin, Daniel, 7, 98, 159

Booth, Charles, 76

Bork, Robert H., 150

Bradford, William, 4–6, 8, 160, 202–3*n*5

Brewster, William, 5–6
Brown, Harold, 170
Buckley, William F., Jr., 109, 172
Bush, George H. W. (1989–93): author's admiration for, xii; election defeat, 150; foreign policy, 29, 111–12, 153, 161, 167, 177, 186
Bush, George W. (2001–9): election and re-election, xv, 112, 126–27, 150, 172, 202*n*31; and executive power, 151, 184; foreign policy and foreign relations, 28, 29, 116, 186–88, 193*n*25; fund-raising, 145; intention to spread democracy, 123–27, 151, 171–72, 175; and the Iraq War, 123–27, 151, 169–72, 175, 187, 204*n*22; and the war on terror, 116, 123–26, 169–70; as "world's sheriff," 28, 193*n*25. *See also* Iraq War (2003–present); neoconservatism; war on terror
Bush, Jeb, 171, 180
business, 106–7, 143–44, 146–47, 149. *See also* capitalism; organized labor
Butler, Benjamin F., 102

Cabot, John, 17
Calhoun, John C., 58, 195*n*40
California, 88
Canada: criminal justice, 130, 131; economy, 135; education, 141; foreign aid (governmental/private), 117, 118; frontier, 65; neoconservative resentment of, 179; and U.S. expansion, 59, 166; voting rights, 37
Canning, George, 20, 54–57
Cannon, Lou, 176–77
capitalism: in Europe, 157, 160–61; finance capitalism, 107; late nineteenth to early twentieth century, 65–67, 156–57; market populism, 106; role in American exceptionalism, 10, 99–100, 160–61; and social issues (*see* poverty; social democracy; the "social question"); unregulated, 12; U.S. duty/destiny to spread, 10, 160–61
capital punishment, 130–32
Caribbean, 59–60, 86–87, 166, 181–82
Carter, Jimmy, 110, 170
Cassidy and Associates, 146
Catholic Church: anti-Catholicism, 48, 93, 174; Catholic immigrants, 41, 48, 93 (*see also* Irish immigrants and Irish Americans); and education, 48, 49
Cazneau, William L., 60
Central Intelligence Agency (CIA), 85, 86–87. *See also* Tenet, George
Chamberlain, Neville, 186
Chateaubriand, Francois-René, 4
Cheney, Dick, 101, 124, 168, 169, 171
Chicago, 108, 141
A Child of the Jago (Morrison), 75
children, 131, 139. *See also* education
Chile, 87, 179
China: capital punishment, 131; and the Cold War, 24–25; economy, 134–35, 185, 199*n*14; lack of realism about, 116, 179; Nixon diplomacy with, 109, 199*n*14; Roosevelt's hopes for, 84, 184; trade and foreign investment, 114; U.S. fears of, 177; after World War II, 183
Christian conservatives, 107, 111. *See also* conservatism
Churchill, Winston, 23, 24, 119, 157
CIA. *See* Central Intelligence Agency (CIA)
cities: growth of, 40, 64, 66, 70; segregation, 108; social inequality and urban poverty, 70, 74–76; worker politics in, 43–44
"Citizen K Street" series (*Washington Post*), 146
"city set upon a hill" metaphor, 1–2, 3, 99
civil rights movement, ix, 96–97
Civil War (U.S), 28, 69–70, 181. *See also* Lincoln, Abraham; slavery

Clarke, Richard, 169–70
class divisions: absence claimed, 11–12; during the Cold War, 91, 95–96, 197*n*22; eighteenth to early nineteenth century, 42–45; and equality of opportunity, 11–12; late nineteenth to early twentieth century, 66, 70–76, 147–48, 156–57; and political ideology, 106, 109; present-day inequalities, xii, 96, 100, 114, 129, 134–37, 142–48; and voting rights, 42; after World War II, 158. *See also* equality
Clemenceau, Georges, 79, 82, 166
climate change, 187
Clinton, Bill: conservatives' reaction to presidency of, 112, 150; on the end of big government, 110; exceptionalist principles, 186; foreign policy, 29, 151, 153, 161, 186; and gun control, 133; international priorities given to Bush, 187, 204*n*22; peace and prosperity lauded, 27, 115
Clinton, Hillary, 140, 145
Cohen, Eliot A., 180–81
Cohn, Jonathan, 140
Cold War: American ideology and, 24–26, 91–98, 161–62, 174; containment policy, 184–85; effect on American society, 89–92; military-industrial complex, 87–90, 97; Miller's ideology and, 7–8; origins, 83–86; overview, 24–25, 153; state making hindered, 167; U.S. power abroad, 86–87
colonialism: American colonialism, 65, 70, 86–87, 91–92 (*see also* westward expansion); American efforts to counter, 153; European colonialism/imperialism, xvi, 16–18, 51, 63–66, 157, 183, 184. *See also* imperialism
colonies, European origins and influences on, 16–19, 175
Columbine High School, 133
Columbus, Christopher, 17, 18
Commager, Henry Steele, 52
communal ownership of property, 160
communism: Cold War tactics of communist states, 24; collapse, in Eastern Europe, 26–27, 113, 167, 179, 185–86; as the Other, 92–93 (*see also* Cold War: American ideology and); spread of, 84–86; U.S. fears about, 83–86, 89–90. *See also* Cold War; Soviet Union; Vietnam War
Congo, Democratic Republic of, 87, 131
Congress: and the Bush election, 127; and Cold War foreign policy, 184–85; and the Iraq War, 126; neoconservative ascendency and, xv; partisan politics, 150–51. *See also* Democratic Party; politics, American; Republican Party
consent of the governed, 10, 12, 13, 36, 60. *See also* democracy
conservatism, 177; Christian conservatives, 107, 111; and the constitutional system, 149–52; of the Democratic Party, 149–50; European conservatism and American exceptionalism, 163–64; intelligentsia, 177–81; liberalism denounced, 101–2; modern ascendancy of, 100–112, 149–51, 177–81, 185–86; and PPP comparisons, 200*n*1; and present-day exceptionalism, 113–15, 117–18, 167–72, 176–81, 185–88; southern conservatism, 104–5, 107–8, 110; and the strength of American society, 162; suspicion of government, 110. *See also* neoconservatism; Republican Party; *and specific individuals*
Constitution, U.S.: abuses of, 149–52; Eu-

ropean influences on, 19; as exceptional document, 34–35; ideology of republicanism refined, 36; individual rights guaranteed, 13; rights threatened by McCarthyism, 86; Second Amendment, 132; and slavery, 31
containment policy, 184–85. *See also* Cold War
corporate management. *See* business
cotton, 56
Crèvecoeur, J. Hector St. Jean, 3–4, 163
criminal justice, 12, 128, 130–33
Croly, Herbert, 72, 81
Cromwell, Oliver, 35
Cuba, 55, 60, 86–87, 139, 167
Cushman, Robert, 39
Czechoslovakia, 85, 186

Danforth, Samuel, 6, 93
Darwin, Charles, 77
death penalty (capital punishment), 130–32
Declaration of Independence, 19, 35–36, 45
Decter, Midge, 180
Defense Department, 85, 90. *See also* military-industrial complex
defense spending, 165
democracy: in Europe, 157; failure of, 149–52; in former communist nations, 186; the frontier and, 11; neoconservative networks and, 181 (*see also* neoconservatism: networks); neoconservative views on foreign democracies, 179; threats to, 149–51, 161–62, 189–90; world admiration for U.S. system, 164–65. *See also* politics, American
democracy, U.S. duty/destiny to spread: from belief to program, 181–82; G. W. Bush administration and, 123, 125, 151, 171–72, 175, 187 (*see also* Iraq War [2003–present]); Clinton administration and, 186; in Germany and Japan, 167; Iraq War and, 123–27, 151, 162, 171–72, 175; origins, 10, 159–60; premise questioned, 151–52, 162; Wilsonian philosophy, 10, 22, 161–62 (*see also* Wilson, Woodrow). *See also* American exceptionalism; capitalism, U.S. duty/destiny to spread; Cold War
Democratic Party: and gun control, 133; and the liberal-conservative divide, 101–5, 107–8, 112, 149–50 (*see also* liberalism); and lobbying firms, 146; move to the left, 107–8; reaction to Reagan, 111; as social democratic party, 73; and the 2004 election, 127; voter identification/allegiance, 103–5. See also *specific individuals*
Denmark, 37, 135, 139
détente, 184–85
Detroit, 68, 108, 196*n*4
Dickens, Charles, 75
Diego Garcia island, 86
discovery of America, 17–18
Disraeli, Benjamin, 75
Donne, John, 163
Dorr, Thomas Wilson, 45
Douglas (aerospace company), 88
Drift and Mastery (Lippmann), 81
Durham, Lord, 59
Dutch settlers, 38

earmarks, 151
economy, U.S.: eighteenth to mid-nineteenth century, 56, 61; late nineteenth to early twentieth century, 21, 64, 65–66, 68–69, 70; during/after World War II, 22–24, 67, 83–84, 91, 157–58; during the Cold War, 91–92, 96, 158–59; late twentieth to

economy, U.S. (*continued*)
early twenty-first century, 113–15, 134–37, 158, 159, 179, 185. *See also* class divisions
education: and class divisions, 137; during the Cold War, 90, 94; eighteenth to mid-nineteenth century, 37, 46–50, 60, 194*n*10; exceptionalism in textbooks, 94–98; higher education, 50, 90, 141–42; recent declines, 140–42, 201*n*22
Egypt, 25, 121
Eichmann, Adolf, 121
Eisenhower, Dwight D., 24, 89, 140, 184
elections, presidential. *See* politics, American; *specific presidents*
electoral college, 112, 150
Eliot, Charles W., 50, 78
Ely, Richard T., 81
Emerson, Ralph Waldo, 77
energy, 115. *See also* oil
England. *See* Great Britain
equality: diminished respect for, xii; exceptionalist claims, 12–13, 96, 147–48; and the meaning of freedom, 13; of opportunity, 12, 148 (*see also* opportunity); present-day inequalities, xii, 96, 100, 114, 129, 134–37, 142–48; U.S. as leader, 13, 133–34. *See also* class divisions
Errand Into the Wilderness (Miller lecture), 6–8, 93–94
Europe: admiration for U.S., 162–64, 203*n*8; American exceptionalism accepted/rejected, 163–65; and the American West, 21; and the Balkan wars, 186; and the Cold War, 84–85, 87; criminal justice, 130, 131; decolonization, 157; defense spending, 165; economy, 134–36, 158, 179, 185; education, 48–49, 194*n*10; expansion and colonization/imperialism, xvi, 16–18, 51, 63–66, 183, 184; health care, 138–40; industrialization, 64, 66–67, 68, 70–71, 196*n*4; land ownership, 33; liberalism, 157; Muslim majority predicted for, 178, 203*n*19; politics and American interests/expansion, 51–60; postwar recovery, 23–24; the Reformation, 18–19; Seven Years' War, 18–19; social issues and social democracy, 32, 72–76, 78–83, 161; struggle for liberty in, 61 (*see also* France: French Revolution); technological development, 68; U.S. criticized, 128–29; and World War I, 21–22, 67; and World War II, 22–24, 67, 83–84. See also *specific countries*
Everett, Edward, 44
exceptionalism, 14–15. *See also* American exceptionalism
executive branch, power of, 151, 184
exemptionalism, 154
exports, U.S., 21, 56, 192*n*19

Fairfax, Lord, 38
fascism, 8, 83, 158, 202*n*2. *See also* the Holocaust; World War II
Federalist party, 53
Feingold, Henry L., 120
feudalism, 11–12, 13
Fichte, Johan Gottlieb, 50, 77
Fiedler, Leslie, 138
finance capitalism, 107. *See also* capitalism
Finland, 37, 135, 136, 141
Florida, 51–52, 57, 88, 131, 166
Ford, Gerald, 110
foreign aid, 116–18, 121
foreign policy and foreign relations: aggression and arrogance in, xiii–xiv, xv, 162, 176, 185, 188–90; Bush (father, 1989–93) and, 29, 111–12, 153, 161, 167, 177, 186; Bush (son, 2001–9) and, 28, 29, 116, 186–88, 193*n*25 (*see also* Iraq War [2003–present]);

Clinton and, 29, 151, 153, 161, 186; Cold War policies, 24–25, 84–87, 184–85 (*see also* Cold War); conservatives and, after Reagan, 161–62, 168–72, 177–81; in the early nineteenth century, 52–54; international system and the U.S. role, 152–54; Israel, 119–22; Nixon and, 109, 199*n*14; Reagan and, 29, 111, 179, 185; recent mistakes and American exceptionalism, 165–72; soft power, 26–27, 193*n*22; state making, 167; unilateralism, 162, 188; U.S. intervention in foreign politics, 86–87; Washington on, 52–53; world perceptions of the U.S., 162–65, 203*n*8. *See also* Cold War; democracy, U.S. duty/destiny to spread; westward expansion; *and specific wars*

Founding Fathers, 19, 173. See also *specific individuals*

Fox, Charles James, 31–32

France: American attitudes toward, 116, 179; criminal justice, 130, 131; economy, 135–36, 158; education, 49; foreign aid, 117; French Revolution, 31–32, 35, 38; industrialization, 70–71; and Israel, 120; land ownership, 38; life expectancy, 139; Napoleonic Wars, 20, 51–54; poverty and alleviation, 76, 148; Seven Years' War, 18–19; social democracy, 80, 82–83, 197*n*13; U.S. popularity in, 203*n*8; U.S. relations with (early nineteenth century), 52–53; women's rights, 31; and World War I, 21, 22, 67; and World War II, 22, 67

Frank, Thomas, 106

Franklin, Benjamin, 4, 19, 48, 51

Free Soil movement, 39–40

freedom (liberty): ideology of, 35–36, 60–61, 69, 92; inevitability of spread, 181–82; military occupation opposed to, 188; multiple meanings, 12–13, 92; U.S. duty/destiny to spread, 10, 23 (*see also* Cold War; democracy, U.S. duty/destiny to spread)

French and Indian War, 19, 33

the frontier: and American democracy, 63; American westward expansion, 39–40, 51–52, 57–61, 63–66, 166; Europe and the American frontier, 20, 21; Europe's frontier, 16–18, 51; Jackson's thesis, 11. *See also* Louisiana Purchase; Mexican War

Fukuyama, Francis, 180–81

Furman v. Georgia, 131

Gaffney, Frank, 180–81

Geiger, Jack, 138

generosity, 116–18. *See also* foreign aid

Geneva Conventions, 126

Georgia (state), 87–88

Germany: Berlin airlift, 85; Berlin-to-Baghdad railway, 65; criminal justice, 131; education (Prussia), 48, 49–50; fascism, 83; foreign aid (governmental/private), 117, 118; health care, 138; immigrants from, 40, 63; industrialization, 70–71; national myths, 14; neoconservative resentment of, 179; post-WWI recovery, 21, 68; poverty intervention in, 78; reunification, 167; socialism in, 43; unemployment, 135; U.S. popularity in, 203*n*8; U.S. role in establishing democratic government, 167; voting rights, 37; and World War I, 67, 152, 182; and World War II, 23, 67, 119, 152 (*see also* the Holocaust)

Gettysburg Address, 69

Gilded Age, 71–72

Gilman, Daniel Coit, 50, 78

Gladstone, William: on the Constitution, 34, 193–94*n*8; Labouchère on, 172; liberalism, 70, 79, 102
Glazer, Nathan, 169
globalization, 64, 66–67
"God Bless America" (Berlin song), 173
Gore, Al, 112
Great Britain: admiration for U.S., 163–64, 203*n*8; and the American Revolution, 31; anti-slavery movement, 31, 192*n*18, 193*n*3; Common Law, 19; constitution, 36; criminal justice, 130, 131; declining power/influence, 21, 23; decolonization, 157; economy, 135–36, 158; education, 48–49; expansion and colonization, 63–65, 193*n*7; foreign aid, 117, 118; gun ownership, 132, 200–201*n*10; industrialization, 64, 70–71; and Israel, 119–20; Labour Party, 83, 102, 157, 163–64, 194*n*24; land ownership, 38–39; Liberal Party, 102, 157, 164; life expectancy, 139; Manchester liberalism in, 102; and the Napoleonic Wars, 52–53 (*see also* Napoleonic Wars); Oregon Territory acquired from, 166; poverty and social inequality, 75–76; private giving, 118; republican Commonwealth, 35; Seven Years' War, 18–19; social democracy in, 79–83; and Texas, 192*n*18; Thirty Years' War (civil war), 7, 9; U.S. relations with, in the early nineteenth century, 52–57; voting rights, 37, 41; women's rights, 31, 37; and World War I, 21, 22, 67, 182; and World War II, 22–23, 67
Greece (ancient), 15, 35, 174, 189–90
Greece (modern), 84
Gregg v. Georgia, 131
gross domestic product (GDP), 135–36, 159
Gulf War (1990–91), 111–12, 153, 167. *See also* Bush, George H. W. (1989–93): foreign policy
gun ownership, 132–33, 200–201*n*10

Hacker, Andrew, 137
Hamilton, Alexander, 52–53
Havel, Vaclav, 164
Hawaii, 167
Hazard of New Fortunes (Howells), 71–72, 74–75
health care, 129, 137–40
Hegel, Georg Wilhelm Friedrich, 50, 77
Hinckley, John, 132
Hispanics, 132, 141
history, American: connected to European/world history, xvi, 16–21; distortions, xvi; exceptionalist textbooks, 94–98; myths taught as, 14
Hofstadter, Richard, 1, 27
the Holocaust, 26, 119–22
home ownership, 91
Homestead Act, 39
How the Other Half Lives (Riis), 72, 74
Howard, John, 193*n*25
Howells, William Dean, 71–72, 74–75
Hudson Valley, 38, 45
Hughes, John, 48
Hugo, Victor, 76
human rights violations, 126, 153–54
Hungary, 37, 186
Huntington, Samuel, 168
Hussein, Saddam: conservatives' interest in removing from power, 126, 170–72, 187, 204*n*22; French attitude toward, 116; Kuwait invaded, 111, 153, 167; U.S. support for, 126; weapons capability, 124. *See also* Gulf War (1990–91); Iraq; Iraq War (2003–present)
Hyndman, Henry, 76

ideological and party identification, 103–5
Ilké, Fred C., 180

immigrants and immigration: Catholic immigrants, 41, 48, 93; Irish immigrants/Irish Americans, 22, 33, 41, 45, 71, 96; Jewish immigrants, 119–20, 173; and land ownership, 38–40; late nineteenth to early twentieth century, 66, 70; material opportunity and success, 11, 134, 173; motives, 175; U.S. as world society due to, 15–16; voting rights, 41; and westward expansion, 39–40, 66. *See also* Irish immigrants and Irish Americans
imperialism, 157; anti-imperialism, xi, xiii, 23, 87; dangers of, xvi; decline and demise of European imperialism, 183, 184; U.S. power likened to, xiii, 86–87. *See also* colonialism; Mexican War
imports, U.S., 114–15
income, 134–37, 143–44, 158, 178–79. *See also* class divisions; poverty; standard of living
independent voters, 103
India, 87, 177, 179, 203*n*8
Indonesia, 87, 203*n*8
industrialization: and the Civil War, 69; in Europe, 64, 66–67, 68, 70–71, 196*n*4; late nineteenth to early twentieth century, 64, 65, 68, 70–71, 196*n*4; U.S. emergence as industrial power, 21, 22–23
industry, and the Cold War, 88–91
inequality. *See* class divisions; equality
intelligentsia, conservative, 177–81
international criminal court, 187
international system, 152–54. *See also* United Nations
Iran: capital punishment, 131; hypothetical attack on, 162; and Iraq, 124, 125; U.S. support for shah, 25, 86
Iraq: capital punishment, 131; Gulf War (1990–91), 111–12, 153, 167; interest in democracy, 175. *See also* Hussein, Saddam; Iraq War (2003–present)
Iraq War (2003–present): Bush administration's motives, 123–27, 151, 169–72, 175, 204*n*22; consequences for America, 188–89; democratic process lacking in pursuit of, 126–27; exceptionalism as root cause, 165–72; human rights violations, 154; Israel and, 25, 124, 125; Sept. 11 attacks and, 115–16, 122–24. *See also* war on terror
Ireland, 37, 38, 130, 135
Irish immigrants and Irish Americans, 22, 33, 41, 45, 71, 96. *See also* immigrants and immigration
Islam, 177. *See also* Middle East; terrorism; war on terror
isolationism: causes, 22; impossibility of, 68–69; new isolationism, 176 (*see also* unilateralism); before World War II, 183
Israel: and the Iraq War, 25, 124, 125; U.S. support for, 25–26, 119–22, 185
Italy, 35, 117, 139, 167

Jackson, Andrew, 57
Jackson, Henry M., 88, 121
James, William, 78
Japan: economy, 135, 136, 158, 185; health care, 138–40; military successes, 183; postwar recovery, 24, 83; trade and foreign investment, 114; U.S. popularity in, 203*n*8; U.S. role in establishing democratic government, 167; and World War I, 182; and World War II, 23, 119, 152
Jaurès, Jean, 80, 197*n*13
Jay, John, 51
Jefferson, Thomas: on American liberty, 10, 173; ancestry, 96; Crèvecoeur and, 4; on education, 45–46; eloquence, 34; European influences,

Jefferson, Thomas (*continued*) 19; and foreign policy, 53; role in exceptionalist tradition, 10; slave vs. free states' conflict foreseen, 20; slaves owned, 31
Jews: American Jews, 121–22, 173; the Holocaust, 26, 119–22; immigration to Middle East, 119–20 (*see also* Israel)
Johnson, Andrew, 39
Johnson, Lyndon B.: and the Cold War, 24, 184; and social reform, x, 73, 100, 106, 173; and Texas military infrastructure, 88
Johnson, Samuel, 60

Kagan, Donald, 180
Kagan, Frederick, 180
Kagan, Robert, 168
Kalilzad, Zalmay, 180
Kemp, Geoffrey, 170
Kennan, George, 184, 185
Kennedy, John F.: Cold War foreign policy, 24–25, 184; ideology and rhetoric, 92, 97, 100, 159, 185; on Jefferson, 46; and social reform, 106
Keyssar, Alexander, 41–42
King, Martin Luther, Jr., ix, 172
Kipling, Rudyard, xiii, 63–64
Kissinger, Henry, 109, 184, 199*n*14
Klaus, Vaclav, 164
Kloppenberg, James T., 81, 82
Koh, Harold Hongju, 130
Korean War, 85–86
Kristol, Irving, 180
Kristol, William, xiii, 168, 180
Krugman, Paul, 129, 143–44
Kyoto protocol, 187

Labouchère, Henry, 172
Labour Party (Britain), 83, 102, 157, 163–64, 194*n*24
Lamarck, Jean-Baptiste, 77
land ownership: communal ownership, 160; in eighteenth- and nineteenth-century America, 37–40, 60; and the Revolution, 33–34; and voting rights, 41; and westward expansion, 39–40
Latin America: democratization, 66, 181–82; European control vs. independence, 54–56; socialism and social democracy in, 161; U.S. influence/intervention in, 25, 86–87. *See also* Mexican War; *and specific countries*
law of unintended consequences, 106, 185–86
League of Nations, 82, 152, 182
Lebanon, 25
the Left. *See* Democratic Party; Labour Party (Britain); liberalism; Liberal Party (Britain); social democracy; socialism
Lenin, Vladimir, 79–80
Lerner, Max, 8, 159
The Liberal Imagination (Trilling), 100–101
liberalism: decline in modern America, 100–108 (*see also* conservatism: modern ascendancy of); European liberalism and American exceptionalism, 163–64; governmental style/methodology, 105–6; history of term, 102; liberal consensus, 92 (*see also* Cold War: American ideology and); Manchester liberalism, 78, 82, 102, 157; in the media and universities, 177; neoconservative crusade against, 187. *See also* Democratic Party; Labour Party (Britain); Liberal Party (Britain); social democracy; socialism; *and specific individuals*
Liberal Party (Britain), 102, 157, 164
liberty. *See* freedom (liberty)
Libya, 25

life expectancy, 139
Limited Contingency Study, 171
Lincoln, Abraham: exceptionalist beliefs, 100, 173; great speeches, 10, 69, 94, 181; role in exceptionalist tradition, 10
Lions International cartoon booklet, 174
Lippmann, Walter, 81
Lipset, Seymour Martin, 42–43, 73
Lloyd George, David, 82, 102, 166
lobbying industry, 146–47
Lockheed, 88
Lodge, Henry Cabot, 172–73
London School of Economics, 79
Long, Breckinridge, 120
Louisiana Purchase, 20, 39, 51, 166
Lowell, James Russell, 63
Lyell, Sir Charles, 77

Mackay, J. H., 75
Madison, James, 19, 34, 46, 173
Mahon, George, 88
Manchester liberalism, 78, 82, 102, 157
Manifest Destiny, 51–52, 57–61, 159, 166. *See also* westward expansion
Mann, Horace, 47, 173
Mansfield, Lord, 31, 193*n*3
manufacturing. *See* industrialization
market populism, 106
Marks, Gary, 42–43
Marshall, George C., 93
Marshall, Thurgood, 172
Marshall Plan, 24, 83. *See also* Europe: postwar recovery
Massachusetts Bay Company, 6–8, 93–94. *See also* Puritans
material exceptionalism, 11, 158–59. *See also* health care; income; productivity (GDP)
Mayflower Compact, 4–6
Mayhew, Henry, 76
McCain, John, 145, 146
McCarthyism, 86, 89–90, 174
McClure, Samuel, and *McClure's Magazine*, 72
McGovern, George, 108
media, 126, 171, 177
Melos, 189–90
Mexican War, 20, 39, 52, 58, 166, 195*nn*39–40
Mexico, 52, 57–58, 192*n*18. *See also* Mexican War
Michigan, education in, 47, 48
middle class, expansion of, 80, 197*n*22. *See also* class divisions; equality
Middle East: anti-American sentiment in, 122 (*see also* terrorism); conservative policy toward, 170–71 (*see also* Iraq War [2003–present]; Israel); geopolitical vulnerability, 185; Jewish immigration to, 119–20 (*see also* Israel); oil, 25, 115, 171; spreading democracy in, 124–27, 162, 171–72 (*see also* Iraq War [2003–present]); U.S.–Israel relationship and, 25–26, 119–22, 185; after World War II, 183. *See also* Gulf War (1990–91); Iraq War (2003–present); *and specific countries*
military-industrial complex, 87–90, 97
military power: defense spending, 113, 165; importance in modern exceptionalism, 100 (*see also* Iraq War [2003–present]); military infrastructure, 86–89, 97, 113, 153; of the U.S., during the Cold War, 86–89, 97, 153; U.S. dominance, 26, 28, 84, 113; U.S. emergence as, 21–22, 26, 28, 193*n*24 (*see also* Cold War; World War II); use of, to spread democracy, 161–62 (*see also* Iraq War [2003–present]). *See also* military-industrial complex; nuclear weapons
Mill, John Stuart, 77–78, 81, 102, 157
Miller, Perry, 6–8, 9, 93–94

missionary exceptionalism, xii, 159–62. *See also* democracy, U.S. duty/destiny to spread
"A Model of Christian Charity" (Winthrop's *Arbella* sermon), 1, 2–3, 176
Monroe, James, 55–56. *See also* Monroe Doctrine
Monroe Doctrine, 20, 54–56
Morgenthau, Henry, 120
Morison, Samuel Eliot, 52
Morrison, Arthur, 75
Morrow, Jeremiah, 39
Moynihan, Daniel Patrick, 101, 163
Murdoch, Rupert, 178, 180
myths, national, 14

Namier, Sir Lewis, 179
Napoleon Bonaparte, 20, 49, 51, 54, 166. *See also* Louisiana Purchase; Napoleonic Wars
Napoleonic Wars, 20, 51–54
nationalism: American exceptionalism as, 10, 14 (*see also* American exceptionalism); in other nations, 14–15; "patriotism" vs., xiv
national myths, 14
National Review (journal), 109
National Rifle Association (NRA), 132–33
National Security Act (1949), 85
Native Americans: and the American Revolution, 96; decimated by disease, 33; driven out by westward expansion, 40; and equality of opportunity, 12; lobbying by casinos, 146, 202*n*29; and the myth of an empty America, 163; as the Other, 92–93
Nazi Germany. *See* Germany; World War II
neoconservatism: anti–social reform stance, 106; and exceptionalist foreign policy, 167–72, 177–79, 185–89; exceptionalist ideology, xiii–xv, 168–69; and the Iraq War, 123–24, 168–72 (*see also* Iraq War [2003–present]); and the law of unintended consequences, 106, 185–86; and the Middle East, 170; military seen as too small, 113; networks, 179–81; rise of, xiv–xv, 109, 177–81. *See also* conservatism; *and specific individuals*
the Netherlands, 22, 117, 135–36
New Deal, 12, 69, 73, 83. *See also* Roosevelt, Franklin D.; social democracy
New Republic (journal), 81, 140
New Statesman magazine, 79
New York City: education, 48, 141; as financial capital, 21, 68; slums, 70–71, 74; working-class movements, 43–44. *See also* September 11 terror attacks (9/11)
New Zealand, 37, 64, 135, 148
9/11 terror attacks. *See* September 11 terror attacks (9/11)
Nitze, Paul, 84, 185
Nixon, Richard: author and, x; on being Keynesians, 101; and the Cold War, 24, 89, 184; McGovern denounced, 108; political career, xii, 109–10, 199*n*14
Norquist, Grover, 146, 181, 202*n*28
Northwest Ordinances, 39, 47
Norway: education, 141; foreign aid, 117; health care, 138, 139; income and productivity, 135, 136; women's voting rights, 37
Novick, Peter, 122
NRA (National Rifle Association), 132–33
NSC (National Security Council), 85
nuclear weapons, 84, 118, 125, 152, 184

Obama, Barack, 148
oil, 25, 115, 171
O'Neill, Paul, 170
opportunity, 11, 12, 134, 148, 173

Oregon Territory, 166
organized labor: early nineteenth century, 44; late nineteenth to early twentieth century, 71; mid-twentieth to early twenty-first century, 91, 106–7, 111, 149
O'Sullivan, John, 50–51, 58
the Other, 92–93; opposition to the, 91–92
Ottoman Empire, 17, 182, 183

Paine, Thomas, 19, 34, 163, 166, 181
Pakistan, 123, 131, 179
party identification, 103–5
peace, American vision of, 97
People of Plenty (Potter), 11, 159
Perot, Ross, 145
Persian Gulf war (1990–91). *See* Gulf War (1990–91)
Pestalozzi, Johan Heinrich, 49
Pew Center political studies, 104–5
Philippines, 86, 167
Phillips, David L., 171–72
Phillips, Kevin, 146–47
Pierce, John D., 48
Piketty, Thomas, 143
Pilgrims, 4–6, 7, 38–39, 160. *See also* Puritans
Pius XII (Pope), 176
Podhoretz, Norman, 180
Poland, 186; women's voting rights, 37
political philosophy: consent of the governed, 12, 13; late nineteenth to early twentieth century, 70, 72–83 (*see also* Progressive era and progressivism; social democracy; socialism); unregulated capitalism, 12 (*see also* capitalism). *See also* politics, American
politics, American: Cold War politics, 85, 87–90 (*see also* Cold War); conservative ascendancy, 100–112, 149–51, 177–81, 185–86; Europe and, 52–54; and growing inequalities, 142–48; money's role, 144–47, 149; negative aspects, 129; party identification, 103–5; polarization (partisanship), 149–51; public participation, 144; southernization of, 107–8; *2000* election, 112, 150, 179, 202*n*31. *See also* conservatism; Democratic Party; liberalism; political philosophy; Republican Party; *and specific individuals*
Polk, James K., 58
popular culture, 118–19, 122, 173–74
popularity of the U.S., 162–64, 203*n*8. *See also* trustworthiness of the U.S.
population, U.S., 62, 159
population, world, 159
"pork barrel" legislation, 87–88, 151
Portuguese exploration, 17–18
Potter, David, 11, 159
poverty, 70, 73–76, 148. *See also* class divisions; social democracy; socialism; the "social question"
PPP (Purchasing Power Parity), 200*n*1
A Preface to Politics (Lippmann), 81
Prescott, Walter, 16
presidential elections. *See* politics, American; *and specific presidents*
prison and imprisonment, 12, 128, 131–32. *See also* criminal justice
productivity (GDP), 135–36, 159. *See also* industrialization
Progressive era and progressivism, 71–72, 80–83. *See also* social democracy; the "social question"
Project for a New American Century, 169, 171, 180–81. *See also* neoconservatism
projection of power, 86–87, 113–14. *See also* Iraq War (2003–present)
Prussia, 48, 49–50
public education. *See* education
public standards, high, 174, 181

Puerto Rico, 55, 167
Purchasing Power Parity (PPP), 135, 200*n*1
Puritans: beliefs formed by European Reformation, 9, 18; Massachusetts Bay Company, 6–8; Mayflower Compact, 4–6; uniqueness challenged, 8–9, 175

Quitman, John, 60

race: criminal justice system and, 131–32; and public education, 141; urban segregation, 108; white reaction to liberal social reforms, 106. *See also* African-Americans; slavery
Radical Republicans, 102
railroads, 21, 64, 65, 71
Rauschenbusch, Walter, 81
Reagan, Ronald: attempted assassination of, 132–33; author and, x, xi–xii; and the conservative ascendancy, 110–11, 177; exceptionalist (patriotic) beliefs, 176–77; foreign policy under, 29, 179, 185; Winthrop sermon quoted, 1–2, 3, 176
Reagan revolution, 111–12, 150. *See also* Reagan, Ronald
Reconstruction, 69–70
redeemer, U.S. as, 22–24, 25–26, 119–22
Reed, Ralph, 146, 202*n*28
Reformation, Protestant, 18–19
Regents of the University of California v. Bakke, 108
religion: and capitalism, 160; and education, 47–48, 49; exceptionalism's religious overtones, 93–94, 99, 111, 187; late-nineteenth- to early-twentieth-century challenges to, 64, 76–78; political rise of evangelical Christianity, 107, 111; religious tolerance, 13, 48
Republican Party: and the Bush presidency, 126–27; and the conservative ascendancy, 103–5, 107–12, 149–51; and early-nineteenth-century foreign policy, 53; and gun control, 133; and the liberal-conservative divide, 101–5, 107, 108–12; and lobbying firms, 146; and southern conservatism, 107; *2004* convention, 172, 174; voter identification/allegiance, 103–5; and voting rights, 41. *See also* conservatism; neoconservatism; *and specific individuals*
republics, 35; ideology of republicanism, 35–36, 60–61; land ownership and, 37 (*see also* land ownership). *See also* American Revolution; Constitution, U.S.; Declaration of Independence
research, 90
Revolution. *See* American Revolution
Rice, Condoleezza, 125, 148, 170, 171–72
the Right. *See* conservatism; neoconservatism; Republican Party
rights, Constitutional, 13. *See also* civil rights movement; slavery, emancipation; voting rights; women's rights
Riis, Jacob, 72, 74
Rodman, Peter, 180–81
Roman Empire, 15
Roosevelt, Franklin D.: fascism avoided, 8, 158; ideological principles, 23, 159, 173; and the New Deal, 83; postwar plans, 84, 184; and World War II, 119–20, 183–84
Roosevelt, Theodore, 28, 72
Ross, Dennis, 170–71
Roszak, Theodore, 169
Rove, Karl, 146, 202*n*28
Rumsfeld, Donald, 101, 124, 168, 169, 171
Rush, Richard, 54–55
Russia: criminal justice, 131; democracy in, 186; eastward expansion, 65; nationalism, 14; Russian Revolution,

82–83, 183; U.S. popularity in, 203*n*8; women's rights, 37; and World War I, 182. *See also* Soviet Union

Saez, Emmanuel, 143
Saint-Simon, Louis de Rouvroy, duc de, 181
Saltonstall, Richard, 9
Saudi Arabia, 25, 121, 124, 131
Scandinavian immigrants, 40, 63
science: Christianity challenged by, 77–78; nuclear weapons development, 84, 118. *See also* technology
Scotland, 14, 38, 49, 194*n*10. *See also* Great Britain
separation of powers, 151
September 11 terror attacks (9/11): American emotional response, 27, 113, 115–16, 122–23; and elections, 112, 144; and the Iraq War, 122–24, 126, 169–70, 187–88. *See also* Iraq War (2003–present); war on terror
settlement houses, 79
Seward, William Henry, 44, 59, 173
Shays, Daniel, 44
Singapore, 139
slavery: American Revolution and, 30, 31, 96; Britain and, 31, 192*n*18, 193*n*3; and the Civil War, 28, 69, 181; emancipation, 181; and the ideology of liberty, 60; Jefferson's concerns about, 20; slaves as the Other, 93; South's expansionist dreams, 59–60; in Texas, 57; and westward expansion, 40; and working-class movements, 43–44
social conservatism, 108
social democracy: conservatives and, 92, 102, 106; importance in American politics, 12, 73; maintained through state regulation, 161; New Deal, 12, 69, 73, 83; origins, 78–80, 102; Progressive era, 71–72, 80–83. *See also* the "social question"
socialism: in France, 80, 197*n*13; origins, 78; in the U.S., 12, 43, 73, 102, 192*n*10
the "social question," 71–76, 78–82, 156–57. *See also* poverty; social democracy; socialism
Sombart, Werner, 73
the South (U.S.): capital punishment, 131; expansion into Caribbean dreamt of, 59–60; southern conservatism, 104–5, 107–8, 110. *See also* Civil War (U.S.); slavery
South Africa, 64, 65, 120
South Korea, 25, 141, 185
South Vietnam, 25, 87. *See also* Vietnam War
Soviet Union: and the Cold War, 24–25, 26, 84–86, 153, 183 (*see also* Cold War); collapse and disintegration, 26, 153, 185–86; emigration of Russian Jews, 121; and Israel, 120; and Middle East oil reserves, 171; Nixon-era relations with, 109; nuclear capability, 84; Reagan-era relations with, 111. *See also* Russia
Spain: and American expansion, 51–52, 166; capital punishment, 130; and the Napoleonic and Mexican Wars, 20, 52, 54; national pride, 14; unemployment, 135
Sparta, 174
Stalin, Joseph, 84–86. *See also* Soviet Union
standard of living, 91, 96, 114, 134–36, 158–59. *See also* class divisions: present-day inequalities
State Department, 125. *See also* foreign policy and foreign relations
"The State of Working America" (Economic Policy Institute), 134–35
Steffens, Lincoln, 72

stock market, 113–14. *See also* economy, U.S.
Storm, Jane Eliza, 51, 58, 60
Strauss, Leo, 168, 180
Suskind, Ron, 170
Sweden, 117, 118, 135, 139, 140
Switzerland, 135, 138
Sybil (Disraeli), 75

Taft, Robert, 73
Taliban, 123, 124
Tarbell, Ida, 72
technology, 68, 90. *See also* industrialization; military-industrial complex; nuclear weapons
Tenet, George, 170
terrorism: September 11 attacks, 27, 112, 113, 115–16, 122–24, 187–88; war on terror, 113–14, 122–27, 153–54, 188. *See also* Iraq War (2003–present)
Texas: annexation, 50–51, 55, 57–58, 166; capital punishment, 131; independence, 20, 192*n*18; military-industrial complex, 88
textbooks, 94–98
Thatcher, Margaret, 100, 164
Thucydides, 189–90
Tocqueville, Alexis de: Crèvecoeur and, 4; on criminal justice, 130; on equality, 13, 70, 71, 100, 130; on voting rights, 40–41
Trilling, Lionel, 100–101
Trist, Nicholas, 58
Trollope, Anthony, 13
Truman, Harry S.: and the Cold War, 24, 85–86, 93, 184; health care reform proposed, 139; ideology, 159; and postwar recovery efforts, 83–84; support for Israel, 120
trustworthiness of the U.S., 152–54. *See also* popularity of the U.S.
tsunami relief, 118
Turner, Frederick Jackson, 11, 51, 63–64, 66
Twain, Mark, 157, 174

unemployment, 135
unilateralism, 29, 162, 188. *See also* Bush, George W. (2001–9); Iraq War (2003–present)
unintended consequences, law of, 106, 185–86
unions. *See* organized labor
United Kingdom. *See* Great Britain
United Nations, xiii, 85, 111, 116–17, 124
United States: emergence as superpower, 21–24, 26; as "lone superpower," 26–27, 113, 153, 167; outsiders' changing views of, 163–65; relationship to rest of the world, 152–54, 175–76, 188–89. See also *specific topics*
universities, 50, 90, 141–42, 177, 180
University of Virginia, 46

van Buren, Martin, 44, 58
Vespucci, Amerigo, 17
Vietnam War: end of, 110, 185; international criticism of, 152; overview, 25; and present-day conservative exceptionalism, 176; Reagan on, 177. *See also* South Vietnam
voter turnout, 144
voting rights, 13, 37, 40–42, 60

Waldeck-Rousseau, Pierre, 80
Walker, William, 60
Wallace, Alfred Wallace, 77
Wallace, George, 109, 172
war on terror, 113–14, 122–27, 153–54, 188. *See also* Iraq War (2003–present); September 11 terror attacks (9/11)
Washington (state), 88–89
Washington, D.C., 141
Washington, George: on alliances (farewell address), 52–53; ancestry, 96; cherry